"The Bruderhof was a community of C[hrist]ians who tried to live a simple life dedicated to the ideal of peace. The [vision]ary [German founder] Eberhard Arnold had started the movement in the wake of the disasters that enveloped Germany after the First World War. . . Ian Randall has written a full, evocative and appealing account of a group who in troubled times 'wanted to follow Jesus and do his will.'"

—David Bebbington
Professor of History, University of Stirling, Scotland

"This detailed narrative fills a longstanding gap in Bruderhof historiography—the story of the Cotswold Bruderhof in England, particularly during the formative years as it took shape between the Nazi confiscation of the Rhoen community in 1937 and the Bruderhof's transition to Paraguay in 1940 . . . As images of refugees, racial violence, and warfare once again dominate the news media, the Cotswold story is powerful and timely testimony to an alternative vision for humanity."

—John D. Roth
Professor of History, Goshen College

"This absorbing book is an important contribution to the history of the Anabaptist movement. Based on thorough research and drawing on a wide variety of sources, it charts the early years of the Bruderhof in Germany and England during a turbulent period of their history and explores the remarkable commitment of the founders and community members to peace witness, shared lifestyle and mission. Through this sympathetic historical study, Ian Randall highlights issues which remain relevant today."

—Linda Wilson
Research Fellow, Bristol Baptist College

"Christians from many traditions have been learning from the Anabaptists in recent years. The Bruderhof communities embody a distinctive and enduring witness to principles and practices inspired by the Anabaptist vision. Ian Randall's detailed study tells the story of the Bruderhof in a crucial early phase of their life in England, inviting us to learn from their faithfulness in the midst of struggles."

—Stuart Murray Williams
Anabaptist Network, Chair, Mennonite Trust, United Kingdom

"In *A Christian Peace Experiment*, Ian Randall offers a scholarly and approachable case study of the Bruderhof, a significant Christian movement, at an important stage in its development and growth when it moved from Germany to England and later to the Americas. Randall offers a fascinating and well-documented account of a pacifist Christian community with a German foundation in England at the start of World War II . . . Randall provides a valuable resource for both scholars interested in Christian social movements and for those of us who are asking ourselves what it means to be a Christian in the world today."

—Kevin Ahern
Assistant Professor, Director of Peace Studies, Manhattan College

"I've long been an admirer of the Bruderhof community and its vibrant commitment to peacemaking, and Ian Randall's book about the community's British history only increases that esteem. *A Christian Peace Experiment* brims with insights into the historical realities faced by peacemakers in a time of war."

—Colman McCarthy
Director, Center for Teaching Peace, Washington, D.C.

A Christian Peace Experiment

To

Rob

with thanks

for years of

rich fellowship

A Christian Peace Experiment

The Bruderhof Community in Britain, 1933–1942

IAN M. RANDALL

Foreword by Nigel G. Wright

CASCADE *Books* · Eugene, Oregon

A CHRISTIAN PEACE EXPERIMENT
The Bruderhof Community in Britain, 1933–1942

Cascade Books
An Imprint of Wipf and Stock Publishers
199 W. 8th Ave., Suite 3
Eugene, OR 97401

www.wipfandstock.com

PAPERBACK ISBN: 978-1-5326-3998-2
HARDCOVER ISBN: 978-1-5326-3999-9
EBOOK ISBN: 978-1-5326-4000-1

Cataloguing-in-Publication data:

Names: Randall, Ian M., author. | Wright, Nigel, 1949–, foreword.

Title: A Christian peace experiment : the Bruderhof community in Britain, 1933–1942 / Ian M. Randall ; foreword by Nigel G. Wright.

Description: Eugene, OR : Pickwick Publications, 2018. | Includes bibliographical references and index.

Identifiers: ISBN 978-1-5326-3998-2 (paperback) | ISBN 978-1-5326-3999-9 (hardcover) | ISBN 978-1-5326-4000-1 (ebook)

Subjects: LCSH: Cotswold Bruderhof (Ashton Keyens, Wiltshire, England) | Peace—Religious aspects—Bruderhof Communities—Case studies. | Bruderhof Communities—History.

Classification: BX8129.B63 R36 2018 (paperback) | BX8129.B63 R36 (ebook)

Manufactured in the U.S.A.   03/13/18

Cover image: Members of the Cotswold Bruderhof, 1940. Photograph © Bruderhof Historical Archive.

All photographs are © Bruderhof Historical Archive.

Contents

Foreword

Among the modest items inherited from my parents is a simple wooden fruit bowl marked on the underside with a motif strangely resembling a bishop's mitre and the words 'Cotswold Bruderhof Handicrafts'. It is a remnant of the time (less than half a year as it turned out) my mother and father spent at the Oaksey Bruderhof community in 1940. Like many such items, it tells a story way beyond its immediate usefulness.

Having met and married in the Salvation Army, my parents, Charles and Muriel Wright, under the pressure of changing religious views, began to meet with the Quakers in Wythenshawe, Manchester. Wythenshawe was an idealistic experiment in social housing (later to become the largest such estate in Europe) and they were among the first pioneering residents. Meeting with the Quakers, they were to encounter an outreach delegation from the Bruderhof and, my father being a conscientious objector and the Second World War being in its first year, they were moved to sell their possessions and against family advice to migrate to the Bruderhof with their three children, my older siblings. Others were doing the same. In the event and although being enrolled in the community's 'novitiate', Charles and Muriel were not to continue in membership. As their views continued to change, and whether because of matters of principle or because they could not contemplate a future in Paraguay, they parted with the Bruderhof and settled less adventurously in rural Cheshire. My father then enlisted in the Non-combatant Corps working on war damage, transferred in time into the military and was finally to serve with the Royal Engineers for three years in Africa and India as a commissioned officer with the final rank of captain. It was no doubt a relief to his conscience that he was never in combat.

It would be an understatement to say that these were disruptive times. Yet I have often wondered how it must have been in wartime to join a community of 'aliens', and, even more so, how those 'aliens' themselves would have coped with the inevitable hostility they encountered even in a country such as the United Kingdom. This thoroughly well-researched and readable book gives us the answers. It is heartening to read about support from official and unofficial sources alongside less welcoming attitudes.

It is not as though everything in the case of my parents was lost. They retained an abiding respect for their experiences in the Bruderhof and were marked by them as by their Salvation Army heritage. Although I was born sometime after the war as their sixth child, the subliminal influences of the Bruderhof remained. Names such as Hardy Arnold, Hans Meier, Arnold Mason and Stanley Fletcher were recalled from time to time along with other aspects of the common life. Working alongside Hans Meier in particular my father picked up a smattering of German which, along with the Swahili he later learnt in the army, he liked to parade. This must have fed into my own consciousness since it was through German in particular (though not Swahili!) that my own lacklustre grammar school education was redeemed and that I went on to university. More significantly I managed to acquire by osmosis (in what had become a family that was not notably religiously observant) an instinct for radical Christian movements that would later become a particular theological interest in the Anabaptists and their descendants. Perhaps these are signs that the influence of a movement such as the Bruderhof rests not only with those who stay the course but also with those on the margins. Seeds sown spring up in unpredictable places. If so, the present volume is likely to have a constructive impact far beyond the immediate community whose early history it relates.

Ian Randall has acquired a formidable reputation as an historian of modern renewal movements and is superbly qualified for the task of researching and presenting this book. He brings a precision of scholarship to the task allied to sympathetic sound judgment and spiritual awareness that together ensure that both reader and the movement about which they read will be well served. It is a privilege to commend book, author and movement

Dr. Nigel G. Wright
Principal Emeritus, Spurgeon's College London and President,
Baptist Union of Great Britain 2002–3.

Introduction

In March 1938, in an article entitled 'In England Now: An Outline of Some Developments towards the Coming Order', Leslie Stubbings, the honorary secretary of the newly formed Community Service Committee, wrote about the significance of contemporary communal living movements. He acknowledged that those who were 'apt to measure the significance of things by their size rather than their spirit' were not 'likely to devote very much attention to community in this country'. In 1938, living in community was not new. Nonetheless, he argued that the times were awakening a fresh interest in communal life.

Stubbings saw the circumstances in the world in 1938 as offering little reason for hope. The quest for wealth had resulted in economic inequality; liberty was overshadowed by dictatorships; a search for peace had brought 'the massacre of innocents'; and a desire for collective security had ended in the breakdown of international law. As he saw it, true hope lay not in dreams that had been fulfilled, but rather in facing reality. 'Disillusionment', he argued, could be 'a highway to wisdom'. For him the route back to reality within the Christian church could be found in a new way of life in which – among individuals, groups, and communities – there was a 'spontaneous coming together'. Through such renewal, a 'new order' could be glimpsed.[1]

Stubbings' article was published in the first issue of *The Plough*, a quarterly journal produced by the Bruderhof community. The Bruderhof ('place of brothers') was a communal Christian movement that began in Germany in 1920 under the leadership of Eberhard and Emmy Arnold. Eberhard Arnold's powerful influence was felt in Germany and elsewhere, especially through his speaking and writing, over the course of

1. Leslie Stubbings, 'In England Now', *The Plough* 1, no. 1 (March 1938), 12–13.

three decades.[2] Three years prior to Stubbings' article, in 1935, Arnold had died suddenly, after a failed leg amputation, at the age of fifty-two.[3] Now, as a result of increasing Nazi pressure, the community had moved from Germany to Wiltshire, England, where it was known as the Cotswold Bruderhof.[4]

The first issue of *The Plough* promised articles on 'the fundamental aspects of the coming order or the conditions which must be fulfilled for it to become reality here and now'. There would also be articles on historical movements or groups that were seen as being of special relevance, and contributions that dealt with contemporary ideas and activities. In addition, there would be commentary, news, and book reviews.[5] As well as publishing the journal, the Cotswold Bruderhof had a small publishing house, the Plough Publishing Company, which produced and disseminated works that reflected the beliefs of the community and the wider communal living movement. For example, in 1938 Plough published *Community in Britain*.[6] Dennis Hardy, in *Utopian England: Community Experiments, 1900–1945*, notes that this particular volume was 'an important review of community ideas and schemes in this period'.[7]

Indeed, the Bruderhof was part of a wider movement in the 1930s that sought to give witness to a 'new order' in the context of deepening crisis in Europe. Leslie Stubbings, although not a member of the Bruderhof, spoke of how news had spread regarding the Cotswold community 'only two years after its foundation'. He considered this 'a sign of the times'. In an evocative comment on the significance of the community, he wrote: 'Like the peace movement, the Bruderhof has released a consciousness that was already latent and growing. Six miles from a railway, in the middle of a field, and in the loneliest of the Southern shires, these grey stone buildings have become a symbol of new life; a national witness to the practical possibility of a life rooted and grounded in love and service.'[8]

The search which led to the establishment in 1936 of this community 'in the middle of a field' was undertaken by Freda Bridgwater

2. Arnold's magnum opus, *Innerland*, absorbed his energies from 1916 to 1935.

3. For Arnold's life see Baum, *Against the Wind*.

4. For the story of the community in Nazi Germany see Barth, *An Embassy Besieged*; and Nauerth, *Zeugnis, Liebe und Widerstand*.

5. The Editor, 'The Task of the Plough', *The Plough* 1, no. 1 (March 1938), 3.

6. *Community in Britain*, 1938.

7. Hardy, *Utopian England*, 188.

8. Leslie Stubbings, 'In England Now', *The Plough* 1, no. 1 (March 1938), 14.

and Arnold Mason, two English members of the Bruderhof, and Hans Zumpe, a German member who was visiting England. The property they selected was Ashton Fields farm, near Ashton Keynes, several miles from Cirencester. Freda Bridgwater later recalled that when the three turned into the drive they saw a beautiful field of wheat on their left. But the buildings looked the worse for wear: doors were off their hinges, furniture had been knocked around, and outhouses were in a similarly poor state. Yet Freda felt the place was so rundown that it was ripe for renewal as a community. Her companions found this hard to believe, but her instinct proved correct.[9]

The Cotswold community soon began at Ashton Keynes, and over the next five years the community experienced considerable growth. Buildings were renovated, and new structures were created. Bruderhof members, now refugees, began to arrive from Germany, where their witness had made them a target of the Nazi regime. As word spread about the Bruderhof, significant numbers of British people joined. The growth resulted in the extension of the community's activities, with the acquisition of additional farms.

Reflecting on twenty years of Bruderhof life, *The Plough*, in summer 1940, recalled that in 1920 a small group of people in Germany, 'deeply disquieted by the horror and injustice of the World War of 1914–18', had embarked on a 'new venture of community living'. Now, in 1940, the people of Europe and people from other parts of the world were caught up in another World War. At this critical moment in history, Bruderhof members wanted to declare again their conviction that 'the common life, community in all its spiritual and material things, is the fruit of love, and as such the only solution for the need of the world. To it belongs the spreading of the good tidings of the coming Kingdom, and the call to repentance throughout the world.'[10] The pressures of war, however, made it difficult for the Bruderhof, forced out of Germany, to maintain the international communal life and witness it had built up in the 1930s.

In May 1940, just four years after finding the site for the Bruderhof, Freda Bridgwater married a German widower in the Cotswold community, August Dyroff. Eight days after the wedding, a plainclothes policeman arrived at the community, and Freda found herself under arrest as an 'enemy alien'. August had previously appeared before a tribunal and

9. Winifred Dyroff (formerly Bridgwater), 'Telling about Cotswold'. BHA Coll. 0066.

10. 'Our Pledge', *The Plough* 3, no. 2 (Summer 1940), 33.

been granted freedom to continue to live in Britain, but Freda, lacking the same exemption, was now regarded as German. With only a few minutes given to her to pack, she gathered her Bible and writing equipment, said goodbye to the community, and was taken to the police station in Swindon where she discovered several other women in a similar plight. Most were refugees from Germany and Austria, and some had children with them. Freda and others were taken to Liverpool and housed in a large building normally used for lodging sailors. After four days, Freda and four thousand others from all over England were told they were going to be interned on the Isle of Man.[11] News of Freda's whereabouts did not reach the community for two weeks, and only then because Freda managed to pass a letter to a local. After six weeks of internment Freda was released.[12] It was becoming clear, however, that Bruderhof life was under threat.

This book examines the development of the Bruderhof in Britain from 1933 and its life in Wiltshire from 1936 to 1942. The community, in which Germans were a significant presence, incurred increasing hostility after the beginning of the Second World War, and this finally – and reluctantly – led to the Bruderhof's move from Britain to Paraguay, and to the establishment of a Bruderhof community in Primavera (Spanish for 'spring'). In chapter 1, this study examines the beginnings of the Bruderhof in Germany, centred on Eberhard Arnold, his wife Emmy, and her sister Else von Hollander. The Bruderhof's early connections in England, in the 1920s and early 1930s, form the subject of chapter 2. With the establishment of the Cotswold community, roots were put down in England, as outlined in chapter 3. Chapter 4 details how the Bruderhof shared in witness alongside other peace movements and communal initiatives in Britain in the 1930s. Chapter 5 offers an analysis of Cotswold communal life. Various influences shaped this life, including the Anabaptist Hutterite tradition, dating from the sixteenth century, and these influences are evaluated in chapter 6. The next chapter examines the community's progress and the pressures it faced, and chapter 8 gives an account of how the Cotswold community came to an end.

While several books have been written about the Bruderhof by investigators from outside the community, the perspective has tended to

---

11. Winifred Dyroff, 'Recollections of My Early Years'. BHA Coll. 0066. For background see Chappell, *Island of Barbed Wire*.

12. Arnold Mason, 'Early Memories'. BHA Coll. 0006. See chapter 7.

be a sociological one.[13] From within the community, Merrill Mow wrote *Torches Rekindled: The Bruderhof's Struggle for Renewal* (1989).[14] The title drew from an earlier book by Emmy Arnold, *Torches Together*, an expanded version of which was published in 1999 as *A Joyful Pilgrimage: My Life in Community*.[15] Faith and struggle were dominant themes in a book published in 2004 by a community member, Peter Mommsen, entitled *Homage to a Broken Man*, a graphic account of the life of Heinrich (Heini) Arnold, one of Eberhard and Emmy's sons.[16]

In 1961, in a time of huge turmoil for the Bruderhof, Primavera was dissolved. Many Bruderhof members left or were put out of the movement. A number of former members wanted to give accounts of what they saw as having gone wrong, and these were published by Carrier Pigeon Press, which had been set up for that purpose. These memoirs included books by Roger Allain, who wrote *The Community that Failed* (1992), and by Elizabeth Bohlken-Zumpe, a granddaughter of Eberhard and Emmy Arnold, who wrote *Torches Extinguished* (1993).[17] Such stories formed the basis of a hostile book on the Bruderhof published in 2000 by Julius H. Rubin, a sociologist who never actually visited the Bruderhof.[18]

In 1996 Yaacov Oved produced a comprehensive account of the Bruderhof, *The Witness of the Brothers*, which included a helpful chapter about the Cotswold years.[19] Oved, a member of Kibbutz Palmachim since 1949, a former professor in Tel Aviv University's history department, and an authority on communal movements, pointed out the significance of the continued existence of the Bruderhof over eight decades: 'From among the many German communities of the [1920s], only the Bruderhof became a communal movement that has survived to this day.'[20] As

13. Zablocki, *The Joyful Community*; Whitworth, *God's Blueprints*; Tyldesley, *No Heavenly Delusion?*.

14. Mow, *Torches Rekindled*.

15. Emmy Arnold, *Torches Together*; Emmy Arnold, *A Joyful Pilgrimage*.

16. Mommsen, *Homage to a Broken Man*.

17. Allain, *The Community that Failed*; Bohlken-Zumpe, *Torches Extinguished*. The press was set up by KIT, a group for ex-members of the Bruderhof. See also Pleil, *Free from Bondage*; Manley, *Through Streets Broad and Narrow*; Holmes, *Cast Out in the World*.

18. Rubin, *The Other Side of Joy*. Rubin's interest was already in what he called 'religious melancholy'. See Rubin, *Religious Melancholy and Protestant Experience in America*.

19. Oved, *Witness of the Brothers*.

20. Oved, *Witness of the Brothers*, 33.

well as dealing with periods of community advance, Oved also gave attention to the painful experiences of former members of the community. He spoke of the years 1959 to 1962 as 'years of great crisis, a dark period in Bruderhof history',[21] although arguably the 'dark period' was a consequence of pre-existing problems.

Benjamin Zablocki, in *The Joyful Community*, took the view that the English period was an 'interlude' in Bruderhof history, and that the mood was 'one of holding together in the face of Arnold's sudden death, the sudden expulsion from the homeland, and the growing hostility due to the heightened emotions of war'.[22] Among Zablocki's sources was a college paper by an ex-Bruderhof member. This unnamed student posited that, despite the large numbers of English participants in the Bruderhof, 'their impact on Bruderhof belief and practice was nil'.[23] John McKelvie Whitworth, in *God's Blueprints*, stated, without offering evidence, that the period from the death of Eberhard Arnold in 1935 to the end of 'the purge', as he called it, in 1962, had come to be regarded in the Bruderhof as 'an era of apostasy'.[24]

Despite these and other publications about the Bruderhof, this is the first to offer a detailed examination of the Cotswold period, and by utilising primary sources, this book will offer a very different interpretation of the period. Writing about the Early Christians, Eberhard Arnold described them as 'revolutionaries of the Spirit. . . Their witness meant they had to reckon with being sentenced to death by state and society'.[25] The Bruderhof lived with this in mind. As a result of the forced ending of their witness in Germany, the Bruderhof community moved to England. Emmy Arnold spoke of 'the loss of everything we had' and added, 'one might well ask how it was possible for us to go on'. Her answer: 'We had heard the call clearly, and there was no choice but to follow it'.[26] I am glad to have been able to explore what was involved in following that call during this important period in the Bruderhof's development.

I wish to thank all those who have helped me with this book. My wife, Janice, and I have been welcomed as guests by Bruderhof communities

21. Oved, *Witness of the Brothers*, 207.

22. Zablocki, *Joyful Community*, 82.

23. 'The Emperor's New Clothes', unpublished college term paper, cited by Zablocki in *Joyful Community*, 83.

24. Whitworth, *God's Blueprints*, 183.

25. Eberhard Arnold, *The Early Christians*, 16–17.

26. Emmy Arnold, *Joyful Pilgrimage*, 167–168.

in England, Germany, and the United States. In particular, we spent an extended time with the community at Fox Hill, in New York State, where the main Bruderhof archive is housed. The archive is an excellent one, and I have based much of what I have written in this book on the material housed there. At all stages in this project I have had unstinting help from Bruderhof community members in Britain and the USA.

In addition to using the Bruderhof archive, I found valuable material in the Cambridge University Library; the Bishopsgate Institute in London, where the Muriel and Doris Lester papers are held; the Fellowship of Reconciliation collection at the London School of Economics; the Friends' Library and Archive in London; and the Angus Library at Regent's Park College in Oxford. I am grateful to the staff in each of these places for their help. I am also grateful to Peter Grace, of Cirencester, for conversation about the Bruderhof on a visit I made to see the buildings that had housed the Cotswold community, and for his unpublished work, 'The Stranger in our Midst' (1990).

Lindsey Alexander, the copy-editor, has worked hard to produce a revised version of this book. One aspect of the way I have written the book should be mentioned here: I have not followed the common academic convention of referring to key figures by their surnames. I concluded that in many cases using first names was more natural.

I

International Beginnings

Eberhard Arnold was born on 16 July 1883 near Königsberg, East Prussia. Eberhard's mother, Elisabeth, née Voigt, was from a family of scholars, and his father, Carl Franklin, was the son of Swiss and American missionaries. Carl Arnold taught theology and philosophy, and in 1888 he was appointed professor of Church History at Breslau University.[1] Emmy von Hollander (later Arnold) was born on 25 December 1884 in Riga, Latvia. Emmy's father was a lawyer and his father had been the last German mayor of Riga, Latvia. The family moved from Latvia to Germany and settled in Halle on the Saale, a university city, in 1897. It was during a spiritual revival there in 1907 that Eberhard and Emmy met and were engaged to be married.

When he was almost sixteen, Eberhard went to stay with his mother's cousin, Lisbeth, and her husband, Ernst Ferdinand Klein. Ernst Klein, a Lutheran pastor in a weavers' village, had taken up the workers' cause in a labour dispute, which had led to his removal by the Lutheran Church to another parish. Later Eberhard would recall his uncle warmly welcoming a Salvation Army member and calling him 'brother'. Many German Lutheran ministers of the time were dismissive of revivalist movements like the Salvation Army,[2] but Klein was keen to hear about their work among the poorest people in Berlin. This impressed Eberhard, as did his uncle's 'courageous, joyful Christianity'.

1. Baum, *Against the Wind*, 2–3.
2. Baum, *Against the Wind*, 8.

After returning from his stay with his aunt and uncle, Eberhard embarked on an intense spiritual search. In October 1899, he visited a young pastor and, after hearing him speak, asked: 'Why do I hear so little from you about the Holy Spirit?' The pastor replied that Eberhard's visit was 'nothing other than the working of the Holy Spirit'.[3] Subsequently, Emmy later recounted, Eberhard 'experienced conversion'.[4] His conversion involved reading the Bible, particularly John 3:3, with its focus on being 'born again'. Several years later, during their engagement in 1907, Eberhard encouraged Emmy in a letter to study scripture 'with eagerness and devotion'.[5] As evidence of his view of the cross, Eberhard wrote in April 1907 of how Christ 'bore humanity's sin—though he himself was sinless—he subjected himself to death for the forgiveness of sins and in order to fulfil the demands of justice'.[6] By eighteen, Eberhard had begun to preach. It was at an event in Halle, in March 1907, at which Eberhard was the speaker, that Emmy felt 'the call to life-long discipleship'.[7]

Evangelical Connections

The Salvation Army was founded by William and Catherine Booth, who had been active within Methodism in England but who saw the need to adopt fresh ways to reach the working-class population.[8] In 1867 they set up the East London Christian Mission, and in 1878 they adopted the Salvation Army name. A decade later the Salvation Army was 'the world's fastest growing Christian sect',[9] but it faced considerable opposition. In Germany open-air meetings were prohibited. At meetings in Stuttgart, authorities even banned open entry, insisting that anyone attending had

3. Clara Arnold, 'His Way'. BHA Coll. 0288_05. Clara Arnold was a sister of Eberhard.

4. Emmy Arnold, *A Joyful Pilgrimage*, 2. This was a classic evangelical conversion experience. Studies of evangelicalism in recent years have generally aligned themselves with David Bebbington's argument that evangelicals are those who stress conversion, the Bible, the cross, and activism: Bebbington, *Evangelicalism in Modern Britain*, 2–17. These came together in Eberhard's experience.

5. Eberhard Arnold to Emmy von Hollander, 31 March 1907, Eberhard Arnold and von Hollander, *Love Letters*, 21.

6. Eberhard Arnold to Emmy von Hollander, 6 April 1907, Eberhard Arnold and von Hollander, *Love Letters*, 30.

7. Emmy Arnold, *Joyful Pilgrimage*, 3, 10.

8. Holmes, *Religious Revivals in Britain and Ireland*, 148–149.

9. Murdoch, *Origins of the Salvation Army*, 136.

to have an admission card signed by a Salvation Army officer. To many, the Army seemed contemptible,[10] but Eberhard Arnold felt at home in their company. Through his connections with the organization he visited some of the poorest areas of Breslau, and at age eighteen he spoke at Army meetings.[11]

These activities were greeted with great dismay by Eberhard's parents, and his father wondered if he would have to resign from his University lecturing post. School authorities stepped in to stop Eberhard's public speaking,[12] but Eberhard continued to take seriously the challenge by William Booth to reach out to the 'submerged tenth', the most desperate people in society. He appreciated the Army's combination of evangelical spirituality and social involvement; as his sister Clara put it: 'Along with the [Army's] sermons on conversion and sanctification, there was a deep social understanding for the outer need of the oppressed masses.'[13]

Despite opposition, the Salvation Army continued to grow and thrive in Germany. On a visit to Stuttgart in 1905, William Booth was deeply moved by the enthusiastic welcome he received.[14] Among the practical ministries being launched were a men's shelter in Hamburg, opened in 1904, and a subsequent shelter in Cologne, paid for by a wealthy lady who had seen three young men who were evidently very poor kneeling at the Army penitent form—the 'mercy seat'.[15]

When Eberhard received a letter from William Booth inviting him to serve in the movement, he wondered if it was 'God who is calling me through his servant Booth'.[16] Eberhard reported to Emmy in June 1907, writing from Breslau, where he was by then a theological student: 'I've just returned from a powerfully blessed Salvation Army meeting. The major allowed me to lead the meeting, and I was greeted with loud hallelujahs and beaming faces by the many members who came.' Eberhard went on to say that he had spoken 'in the strength of the Spirit' from the book of Romans and that many had broken down sobbing. Eberhard ultimately concluded that the Army 'lacked a certain depth in the way they handled

10. Page, *The Christianity of the Continent*, 56–57.
11. Emmy Arnold, *Joyful Pilgrimage*, 3.
12. Baum, *Against the Wind*, 13–14.
13. Clara Arnold, 'His Way', BHA Coll. 0288_05.
14. Begbie, *The Life of General William Booth*, 360.
15. Sandall, *The History of the Salvation Army*, 117.
16. Clara Arnold, 'His Way' BHA Coll. 0288_05.

the various social problems with which they were confronted', but he al-
ways retained a special sense of friendship and love for Army members.[17]
Emmy, too, continued to speak warmly of the Salvation Army, telling
Eberhard in May 1909 of her desire to 'become a truly blessed witness for
Jesus, like Catherine Booth'.[18]

As well as making connections with evangelical life in England
through the Salvation Army, Eberhard and Emmy became involved in
the Young Men's Christian Association (YMCA) and the Young Women's
Christian Association (YWCA) respectively. These organisations began and grew in England in the 1840s and 1850s, eventually spreading
throughout Europe and the United States. While he was a student in
Breslau, Eberhard Arnold led a group of about thirty young men under
the auspices of the local YMCA. A number of these made a commitment to follow Jesus.[19] In Halle, Emmy joined the Young Women's Union,
an association linked with the YWCA, and although she was aware of a
mixture of views in the Union, she found there young women who were
'sisters in Jesus'.[20] Eberhard affirmed her work in the Union, while at the
same time encouraging her to keep in close contact with what they both
saw as a deeper spiritual fellowship to be found in another international
movement, the Evangelical Alliance.[21]

Renewal and Revival Movements

The Evangelical Alliance, which began in London in 1846 as a new endeavour aimed at fostering international and interdenominational Christian unity, spread across mainland Europe and contributed to a vision for
spiritual renewal across denominations.[22] In the 1890s F. B. Meyer, a well-
known English Baptist and the most prominent international figure in
the Keswick Convention holiness movement (the Convention was held

17. Emmy Arnold, *Joyful Pilgrimage*, 4.

18. Emmy von Hollander to Eberhard Arnold, 18 May 1909, Eberhard Arnold and
von Hollander, *Love Letters*, 266.

19. Baum, *Against the Wind*, 43.

20. Emmy von Hollander to Eberhard Arnold, 7 March 1908, Eberhard Arnold
and von Hollander, *Love Letters*, 190.

21. Eberhard Arnold to Emmy von Hollander, 8 March 1908, Eberhard Arnold
and von Hollander, *Love Letters*, 193.

22. For the Evangelical Alliance in Europe see Randall, *One Body in Christ*,
159–182.

annually in the English Lake District town of Keswick), spoke at the German Evangelical Alliance conferences in Bad Blankenburg, south-east of Erfurt.[23] Like other speakers there, he stressed the 'deeper' spiritual life. Meyer was impressed by the remarkable *Gemeinschaftsbewegung* or 'Fellowship meeting' movement in Lutheranism, wondering if it would revive or split the Church.[24]

In Halle, a revival 'Fellowship' had formed, which met on the Alte Promenade (now Paracelsus-Strasse) in the reconstructed studio of a painter. Eberhard Arnold seems to have founded or co-founded this Fellowship. One of the frequent speakers at the Alte Promenade Fellowship was Bernhard Kühn, the secretary of the Evangelical Alliance House in Bad Blankenburg, whose presence in any group brought inspiration. Kühn was a somewhat controversial editor of the *Evangelical Alliance* magazine (*Evangelische Allianzblatt*), at times voicing severe criticisms of the Lutheran Church. Eberhard began to write for the magazine in 1907. In that year he also spoke at the Blankenburg conference.[25]

Along with Kühn, German-born F. W. Baedeker, who had experienced evangelical conversion and become associated in England with the lay-led, non-liturgical Open Brethren assemblies, was also influential in the Blankenburg movement. Kühn, who was also with the Open Brethren, eventually wrote a biography of Baedeker, tracing his remarkable contribution to evangelism and revival in Russia and Germany. Baedeker's assistance in the development of Blankenburg led to his being called the 'Father of the Alliance House'.[26]

German evangelicals also felt the impact of the Welsh Revival, from 1904 to 1905.[27] In 1905 a number of people who were well known in Blankenburg circles visited Wales and were impressed by the prayer, praise, and testimonies there. Among them were Jakob Vetter, a leading tent mission evangelist, and Eva von Tiele-Winckler, a woman from a successful business family who had committed herself to care for homeless children in the Friedenshort (Refuge of Peace).[28] Inspired by his

23. Minutes of the Evangelical Alliance Executive Council, 11 July 1895.

24. Minutes of the Evangelical Alliance Executive Council, 11 July 1895; *Evangelical Alliance Quarterly*, 2 October 1899, 20.

25. Baum, *Against the Wind*, 25–26.

26. See Holthaus, 'Friedrich Wilhelm Baedeker (1823–1906): His Life', in Grass, ed., *Witness in Many Lands*, 59–72.

27. See Evans, *The Welsh Revival of 1904*.

28. Gibbard, *On the Wings of the Dove*, 36–39.

experience in Wales, Vetter held a tent mission in the Ruhr Valley mining area and saw three thousand people profess conversion. When an associate of Vetter's, a fellow German evangelist named Veller, came to visit Halle in March 1908, Emmy reported, 'We distributed about fifty invitations for him in the vocational school today.'[29]

The emergence of Pentecostalism, which emphasised the baptism of the Spirit and gifts such as speaking in tongues, also influenced the Blankenburg movement. The 'father' of continental European Pentecostalism, Thomas B. Barratt, was a British Norwegian Methodist minister and head of the City Mission in Oslo (then Christiania), Norway. Moved by the Welsh Revival, Barratt believed Norwegians, too, longed for the power of the Holy Spirit.[30] In 1906 Barratt encountered Pentecostal spirituality first hand in the United States, and when he returned to Oslo, he arranged Pentecostal meetings at which speaking in tongues and ecstatic experiences produced a considerable stir.[31] The news of what was happening in Oslo caused excitement in Germany, and Jonathan Paul, a Lutheran pastor and tent mission leader who was well respected in the *Gemeinschaftsbewegung*, went to Norway to meet Barratt.[32] After his return, at an evangelistic conference in Brieg in April 1907, Paul reported positively on his experiences while also warning of the need to be discerning.[33] As an indication of how close Eberhard and Emmy were to these developments, in a letter on 4 April, over two weeks before the Brieg conference, Eberhard wrote of how Jonathan Paul had returned from Oslo and had 'told us now about the wonderful revival movement there' in which the Spirit had 'come down with a power as at Pentecost in the Acts of the Apostles; thus people there today speak in strange tongues'. Eberhard continued: 'We—like the brothers and sisters in Norway too—do not want to wish for signs and wonders, but always only for the one thing, that Christ alone be glorified in every way.'[34]

Pentecostalism soon became an international movement, with conferences being held in Sunderland in the north-east of England which

29. Emmy von Hollander to Eberhard Arnold, 7 March 1908, Eberhard and Arnold and von Hollander, *Love Letters*, 190.

30. Barratt, *When the Fire Fell*, 95–97.

31. Bloch-Hoell, *The Pentecostal Movement*, 66–68.

32. Paul Schmidgall, *European Pentecostalism*, 128–129.

33. Simpson, 'The Development of the Pentecostal and Charismatic Movements in the Germanic Countries', in Kay and Dyer, eds., *European Pentecostalism*, 63.

34. Eberhard Arnold to Emmy von Hollander, 4 April 1907. BHA Coll. 0288_02.

drew together leaders from across Europe. The movement, however, was divisive. In Germany, opposition was precipitated by meetings in Kassel in June 1907 at which two young Scandinavian Pentecostal women spoke. There were emotional outbursts which Heinrich Dallmeyer, the evangelist in charge, later said were diabolically inspired.[35] Emmy described in August 1907 how four Swedes 'said they had been urged to come to Halle by the Holy Spirit though they had not even known there was such a town as Halle'. Emmy and her sister, Else, were concerned that the Swedes were focussed not on the cross of Christ but on being filled with the Spirit, an experience which, it seemed to Emmy, 'they try to force'.[36] Yet she told Eberhard: 'We were both blessed!'[37] Eberhard, meanwhile, had been discussing speaking in tongues with 'an older brother from Kassel', who urged caution and considered that the new movement contained 'a mixture of God's and Satan's work'.[38] Two years later, in 1909, leaders in the *Gemeinschaftsbewegung* gathered in Berlin and issued the 'Berlin Declaration', which condemned the Pentecostal movement as 'from below'.[39] Eberhard Arnold, however, never associated himself with this negative view, and continued to stress the power of the Holy Spirit.

Student Ministry

When Eberhard began his theological studies at Breslau, significant Christian student organizations in operation included the German Student Christian Movement (SCM) and the World's Students Christian Federation (WSCF). The German SCM (or DCSV, *Deutsche Christliche Studenten Vereinigung*) was founded in 1885 with the guidance of Count Edouard von Pückler, a lawyer. In 1905, at Breslau University, Eberhard immediately became a member of the SCM, and his involvement continued when he later moved to Halle. Although Pückler was wary of Germans attending international SCM conferences, which he saw as Anglo-Saxon in their ethos, important links were being made across national boundaries. In May 1905 an important conference of the WSCF

---

35. Hollenweger, *The Pentecostals*, 223.

36. Emmy von Hollander to Eberhard Arnold, 9 August 1907. BHA Coll. 0288_02.

37. Emmy von Hollander to Eberhard Arnold, 11 August 1907. BHA Coll. 0288_02.

38. Eberhard Arnold to Emmy von Hollander, 11 August 1907. BHA Coll. 0288_02.

39. Simpson, 'The Development of the Pentecostal and Charismatic Movements in the Germanic Countries', in Kay and Dyer, eds., *European Pentecostalism*, 65.

was held in Zeist in the Netherlands, at the Moravian community head-quarters, where it was decided that the next conference would be held in Japan. Despite resistance from some, the international student vision was gradually being realised.[40]

Eberhard attended his first SCM conference in August 1905 in Wernigerode (about seventy miles north-west of Halle), with his sister Clara. German universities had only begun to accept women four years previously, and at this conference a women's branch of the SCM was formed. Clara Arnold spoke of the 'enthusiastic love of Jesus' and the 'deep unity' among the students at Wernigerode. Memorable addresses were delivered by Karl Heim, later a professor of Dogmatics at Münster and Tübingen Universities, and by R. A. Torrey, an American evangelist and writer who undertook evangelistic campaigns similar to those of D. L. Moody in the nineteenth century. Torrey spoke of 'the personal experience of the Spirit's power' and of the experience of 'baptism by the Spirit', giving examples from Moody's life and ministry in America and Britain.[41] Later Eberhard encouraged Emmy to read Torrey 'over and over again with much praying'.[42] Emmy immediately took his advice and found Torrey's book *How to Obtain Fullness of Power* a great help.[43] Eberhard considered books written by Torrey and by an earlier American evangelist and social reformer, Charles Finney, as among those that had 'meant most blessing for my life'.[44]

In 1906, Eberhard was elected chairman of the Halle branch of the SCM, and in his inaugural address, on 26 April, he set out in powerful terms his vision, one that was not his own construction but expressed the heart of his evangelical spirituality. 'We ourselves have experienced', he stated, 'that Jesus has taken away our sins and given a new strength. He alone is the firm, saving ground for the anchorless wrecks that are flung back and forth by the opinions and currents of the present day.' The task was 'to place Him in the midst of the world that ridicules Him and says He is finished'. Eberhard's vision went beyond Germany, as he asserted: 'Many thousands of students on all continents gather around the cross of Jesus and spur one another on to be faithful and resolute in the great

40. Rouse, *The World's Student Christian Federation*, 106–107.

41. Baum, *Against the Wind*, 19.

42. Eberhard Arnold to Emmy von Hollander, 4 April 1907. BHA Coll. 0288_02.

43. Emmy von Hollander to Eberhard Arnold, 7 and 8 April 1907. BHA Coll. 0288_02.

44. Eberhard Arnold to Emmy von Hollander, 25 April 1907. BHA Coll. 0288_02.

struggle of the great King.' In Germany, the challenge was for the SCM to avoid being another Christian sect. Rather, the goal was to be 'a missionizing power for every circle of our universities' and to 'unite Christians of all shadings under the banner of Jesus'. Eberhard concluded in stirring tones: 'The whole Christ of the whole Scripture is the one whom we want to serve with whole hearts! Jesus alone! is the motto of our Union. We know that we no longer belong to ourselves, but that He has bought us for God with his blood!'[45] Eberhard was soon speaking at conferences across Germany. At the SCM conference in August 1907, he spoke on Jesus as Son of God, demanding submission and faith, and Jesus as Son of Man, demanding discipleship. However, he was dissatisfied with how he communicated, telling Emmy that 'I fell into my old excitement. . . and therefore left out half of what I wanted to say'.[46]

As well as being offered speaking opportunities, Eberhard was asked to become a student member of the German SCM's national executive committee. In it he worked closely with Ludwig von Gerdtell, a strongly evangelistic travelling secretary for the German SCM from 1902 to 1908. Eberhard was impressed by the way in which talks by von Gerdtell were bringing about profound changes in the lives of students. Von Gerdtell also spent time in personal conversation with students who wanted spiritual and theological guidance. Within SCM there were different approaches to theological issues, and Eberhard admired von Gerdtell's uncompromising stance. (By contrast, Eberhard found the more eminent Karl Heim, whom he also came to know, overly willing to accommodate a variety of viewpoints.[47]) Committed to evangelism in Germany, von Gerdtell also wished to bring the challenge of world mission, a theme that was close to the centre of the student movement.

In 1901, in Halle, the SCM had held a remarkable missionary convention. Von Gerdtell later visited the Far East, and in 1907, at what Eberhard called 'a splendid mission meeting', there were reports on missionary work by speakers from America, China, and Germany, including von Gerdtell. The challenge of China was especially strong, not least because the student world was aware of the 'Cambridge Seven', who had

45. Eberhard Arnold, Inauguration speech on taking over the chair of the Halle DCSV, 26 April 1906, enclosed with letter Eberhard Arnold to Emmy von Hollander, 2 July 1907. BHA Coll. 0288_02.

46. Eberhard Arnold to Emmy von Hollander, 9 August 1907. BHA Coll. 0288_02.

47. Eberhard Arnold to Emmy von Hollander, 23 June 1907. BHA Coll. 0288_02; Eberhard Arnold to Emmy von Hollander, 12 August 1907. BHA Coll. 0288_02.

joined the China Inland Mission in the 1880s. Eberhard was open to the possibility of going to China. However, General von Viebahn, an evangelist connected with Blankenburg and the SCM who knew of Eberhard's ambitions, urged him 'for now to remain faithful to the student work'.[48]

Being faithful turned out to be difficult. Tensions were building in August 1907 at SCM meetings chaired by Count Pückler. Eberhard was concerned that the German SCM would move away from the 'clear witness'—including, especially, witness to the authority of scripture—which he saw as vital. In words that echoed the Moravian motto, Eberhard averred that 'we are going on staunchly, following the Lamb wherever He goes'.[49] Tension within the SCM came to a head in October 1907. Eberhard wrote to Emmy on 9 October to inform her of the 'colossal struggle' ahead in the near future in the SCM and the possibility that he and others might be forced 'by the dishonest position of the others in regard to the basis and to the Bible, to make a complete break. . . and to form a new Executive Committee'. He realised that this episode had the potential to divide the whole national movement. In addition, some wanted Eberhard to succeed Count Pückler as chairman.[50]

Eberhard sent a strongly-worded statement to the SCM's Executive Committee members alleging that 'the absolute authority of Scripture has been attacked by some members of the Committee'. The statement argued that 'if the Second Letter of Peter could have been composed by an impostor, if no definite limits are set by us to Old Testament criticism, our confessional adherence to the basis will then be merely a matter of form and will lead to an insincerity and hypocrisy which must frighten the Spirit of God away from our work'.[51]

Similar tensions were evident in this period in the SCM in Britain. The Cambridge Inter-Collegiate Christian Union (CICCU), which had been influential in student ministry since its beginning in 1877, split from the national SCM body in 1910. CICCU was opposed to higher criticism of the Bible, looked for spiritual inspiration and a spiritual challenge to the Keswick Convention, and saw student evangelism as its

---

48. Eberhard Arnold to Emmy von Hollander, 11 August 1907. BHA Coll. 0288_02.

49. Eberhard Arnold to Emmy von Hollander, 11 and 12 August 1907. BHA Coll. 0288_02.

50. Eberhard Arnold to Emmy von Hollander, 9 October 1907. BHA Coll. 0288_02.

51. Statement to the Executive Committee of the DCSV, enclosed with letter, Eberhard Arnold to Count Pückler, 8 October 1907. BHA Coll. 0288_02.

primary objective.[52] All these sympathies were present in Eberhard Arnold, who resigned from the Executive Committee of the German SCM, but continued to work within the movement.

In January 1908, as Eberhard prepared to submit his doctoral thesis in theology, a number of Blankenburg leaders gave him their united opinion that he 'must work in Germany, as an evangelist or student leader or student worker'.[53] Several options were put to him, and Eberhard accepted a part-time position as the secretary of the SCM in Halle. The work he did among students and others grew, and between 1910 and 1913 he travelled extensively, often for a week or more at a time, giving very effective evangelistic lectures in cities such as Hamburg, Leipzig, Magdeburg, and Erfurt. It was not unusual for hundreds of people to attend his lectures. He also continued to publish articles in the *Evangelical Alliance* magazine.[54] Eberhard seemed destined to play a major role in evangelical life in Germany and perhaps beyond.

Church Commitment

While Eberhard had wished early on to study medicine and become a doctor, Eberhard's father felt strongly that his son should study theology and become a Lutheran pastor. Carl Franklin's insistence sowed, in part, the seeds of what would become Eberhard's dissent from the state church. In 1901 Eberhard began to take an interest in movements of renewal and change in church history, especially the sixteenth-century Reformation, and this study of church history was something his father encouraged. The movement that most attracted Eberhard was, however, a radical one: Anabaptism. Although Anabaptist groups differed somewhat, nearly all advocated re-baptism—based on the rejection of the validity of infant baptism—and rejected a state church in favour of a community of committed disciples. Eberhard became especially interested in a communitarian Anabaptist movement led by Jakob Hutter. Eberhard found in Anabaptism a movement that spoke to him about how to follow Jesus.

52. Goodhew, 'The Rise of the Cambridge Inter-Collegiate Christian Union, 1910–1971', 64; Barclay, *Whatever Happened to the Jesus Lane Lot?*, 69–70.

53. Eberhard Arnold to Emmy von Hollander, 26 January 1908. BHA Coll. 0288_02.

54. Baum, *Against the Wind*, 63, 76.

Anabaptism's view of the church as a community of committed disciples also cast doubt on the idea of a state church.[55]

The revival in Halle in 1907 further challenged Eberhard's thinking about the church and in particular about the sacraments. A number of those affected by the revival began to question infant baptism and to promote the baptism of believers as the true expression of baptism. In their correspondence, Eberhard and Emmy wrote about the relationship of conversion to baptism and the nature of a church community. In May 1907 Eberhard saw infant baptism as 'willed by Jesus and God'.[56] In mid-June 1907, however, he told Emmy that through his further reading of scripture he could no longer find 'compelling proof *for* infant baptism'.[57] Writing again to Emmy later in June he emphasised that he wanted to reach a 'calm, clearly reasoned conviction' on the issue. As he saw it, if he was suddenly baptised (or re-baptised, as the Lutheran Church viewed it) as an adult, people would say, 'First the Salvation Army and now baptism. He's always going to extremes! It's because of his temperament!'[58] On 4 September 1907, he told Emmy that he had 'been convinced by God, with quiet and sober biblical certainty, that baptism of believers alone is justified'.[59] On 13 September Eberhard wrote to Emmy to say that he was going to 'withdraw from the established [Lutheran] church since I consider it as dishonest through and through and contrary to the spirit of the Bible'. He wished instead to embrace 'church communities of believing, baptized children of God, with church discipline and the Lord's Supper'.[60]

Eberhard's new position meant that he would not enter the Lutheran Church ministry. This aroused considerable hostility towards him from his own parents and from Emmy's parents. Unwilling to be a Lutheran pastor and wanting to be baptised as a believer, he was disqualified, in 1908, from sitting his doctoral examinations in theology. Eberhard

55. Baum, *Against the Wind*, 14–15.

56. Eberhard Arnold to Emmy von Hollander, 11 May 1907, Eberhard Arnold and von Hollander, *Love Letters*, 56.

57. Eberhard Arnold to Emmy von Hollander, 16 June 1907, Eberhard Arnold and von Hollander, *Love Letters*, 91–92.

58. Eberhard Arnold to Emmy von Hollander, 29–30 June 1907, Eberhard and Arnold and von Hollander, *Love Letters*, 103.

59. Baum, *Against the Wind*, 33–35. Eberhard to Emmy, 4 September 1907, Eberhard and Arnold and von Hollander, *Love Letters*, 132–133.

60. Eberhard Arnold to Emmy von Hollander, 13 September 1907, Eberhard and Arnold and von Hollander, *Love Letters*, 145.

thought about joining a Baptist congregation and told Emmy: 'I shall seek to get to know the German Baptist churches since they have very biblical principles, and shall perhaps, even if not very probably, join them later, since their confession, and to a lesser extent their life, is very much in keeping with my ideal.'[61] He wrote about being 'deeply refreshed' by *All of Grace*, a book by the leading English Baptist pastor, C. H. Spurgeon. But Emmy pointed out that baptism was required for every Baptist member, and Eberhard concluded that although this was the position in the early church, with the variety of views that now existed such a requirement was sectarian. Baptism, as he saw it, was part of the response to Jesus by an individual, but should only happen when a person recognised this as their pathway.[62] Else von Hollander, Emmy's sister, was baptised in August 1908, and in October Eberhard—in spite of strong opposition from his family—was baptised in Halle, in the White Elster River, by a Leipzig doctor, Gotthelf Müller.[63] Emmy's baptism took place in December, in the Blücher Fellowship in Berlin, which had close links with the Evangelical Alliance.[64] Their baptisms represented a public break with the Lutheran Church.

The sense of unity between British Baptists and German Baptists was growing in this period. A conference of European Baptists was held in Berlin in 1908, the first of its kind. It attracted eighteen hundred people. In the lead-up to the conference, an English Baptist minister, Newton Marshall, preached a sermon in his church in London on 'Europe—the Desire of the Christ', speaking about the great history of Europe and the sad reality that the 'real gods of the people' now seemed to be militarism, which he called 'the spear that stabbed Jesus Christ', and 'mammon'. His sermon was published and widely read.[65] Eberhard, meanwhile, was forming his own opinion of German Baptist life. He reported to Emmy on 7 October 1907 that one friend from the SCM had 'told me deeply sad things about conditions among the Baptists'. It was enough to convince

61. Eberhard Arnold to Emmy von Hollander, 13 September 1907. BHA Coll. 0288_02.

62. Eberhard Arnold to Emmy von Hollander, 16 September 1907. BHA Coll. 0288_02.

63. Emmy von Hollander to Eberhard Arnold, 19 October 1908, cited by Baum, *Against the Wind*, 49.

64. Emmy Arnold, 'From our Life', unpublished memoirs, cited by Baum, *Against the Wind*, 51.

65. Marshall, *Baptist Times*, 20 September 1907, 691.

him that he could not belong to their movements.[66] Two days later he was pleased to tell Emmy that in the Baptist newspaper *Witness to Truth* there was an account of Eberhard speaking at Blankenburg. The newspaper approved of Eberhard, who was described as a 'fiery, Christocentric speaker'.[67]

In 1909, Eberhard completed a philosophy doctoral thesis, on Friedrich Nietzsche, and graduated *summa cum laude*. Soon he and Emmy were married and set up home in Leipzig.[68] After their marriage, they held a weekly Bible study meeting attracting up to twenty people in their home. There was also part-time work for Eberhard in the Alte Promenade Fellowship in Halle. In addition, there were opportunities to undertake pastoral ministry and give sermons and lectures to groups linked to Gotthelf Müller, who had baptised Eberhard. In 1910 the couple moved to Halle, so that they could give more time to the Alte Promenade Fellowship. For the next three years Eberhard combined this ministry with a demanding schedule as a travelling evangelist.[69]

In the spring of 1913, Eberhard became seriously ill with tuberculosis, and for the sake of his health, he and Emmy and their children, Emi-Margret and Eberhard (Hardy), who would later be joined by Heinrich (Heini), Hans-Hermann, and Monika, moved to the Tyrol. There had been Anabaptist communities in the region since the early sixteenth century, and the Arnolds began to pay greater attention to Anabaptist figures such as Hans Denck, Balthasar Hubmaier, and Jakob Hutter.[70] Many Anabaptists, including the Mennonites (named after their leader, Menno Simons), encouraged mutual aid within communities, but it was the Hutterites (called after Hutter) who implemented community of goods.[71] In his *Confession of Faith*, Peter Riedemann, a successor of Hutter, argued that those freed from 'created things' could grasp 'what is true and divine'.[72] Eberhard and Emmy were fascinated by this thinking and by Anabaptist stories. They studied records relating to Hutter preserved

---

66. Eberhard Arnold to Emmy von Hollander, 7 October 1907. BHA Coll. 0288_02.

67. Eberhard Arnold to Emmy von Hollander, 9 October 1907. BHA Coll. 0288_02.

68. Emmy Arnold, *Joyful Pilgrimage*, 13–15.

69. Baum, *Against the Wind*, 59–63.

70. Emmy Arnold, *Joyful Pilgrimage*, 17–18.

71. For the early Hutterites see Hutterian Brethren, *The Chronicle of the Hutterian Brethren*; Stayer, *The German Peasants' War and Anabaptist Community of Goods*; Packull, *Hutterite Beginnings*.

72. Riedemann, *Confession of Faith*, 90.

in local archives.[73] At the time they did not know that the Hutterites still existed as communities in America; within two decades, Eberhard would be a Hutterite elder based in Europe.

Justice and Peace

Eberhard Arnold wrestled not only with the issue of authenticity in church life, but also issues connected with society. His social conscience had been stirred through his involvement with the Salvation Army and also through reading about the faith of George Müller and his extensive orphanage work in England. Having read a biography of Müller—which Eberhard called 'a glorious, deep book'—Eberhard said in 1908 that he wanted to live 'from faith alone'.[74] Two years later he was decisively affected by reading the book *They Must!* by Hermann Kutter, a Reformed Church pastor in Zürich. Eberhard resonated with the idea that inner spiritual life thrives and blossoms in practical life, and with the vision of the kingdom of God as an expression of God's concern for a just society.[75] In the same year that Eberhard read Kutter, a British Baptist, Richard Heath, produced English translations of three of Kutter's works under the title *Social Democracy*. Heath affirmed Kutter's challenge to the churches to seek a 'just society' along with seeking individual conversions. Heath's own work wedded an Anabaptist ideal of church as community 'to the goal of creating a democratic socialist society'.[76]

In the 1910s, the international student movement stressed not only evangelism but also social issues. Following on from the historic World Missionary Conference in Edinburgh in 1910, an international student conference was held in Liverpool in 1912 on 'Foreign Missions and Social Problems'. Its report was entitled *Christ and Human Need*.[77] Co-operation between Christian leaders in Germany and England was increasing even in the face of growing political tensions. By 1914, *The Peacemaker*, edited by Baptist leader J. H. Rushbrooke, had achieved a circulation of about

73. Baum, *Against the Wind*, 73.

74. Eberhard Arnold to Emmy von Hollander, 31 August 1908, Eberhard and Arnold and von Hollander, *Love Letters*, 232.

75. Baum, *Against the Wind*, 67–69.

76. Heath, *Social Democracy*, 9; Heath, *Anabaptism*, 193. See Briggs, 'Richard Heath, 1831–1912', in Briggs and Cross, eds., *Freedom and the Powers*, 69–84.

77. Rouse, *The World's Student Christian Federation*, 136–139.

sixty-seven thousand and was a mouthpiece for those concerned about international peace and reconciliation.[78] The war's outbreak, however, brought almost all peace initiatives to an end.

One of those most involved in arranging significant church delegations from Germany to Britain and vice versa was Friedrich Siegmund-Schultze, whom Eberhard knew from his student days. When war was declared, Siegmund-Schultze was among 150 delegates at an international conference in Constance intent on establishing a 'World Alliance for Promoting International Friendship through the Churches'. The conference had to be hurriedly abandoned as European borders began to close. Siegmund-Schultze said farewell to Henry Hodgkin, the secretary of the Quaker body, the Friends' Foreign Missionary Association, who was leaving Constance to return to England. The assurance mutually given was that 'nothing is changed between us. We are one in Christ and can never be at war.'[79]

Eberhard Arnold, however, did not at that time share these sentiments. In 1914 his book, *Inward Life* (which eventually became *Innerland*), was nearing publication, but in view of the war he revised it, introducing patriotic themes and changing the title to *The War: A Call to Inwardness*. The cover design and, in part, its contents aligned it with books being produced to support what was seen as Germany's 'just and righteous war'.[80] Eberhard expressed a willingness to join a German reserve unit in August 1914, but his health was not strong enough. In the early stages of the war Eberhard voiced strident anti-English and anti-American sentiments. He spoke of 'inward powers collapsed and buried in England and America'. England, as he saw it, was a place of 'greed and envy', characterised by living for 'advancement, pleasure and enjoyment'. He rejoiced that the war had made possible a 'release from the superficiality of English hymns'. His earlier appreciation of evangelical authors from England and America seemed to vanish, as did his sense of being spiritually helped through the many hymns sung at Blankenburg that had been translated from English.[81]

---

78. *Baptist Times*, 6 January 1914, 24; Clements, 'Baptists and the Outbreak of the First World War', 80.

79. Wallis, *Valiant for Peace*, 3–5; cf. Clements, 'An Alliance for International Friendship', in Fiddes, ed., 'A World-Order of Love', 9–29.

80. Baum, *Against the Wind*, 80–81.

81. Baum, *Against the Wind*, 83–85.

Eberhard's strongly patriotic sentiments were typical of most SCM leaders and members in Germany. In September 1914 Tissington Tatlow, general secretary of the British SCM, received a strongly nationalistic letter from his German counterpart saying that all German Christians were ready to give their lives for this 'just war' and that 60 percent of SCM members were already fighting. The British nation, in their eyes, had 'betrayed the white race' by supporting Russia. Nonetheless, this letter, which had been approved by the head of the German SCM, Georg Michaelis, an academic and government official, hoped that international brotherhood could continue.[82]

In late summer of 1915, Michaelis asked Eberhard to serve SCM in several capacities: as SCM's literary adviser; as an editor for the movement's magazine, *Die Furche* (The Furrow); and in developing the Furche Publishing House. Siegmund-Schultze, the previous SCM editor, had recommended Eberhard. The SCM rented a house for the Arnold family in Berlin. The scope of the work was considerable. SCM was producing hundreds of thousands of copies of books and other publications going to readers all over Germany, to those fighting at the front, and to German prisoner of war camps in other countries. The SCM conferences at Wernigerode continued, although on a smaller scale.

It seems, however, that in 1917 Eberhard's nationalistic sentiments began to fade. At revival meetings in Berlin he began to speak of the human condition of suffering in all countries, not only in Germany. As he now saw it, everyone needed to experience love and unity, not division.[83] Before the end of 1917 he began to revise his book, which he retitled *Innerland*. The revised version of the book, a journey into the 'inner land of the unseen, to God and the Spirit' and a 'guide into the soul of the Bible', incorporated ideas designed to promote peace and reconciliation. It was published by SCM in July 1918 and revision would continue. The nationalistic sections had been removed, and the text that remained offered a preview of Eberhard's future as an advocate of Christian communal life that transcended boundaries of class and country.[84]

---

82. Tatloe, *The Story of the Student Christian Movement*, 519–20. Michaelis was German chancellor for four months in 1917.

83. Baum, *Against the Wind*, 85–91.

84. Baum, *Against the Wind*, 93.

2

Connections in England after WWI

After the horrors of the First World War, Eberhard Arnold's thinking moved decisively in the direction of a Christian witness that prioritized peace and community. In July 1919, he wrote from Berlin to Otto Herpel, a Lutheran pastor in Lissberg, to say that he was finding 'the Jesus of the Sermon on the Mount' to be 'closer and more real'. He continued, with the war and its aftermath very much in mind: 'What though the whole world around us is full of murderous intent and mammonistic injustice—we oppose the militaristic and capitalistic abuses with the spirit of love and justice.' Eberhard knew that Herpel had embraced pacifism. A movement seemed to be taking shape which was larger than a few individuals. Eberhard was delighted to inform Herpel that he was in touch with 'several hundred' people who were thinking in the same way, and who had come 'very near founding an actual community'. Meanwhile Eberhard attempted to convey 'this new awakening of the Spirit of Jesus'.[1]

Eberhard's evolving perspective caused tensions in his role within the German SCM. Some opposed him, while to others his message was liberating. As well as connecting with Germans who shared his vision, Eberhard and Emmy were renewing their international networks, which had been a valued part of their lives before the war. They hosted SCM members, people from revival fellowships, members of the youth movement, and English Quakers at their house in Berlin in 1919.[2] These

1. Eberhard Arnold to Otto Herpel, 2 July 1919. BHA Coll. 0288_02.
2. Emmy Arnold, *Joyful Pilgrimage*, 26; Baum, *Against the Wind*, 100, 148.

connections would form the basis for a Bruderhof community beginning in 1936 in Wiltshire—the Cotswold Bruderhof.

Common Ground

On 1 April 1920, Eberhard Arnold wrote to Otto Herpel about an important recent development, which was a publishing agreement he had made with English members of the Society of Friends, the Quakers.[3] In October 1919 Eberhard had taken up the post of full-time SCM secretary and continued—as he had done since 1915—to work as editor of *Die Furche*. He regularly spoke at conferences, and at one event organised by Herpel, in September 1919, in Tambach, Eberhard followed Karl Barth, the Swiss theologian. While Eberhard stressed the possibility of taking action in the world, for Barth the task of the Christian was simply to 'pay careful heed to what God is doing.'[4]

Eberhard resigned as SCM secretary in January 1920, effective from 1 April. He explained: 'I could not see the possibility of carrying out my literary plans while working for the Furche Publishing House, especially in so far as these plans had a socialist and pacifist tendency.' He felt he could now be 'free and undisturbed in representing the living, free Christianity which means both personal salvation and God's will in action for our fellow men'. Eberhard wished to 'strengthen the inwardly free, living movement for Christ' within the student movement.[5] However, his priority became working with Otto Herpel in producing a newspaper, *Das Neue Werk* (The New Work), and in the Neuwerk Publishing House which Herpel had set up in Schlüchtern, about forty miles north-east of Frankfurt.[6]

The Society of Friends stated that they would consider Neuwerk their publishing house in Germany. Eberhard wanted to publish an article by a leading English Quaker, Joan Mary Fry, entitled 'Friendship and Freedom'. An extra 3,000 copies would be printed for use by the Quakers.[7] Fry, an important figure in early twentieth-century Quaker life, had

3. Eberhard Arnold to Otto Herpel, 1 April 1920. BHA Coll. 0288_02. Quakers in Britain numbered about 20,000.

4. Vollmer, *Neuwerk* , 21.

5. Eberhard Arnold to Karl Müller, 20 April 1920. BHA Coll. 0288_02.

6. Baum, *Against the Wind*, 112–114.

7. Eberhard Arnold to Otto Herpel, 1 April 1920. BHA Coll. 0288_02. The title in

served as a prison chaplain during the First World War and had helped conscientious objectors. After the Treaty of Versailles was signed in June 1919, Fry and three other Quakers from England made their way to Germany. This group, together with Quakers from the United States, were the first from 'enemy countries' to visit Germany. In Britain their desire to help Germany was met with hostility, and in Germany they initially encountered suspicion. Friedrich Siegmund-Schultze, who was committed to communal Christian social action, became their advocate.[8] Elizabeth Fox Howard, one of the English Quakers in Berlin, spoke of how, alongside relief work, the Quakers tried to carry 'a quiet and unostentatious message of friendship and reconciliation'.[9] The Berlin Quaker team provided basic help for students and assisted with food distribution. The Arnold family's children were among those who received food through the Quakers' programme.[10]

Eberhard was keen to promote the work Fry was doing in Germany. He hoped that contacts he had in Marburg would arrange meetings for Fry, who planned to visit in April 1920. In writing to them he was enthusiastic in his description of the Society of Friends, 'this mighty Christian movement of spiritual awakening' which for several centuries had 'fought for peace and justice, and is now doing an immense amount of good work throughout Germany, chiefly for women and children and sick people'. With his SCM involvement in mind, Eberhard suggested that a meeting for students could be arranged in Marburg, at which Joan Mary Fry could 'tell them about the Quaker movement in England, and about the extensive relief work it is carrying out in Germany'. His consciousness of being part of something emerging and his developing transnational sense were clear when he spoke enthusiastically of the Quakers as standing 'very close to our movement'.[11]

English was *For Fellowship and Freedom: Some Aspects of the Society of Friends* (1908). It was published in German as *Freundschaft und Freiheit: einige Gesichtspunkte zum Verständnis der Gesellschaft der Freunde.*

8. For her experiences see Fry, *In Downcast Germany*. See also Schmitt, *Quakers and Nazis*, 13–14.

9. Cited by Borries, *Quiet Helpers*, 26. Fawell, *Joan Mary Fry*, 38, also speaks about the Friends arriving quietly in Germany.

10. Mommsen, *Homage to a Broken Man*, 16.

11. Letter written on behalf of Eberhard Arnold to Karl Sommer, Marburg, 14 April 1920. BHA Coll. 0288_02.

Seeking common ground with international movements, Eberhard hoped that Neuwerk could become known in Germany for 'representing related movements in England'. He was interested in forging a connection with Wilfred Wellock, a Methodist lay preacher in England who had launched, in 1916, a Christian revolutionary journal, the *New Crusader*, published by 'the Committee for the Promotion of Pacifism'.[12] Eberhard's connections with Fry would prove much stronger than those with Wellock, but the Peace Pledge Union (PPU) in England, which Wellock had co-founded, would be significant for the Cotswold Bruderhof.[13]

In an invitation Eberhard Arnold sent out for a mountaintop conference on the Inselberg in March 1920, he said that he wanted to encourage a 'free movement of young people for Christ'.[14] Following this March conference, which gathered members of the Youth Movement, SCM members, and those from revolutionary and workers' groups, another important conference took place, a Whitsun (Pentecost) conference at Schlüchtern. Along with Otto Herpel, a friend of Eberhard's in Schlüchtern, Georg Flemmig, a schoolteacher, had been seeking to pioneer an 'early church' movement. This had attracted the interest of Eberhard, Emmy, and Else. At the conference, Eberhard took up the themes of the 'Mystery of the Early Church' and linked with that the spirit of Pentecost.[15] The influence of another English Quaker, John Stephens, was apparent during the conference. Stephens had studied in Frankfurt and visited France, Holland, Czechoslovakia, Poland, and Italy, seeking to understand more of the European situation. He suggested—from his Quaker spiritual tradition—a silent meeting as part of the conference, commenting, 'You Germans still talk far too much'. His suggestion was half an hour of silence 'to listen to the Spirit'. Immediately an elderly academic present began a long speech, to which Stephens replied 'Hush', which was not well received by the professor but provoked general mirth among the young people.[16] In Eberhard's experience, the feeling of 'inner contact' with the Quakers was growing.[17] Stephens, who would take up

12. Eberhard Arnold to Otto Herpel, 1 April 1920. BHA Coll. 0288_02. For his story see Wellock, *Off the Beaten Track*.

13. See chapter 3.

14. Baum, *Against the Wind*, 117.

15. Eberhard Arnold, 'Das Geheimnis der Urgemeinde', printed in *Das Neue Werk*, no. 20–21, 160; cf. Baum, *Against the Wind*, 123.

16. Emmy Arnold, *Joyful Pilgrimage*, 34–35.

17. Eberhard Arnold to Max Luckow, 2 June 1920. BHA Coll. 0288_02.

a post as lecturer in history at Birmingham University, would become a significant Bruderhof contact.

Following the conference, Eberhard and Emmy and some young people walked from Schlüchtern to nearby Ahlersbach. They stopped at the village of Sannerz, to make enquires about a house that they had heard might be available which they hoped might be suitable for a community. They were directed to a fifteen-room brick villa, and after weeks of discussion a rental agreement for ten years was signed. The community life they had envisaged took concrete form in Sannerz in June 1920. Initially the core group was small: Eberhard and Emmy, with their five children; Else von Hollander; and also Suse Hungar, a Salvation Army captain and teacher. Others visited and some soon joined. The community was dedicated to work and worship, with the first celebration of the Lord's Supper taking place on 26 September 1920.[18]

Meanwhile, in England there was more and more interest in Eberhard's work. He told Herpel on 9 June 1920 that he had been invited to England 'for an interdenominational Christian gathering', at which twelve denominations would be represented, to discuss topics connected with 'socialism and pacifism'. In addition, he had been invited by the Quakers to their important Yearly Meeting in England. He was disappointed that he was not going to be able to accept these invitations as the local work based in Sannerz was 'growing all the time'. Eberhard hoped that Elizabeth Staiger, who had written a report about the Schlüchtern conference, might be invited by the Quakers in his place.[19]

Eberhard Arnold also found common ground in the years after WWI with the Fellowship of Reconciliation (FoR), which had started in England in December 1914, in part as a follow-up to the conference in Constance in August of that year. With Henry Hodgkin's encouragement, Quakers drew up a 'Message to Men and Woman of Goodwill' that appeared in leading newspapers and was printed widely. In Germany it was circulated by Siegmund-Schultze.[20] The December 1914 conference which launched FoR, held in Cambridge over four days, was attended by 130 people, invited 'to consider the basis from which all our discussions will start, namely that intuitive certainty which we share that all war is contrary to the mind of Christ'. The prime movers at this stage

18. Baum, *Against the Wind*, 123–30. Emmy Arnold, *Joyful Pilgrimage*, 36–40.
19. Eberhard Arnold to Otto Herpel, 9 June 1920. BHA Coll. 0288_02.
20. Brittain, *Rebel Passion*, 31.

were Hodgkin; Richard Roberts, a London Presbyterian minister; Lucy Gardner, a Quaker; and Maude Royden, a pioneer of women's roles in church ministry. Joan Mary Fry edited the main conference papers.[21] FoR's principles included the belief that 'as Christians, we are forbidden to wage war, and that loyalty to our country, to humanity, to the Church Universal, and to Jesus Christ, our Lord and Master, calls us instead to a life-service for the enthronement of Love in personal, social, commercial and national life'.[22] The movement was 'open to all . . . who wished to promote a spirit of Christian Reconciliation', and it grew steadily. By November 1915, 1,550 had registered as members; there were nearly 7,000 members by the end of the war.[23]

The British FoR led to the creation in 1919 of the International Fellowship of Reconciliation (IFoR), known initially as the 'Movement towards a Christian International'. The first conference attracted fifty people from ten countries and was held at Bilthoven, near Utrecht, in the Netherlands. Henry Hodgkin was again central, together with Kees Boeke, a Dutch violinist from a Mennonite background who had joined the Quakers in England. Boeke was married to Beatrice ('Betty') Cadbury, the daughter of Richard Cadbury, one of two Quaker brothers who had established a chocolate business in Birmingham and who sought to provide good working and living conditions for their employees. Betty and Kees spent time in Syria, in education, and later founded Brotherhood House in Bilthoven, where the IFoR conference was held. Among the participants were Siegmund-Schultze; Mathilda Wrede, a Finnish baroness known for her evangelistic work and her involvement in rehabilitation of prisoners; Pierre Cérésole, a Quaker from Switzerland who founded the International Voluntary Service for Peace; and Lilian Stevenson from England, who said: 'We met as strangers; we parted a Fellowship.'[24]

Eberhard was invited, but the invitation never reached him, and when he received an invitation to a second IFoR conference in the following year it was too late to arrange a travel permit. However, in June 1920

21. Fry, ed., *Christ and Peace.*

22. Holliday, ed., *FoR: 100 Years of Nonviolence*, 8.

23. Wallis, *Valiant for Peace*, 7–8; Brittain, *Rebel Passion*, 33–36. Baum, *Against the Wind*, is incorrect in saying that it was Quakers who formed FoR, 148.

24. Brittain, *Rebel Passion*, 43–44. For Betty Cadbury see Joseph, *Beatrice: The Cadbury Heiress Who Gave Away Her Fortune.* For Mathilda Wrede see Stevenson, *Mathilda Wrede of Finland.*

Lilian Stevenson, who had been active in SCM and who had pioneered SCM work among art students, attracted the FoR's attention to *Das Neue Werk*, stating that in a number of its articles it 'breathed the same spirit and stood for the same ideals as the Fellowship'.[25] Eberhard responded by welcoming FoR's 'clear expression of the Spirit at work in us; we have scarcely ever met with such a clear expression apart from our own circles'. He expressed eagerness to publish FoR material and invited those at Bilthoven in 1920 to a forthcoming Neuwerk conference in Marburg.[26]

John Stephens and Joan Mary Fry, meanwhile, were making contacts in SCM and Evangelical Alliance circles. Stephens described meeting one young pastor, Otto Roth, who had come back from Bilthoven 'full of enthusiasm'. Stephens commented that Roth would suffer for his new-found pacifist faith.[27] Walther Koch, a German Quaker, sought ideas from Eberhard about those in the Neuwerk circle who might support FoR, and in August 1920 Eberhard suggested people from SCM; from Bible groups; from Lutheran, Baptist, and Mennonite churches; and from the Evangelical Alliance. Eberhard particularly emphasised the role of the Evangelical Alliance, which, he said, 'stands for Christianity in the sense of the mystical Body of Christ, in the sense of the unity of true believers', and he spoke warmly of the Blankenburg conferences, saying that he had spoken there several times and that they attracted people from England, Russia, and America.[28]

On the same day as he wrote to Koch, Eberhard wrote to Lilian Stevenson with the hope that 'the financial basis of the [Neuwerk] publishing house should be laid by brothers and sisters who are of one mind with us'.[29] He was probably aware that Stevenson, a wealthy woman, gave generously to FoR.[30] A letter to Corder Catchpool, an English Quaker working in Berlin, followed, again mentioning financial needs. Eberhard ended his letter to Catchpool: 'Heartfelt greetings in the fellowship of

25. Minutes of the International Committee of FoR, 1 June 1920, COLL MISC 0456/5/5, FoR Archive, London School of Economics.

26. Eberhard Arnold to the Bilthoven conference for a Christian International, Bilthoven, Holland, 20 July 1920. BHA Coll. 0288_02.

27. John Stephens, 26 October 1919, to Friends. 'Relief Mission Germany', FEWURC/MISSIONS/10/1/6/11, Friends Archive, London.

28. Eberhard Arnold to Walther Koch, 16 August 1920. BHA Coll. 0288_02.

29. Eberhard Arnold to Lilian Stevenson, 16 August 1920. BHA Coll. 0288_02.

30. Brittain, *Rebel Passion*, 80–81.

the same Spirit'.[31] Catchpool had suffered in prison during the war as a conscientious objector. Like Joan Mary Fry, he had moved to Berlin afterwards to undertake relief work.[32]

Lilian Stevenson and Corder Catchpool both purchased shares in the Neuwerk Publishing Association, the first people from outside Germany to do so. Writing to Catchpool in September 1920, Eberhard made a point of stressing that 'we are one with you [Quakers] in everything essential' and spoke of his appreciation of the Quaker publication, *Schweigende Andacht* (Silent Worship).[33] At the end of January 1921, Eberhard participated in meetings of the IFoR, of which he was now a committee member. He reported in *Das Neue Werk* on the growth of FoR and the appointment of Stevenson as international secretary of the movement. He noted that she was 'well-known in German Christian and pacifist circles'. Eberhard was encouraged that the peace movement in England was 'on the increase among student groups' and that in the SCM in Britain 'there are quite a few convinced pacifists who take a stand as followers of Jesus, in opposition to militarism, power politics, and capitalism'. By contrast, in the United States, he added, 'the newly imported, powerful spirit of militarism has fully captured public opinion'. Eberhard's vision was to see that 'a common cause is established through which the message of peace is spread abroad' and he saw the Church as an 'Embassy' of a different kingdom.[34] After the ravages of war in Europe, an international mission of peace seemed to offer hope.

'Different Ways of Thinking'

Although Eberhard Arnold was excited that the mission to which the growing Sannerz community was committed had 'received a special strengthening' through IFoR and the discovery of 'the same spirit of willingness for unconditional love and peace',[35] he was aware after being at Bilthoven of what he described, in February 1921, as 'the different

31. Eberhard Arnold to Corder Catchpool, 21 August 1920. BHA Coll. 0288_02.

32. See Hughes, *Indomitable Friend*.

33. Eberhard Arnold to Corder Catchpole, 22 September 1920. BHA Coll. 0288_02.

34. Eberhard Arnold, 'Reconciliation Work' [in German], in *Das Neue Werk*, 16 February 1921, 2. Jahrgang Nr. 22, 576–584. Also retained as BHA EA 21/05.

35. Eberhard Arnold to Paul Wetzel, 12 February 1921. BHA Coll. 0288_02.

ways of thinking of people from different nations'. He instanced the 'very revolutionary-minded French pacifists'. Eberhard was, however, happy to be on the IFoR committee so that he could 'show the organic link our Neuwerk cause has with this whole world-movement'.[36] There were differences within the Sannerz community, which was attracting people from very diverse backgrounds, but interacting with allies across Europe presented larger challenges.

At Eberhard's request the IFoR decided to bring together a group to discuss peace witness in Germany. This ecumenical and international group included Oliver Dryer, a Presbyterian minister and leader in the British FoR; Kees Boeke from the Netherlands; Walther Koch; and Max Josef Metzger, a Catholic priest in Vienna who was an influential advocate of ecumenism and pacifism. Eberhard commented in February 1921 to Else von Hollander that 'contrary to Walther Koch's suggestions', the thinking of the group was 'to be as concentratedly Christian as possible!'[37] With Kees Boeke, Eberhard 'found a relationship of the deepest and innermost nature'.[38] By contrast, Eberhard felt there was a lack of engagement internationally by some leaders within the German SCM. He was disappointed that an invitation to a major World's Student Christian Federation conference in Glasgow in 1921, dealing with important issues of racial, economic, and political relationships across the world, was not publicised in Germany.[39] On the other hand, as Eberhard reported to Lilian Stevenson, student meetings he had addressed in Frankfurt had produced a desire for community, peace, justice, and love.[40]

Meanwhile, work took place on the translation of a book by Joan Mary Fry, *Communion of Life*, with the intention of conveying her message 'in today's German'.[41] The book was published in the summer of 1921. Neuwerk saw 'the essential basic character of Quakerism as identi-

36. Eberhard Arnold to Max Wolf, 22 February 1921. BHA Coll. 0288_02. Wolf was the owner of a Schlüchtern factory.

37. Eberhard Arnold to Else von Hollander, 28 February 1921. BHA Coll. 0288_02. Metzger set up a secretariat for peace work in the Catholic Church. He was executed by the Nazis in 1944.

38. Eberhard Arnold to Jacob Kröker, 7 February 1921. BHA Coll. 0288_02.

39. Eberhard Arnold to Johannes Weise, 23 February 1921. BHA Coll. 0288_02; cf. Rouse, *The World's Student Christian Federation*, 269.

40. Eberhard Arnold to Lilian Stevenson, 28 April 1921. BHA Coll. 0288_02.

41. Eberhard Arnold to Joan Mary Fry, 7 March 1921. BHA Coll. 0288_02.

cal with our own'.[42] But relationships with the English Quakers and FoR were threatened in the same period by one of Eberhard's circle, Heinrich Schultheiss, a militant socialist who gave up his position as a Lutheran pastor to become part of the Sannerz community.[43] Eberhard was not able to attend the main IFoR conference in Bilthoven in 1921; Schultheiss went instead. Schultheiss presented to the conference a positive letter from Sannerz, which stated that 'many of us in Neuwerk belong to the [German] Fellowship of Reconciliation as it has been led up to now by Siegmund-Schultze and Otto Roth',[44] but Schultheiss' own reaction to the IFoR conference was entirely negative. On 12 July 1921, he wrote to Eberhard in highly exaggerated tones to say that he had 'seldom—no, I must say never—seen such dreadful things as I saw there [at Bilthoven]'. He continued: 'Typically, only the English and Americans were sitting in the centre of the conference table', along with the 'subservient' Pierre Cérésole.[45] Perhaps without thinking of the implications, Eberhard published an account, 'Impressions from Bilthoven', by Schultheiss in *Das Neue Werk*. Siegmund-Schultze and a colleague, Alfred Peter, expressed sadness about the divisions fomented by this report.[46]

Eberhard was committed to maintaining contact with as many people in England as possible. He wrote letters to Quakers such as Alfred Lyles in Yorkshire to greet 'the Friends [Quakers] in England, who, like us, want to stand for unconditional peace and the work of love as Jesus taught us',[47] but at the same time Schultheiss' attitude placed Sannerz in a difficult position. However, Lilian Stevenson was determined to rebuild bridges. She wrote to Eberhard in September 1921 to say she was in Switzerland and would like to visit 'the Neuwerk Settlement', in particular to discuss Schultheiss' piece. Stevenson believed Schultheiss had 'not grasped the essence of the Christian International'. She suggested this may have been because he left before the end of the conference and therefore missed the last session, which was 'by far the best'. Stevenson also offered to write an article about the meaning of IFoR, as she saw it,

42. The *Neuwerk* Movement to the Quakers, 13 July 1921. BHA Coll. 0288_02.

43. Baum, *Against the Wind*, 114, 135.

44. Eberhard Arnold to the Directors of the Christian International in Bilthoven, c/o the Secretary, Lilian Stevenson, 30 June 1921. BHA Coll. 0288_02.

45. Heinrich Schultheiss to Eberhard Arnold, 12 July 1921. BHA Coll. 0288_02.

46. Alfred Peter to Oliver Dryer, 9 August 1921. BHA Coll. 0288_02.

47. Eberhard Arnold to Alfred Lyles, Bradford, 15 July 1921. BHA Coll. 0288_02.

for *Das Neue Werk*.[48] Hubert Parris, a Baptist from England (and later a Baptist missionary in Africa), who had been involved in post-WWI reconstruction in France and was well respected in IFoR, felt that Schultheiss' 'unfortunate lack of knowledge of any foreign language prevented him from perceiving much of the truly fine spirit of the meeting'.[49] After Stevenson's visit to Sannerz, she informed the International Committee of FoR in England that she had 'tried to clear up misunderstandings which had arisen in the minds of Dr Arnold and his circle'.[50]

Das Neue Werk readily agreed to publish Lilian Stevenson's article, but it was decided that it would appear with a response from Schultheiss, who was not impressed by Stevenson's approach, complaining bitterly to Eberhard that the 'whole idealistic democratic direction' represented by FoR was 'soft as wax'. He believed that 'just because everything they say is so totally right, it is absolutely wrong. In this reconciling thinking I sense the Antichrist so strongly'.[51] This was certainly not a fair assessment of the work of the Fellowship, but it was an indication of the deep dissatisfaction Schultheiss was feeling. Eberhard explained to Lilian Stevenson that in the Christmas issue of *Das Neue Werk* she would find her essay, with the title 'Movement and Organization', translated into German. He mentioned that Schultheiss had written his reply under the title, 'No, that is just not how it is!' (*Nein, gerade so ist es nicht*). For Eberhard this was simply a welcome discussion, but it made it seem that Schultheiss was being given the last word. Eberhard suggested to Stevenson that her support of 'organisation' in a movement was not readily understood in Germany. In conversations Eberhard had with John Stephens, they had agreed that in IFoR what was to be avoided was not 'organisation' as such but rather 'inflexible' and 'mechanical' organisation. Eberhard added that it was a bad sign when 'a living movement that was carried by a strong spirit needs outer forms to guide it back into the right stream'. He was, nonetheless, thankful for Stevenson's 'lively and descriptive essay'.[52]

This discussion might have carried on, but in the summer of 1922, when the Arnold family was spending time in Bilthoven, at the

48. Lilian Stevenson to Eberhard Arnold, 26 September 1921. BHA Coll. 0288_02.

49. Hubert Parris to Eberhard Arnold, 11 October 1921. BHA Coll. 0288_02.

50. Minutes of the International Committee of FoR, 7 November 1921. COLL MISC 0456/5/5, FoR Archive, London School of Economics.

51. Heinrich Schultheiss to Eberhard Arnold, received 19 December 1921. BHA Coll. 0288_02.

52. Eberhard Arnold to Lilian Stevenson, 22 December 1921. BHA Coll. 0288_02.

Brotherhood House where Kees and Betty Boeke lived, matters came to a head. The Sannerz community began to lose its way. The upshot, due to several interlocking areas of tension, including financial issues, was that most of the community of thirty adults left, with only seven remaining.[53] Eberhard Arnold's involvement in *Das Neue Werk* ceased. All of this constituted an enormous blow to Eberhard's vision.

Gradually, however, the community recovered. Significantly, Adolf and Martha Braun, who had a leadership role in German Baptist youth ministry, arrived in 1924. Eberhard had challenged Adolf to become involved in serving 'the little circle' at Sannerz, helping with publishing and evangelism.[54] Not only did he and Martha respond, but they also brought to Sannerz a range of other projects, including the publication of the German Baptist Youth magazine. In July 1925 Eberhard told Lilian Stevenson that Sannerz was due to welcome twenty Americans, including African Americans, and the community would 'ever so much like to have you here in our midst for that'. He was also going to speak to French and German FoR members, and the community would be singing 'songs about peace' from their *Sonnenlieder* (Songs of the Sun) song book—'for us a special joy!'[55]

In August 1926 Eberhard and Emmy attended an international peace conference in Oberammergau. They reported to Sannerz that the conference was 'quite good as far as what is spoken, but there is no life'. Meeting a range of people—who came from twenty-five countries—was enjoyable, and they appreciated talks by John Stephens and by Siegmund-Schultze, who 'spoke very well about England as seen from a German viewpoint!' Eberhard spoke on the German FoR.[56] But Eberhard's thinking was gradually becoming more aligned with the Anabaptist group he thought embodied the communal vision embraced at Sannerz—the Hutterites.

In 1921 Eberhard had learned about the existence of contemporary Hutterite communities in North America. They had migrated from Germany to Russia and then in the 1870s had left Russia and settled in South Dakota. Eberhard's information about the contemporary Hutterite

---

53. Baum, *Against the Wind*, 134–140.

54. Eberhard Arnold to Adolf Braun, 26 April 1924. BHA Coll. 0288_02.

55. Eberhard Arnold to Lilian Stevenson, 4 July 1925. BHA Coll. 0288_02. Emmy Arnold was the principal compiler of the song book.

56. Emmy and Eberhard Arnold to Monika von Hollander and Trudi Dalgas, 17 August 1926. BHA Coll. 0288_02.

communities came from J. G. Evert, a professor at Tabor College, a Mennonite Brethren College in Kansas. In April 1921 Evert told Eberhard
that the Hutterite and Amish communities he knew were 'not very sympathetic to me, as they reject culture'.[57] Evert, who was committed to
socialism and pacifism and was editor of a German-language magazine,
Vorwärts (Forward), was enthusiastic about *Das Neue Werk*. Eberhard
went on to publish Evert's articles about punishments inflicted on pacifist
American Hutterites during WWI.[58] Eberhard made no attempt initially
to contact the Hutterites, but in 1926 he began referring to the community as a 'Bruderhof', borrowing a term used by the Hutterites. That same
year, in November, Eberhard reported: 'We have bought a Bruderhof in
the Rhön mountains on the Black hills among the Sparhof farms'.[59] The
growing community's new home—moving on from Sannerz—was a large
but neglected farm.

The Rhön Bruderhof grew from thirty to seventy people from 1926
to 1930. Members farmed, published, educated children, and took care
of orphans. These developments were paralleled by Eberhard's deepening interest in the Hutterites. In January 1927 Eberhard wrote to Ludwig
von Gerdtell, with whom he had worked closely in the SCM twenty years
before, to explain about Hutterite history 'in south Germany, the Tirol,
Bohemia, Moravia and Hungary, later in Russia and in the present day in
America and Canada'. He saw the Rhön community as embracing 'this
living witness and this attitude of life, especially in our resolute biblical and early Christian position'. This set it apart 'strongly' from German
Baptists, Mennonites, Exclusive and Open Brethren, Quakers and 'Christian fellowships'.[60] Despite such trenchant expressions of separation, in
correspondence with two American Mennonite historians, John Horsch
and his son-in-law, Harold Bender, Eberhard stated that the spiritual
roots of the Sannerz/Rhön Bruderhof included revival movements, Baptists and the Salvation Army, Quakers, youth movements, and workers'
movements. He wanted to discuss 'the task of mission and evangelizing',
commenting that Hutterite communities in North America did not seem
to be undertaking mission 'comparable to what happened so powerfully

57. J. G. Evert to Eberhard Arnold, 20 April 1921. BHA Coll. 0288_02.

58. Baum, *Against the Wind*, 134.

59. Eberhard Arnold to Walter Jack, 19 November 1926. BHA Coll. 0288_02.

60. Eberhard Arnold to Ludwig von Gerdtell, 12 January 1927. BHA Coll.
0288_02.

in Moravia' through early Hutterites.[61] Despite this reservation, in a letter to a Hutterite elder in Canada, Elias Walter, Eberhard expressed the determination of the Rhön Bruderhof to join the Hutterites.[62]

The Rhön community was now focussed on what was seen as its Hutterite identity. In August 1929 it was decided 'by unanimous Brotherhood decision' that Eberhard should visit the United States and Canada and seek to unite their community with the Hutterites.[63] In June 1930 Emmy Arnold wrote to John Stephens in England and explained that Eberhard had just gone to America, as Emmy put, 'to visit friends and get to know Christian brotherhoods there and to learn from them'. Emmy told Stephens that the Bruderhof was 'full to overflowing' with more than seventy people. She was willing to try to accommodate a student recommended by Stephens, but was disappointed that Stephens had not offered financial help. She pointed out that the Bruderhof was fully extended looking after and educating—'under the leadership of three state-certified teachers and one handicraft teacher'—more than twenty children who had come from needy situations in German cities. However, for Emmy the ultimate reality was God's provision: 'We have been living here in this sense for ten years, and God has helped us again and again to continue when we [came] to a difficult corner'.[64] It is evident from this letter that Emmy did not want to spell out the firm intention of the Rhön community to join the Hutterites. The decision to maintain a relationship with the Quakers would prove wise, but the letter reflects a degree of disappointment. The perspective that had prevailed in 1920, of the Quakers standing 'very close to our movement', was notable by its absence. Hutterite connections had produced a different way of thinking.

A Bridgehead in Britain

The early 1930s, with Hitler's rise to power in Germany, were years of growing crisis for the Bruderhof. In June 1932, Hans-Hermann, the Arnolds' youngest son, who was then only sixteen, wrote to his older

61. Eberhard Arnold to John Horsch, 9 January 1928, in Eberhard Arnold, *Brothers Unite*, 2.

62. Eberhard Arnold to Elias Walter, 6 November 1928, in Eberhard Arnold, *Brothers Unite*, 6–9.

63. Community meeting, 11 August 1929, in Eberhard Arnold, *Brothers Unite*, 37.

64. Emmy Arnold to John Stephens, 10 June 1930. BHA Coll. 0288_02.

brother, Hardy (Eberhard): 'At the moment we live in a very difficult time that could spell disaster for us. I am thinking of the political situation and National Socialism. . . I have a feeling that the time of our expulsion and emigration is near.'[65] Hardy was at the time a student in Tübingen, and he arranged for his father to come and lecture in the university. Although the mood of the student body was militaristic, Eberhard's speech made an impact on some students. One of them, Edith Boecker, a theology student, joined the Bruderhof and later married Hardy. In April 1933, Hardy transferred to Zürich University, and from Switzerland he was able to send letters abroad about the German situation, something which was by then impossible in Germany because of police surveillance. On 27 April 1933, Hardy wrote to Elias Walter in Canada describing govern- ment harassment of the Bruderhof. At the same time, Hardy reported that 'our church continues to gather and increase in inward strength and in mission. This was shown at our Easter celebration when more were baptized, and more were present at the Lord's Supper, than we ever had.' However, Hardy asked Walter to 'please be on the lookout for a place for a hundred and twenty or more of us to come to you in America before long'.[66]

Hardy Arnold was the first member of the Bruderhof to live in Eng- land. With financial help from Kees and Betty Boeke and an offer of hos- pitality from John Stephens, he moved to England in September 1933 to continue his university studies, at the University of Birmingham. Hardy's letters from England, especially to Edith Boecker, to whom he had be- come engaged, give a vivid impression of his experiences in this period. Emmy Arnold asked Hardy to greet John Stephens 'very warmly from us all'.[67] Hardy's initial meeting with Stephens, however, did not go well. Hardy told Edith that Stephens had 'hardly any understanding for the social problem and the great guilt of all so-called Christians, who have become the greatest supporters of wealth'. It seems that Hardy had little awareness of the social work Stephens and other Quakers had done in Germany after the war. Hardy was not impressed by Quaker pacifism. He considered that it tended to take on 'fatalistic, passive forms, somewhat in the sense of Gandhi and Tolstoy'. Hardy found this attitude 'basically

65. Hans-Hermann Arnold to Hardy Arnold, 24 June 1932, in Barth, *An Embassy Besieged*, 24.

66. Hardy Arnold to Elias Walter, 27 April 1933, in Barth, *An Embassy Besieged*, 52–53.

67. Emmy Arnold to Hardy Arnold, 20 September 1933. BHA Coll. 0288_02.

different from the fighting one of the Hutterites.'[68] In fact, the Hutterites were largely passive in their approach to the issues of wider society, while the Quakers and Gandhi were heavily involved. Stephens himself was among those writing about the Nazi threat.[69]

By the beginning of October 1933, Hardy was beginning to relish student life in Birmingham, which was Britain's second-largest city after London and had a population of about one million. Hardy told Edith of his 'joyful surprise' in finding almost all the books he needed in the Birmingham University library, and he admitted that the university was 'not so primitive in this regard as I thought'. He noted that the German books he found had 'probably not been used for years, and for the same length of time not dusted. And now the entire coal dust of this industrial city is clinging to them'. Hardy enjoyed 'discussions, disputes of the most weighty and deep-going kind with John [Stephens] and his friends'.[70]

Much of Hardy's time was taken up with university classes and discussions. He had tutorials on Milton and Shakespeare—'in a single week I am supposed to read all of Hamlet (in English, of course!) and work out the main ideas'. Hardy was especially impressed by Jack (John) Hoyland, a friend of Gandhi's and a lecturer at Woodbrooke, the Quaker study centre. Hardy was invited to tea with Hoyland and his wife, who had both—Hoyland told Hardy—been entertaining thoughts of community for years. Hoyland had at one time written to the Hutterites in America. Their correspondence had left Hoyland feeling that Hutterite Christianity was 'too literal and legalistic and their style too old-fashioned and conservative'. Hardy tried to explain that the Hutterites spoke in 'very plain, simple language', which could be a barrier for modern people, and Hardy also commented that the modern desire for complicated theories—he referenced Marxism and (rather bizarrely) the theology of Karl Barth—made 'the plain truth of the Bible' hard to understand. Jack Hoyland asked Hardy to give a full account of the Bruderhof, and in trying to do so Hardy emphasised 'that everything we do is done only from the Spirit'.[71]

As the university term progressed, Hardy gained a deeper understanding of what he needed to convey in explaining his community. He

68. Hardy Arnold to Edith Boecker, 23 September 1933. BHA Coll. 0304.
69. John Stephens to the editor, *The Friend*, 19 May 1933.
70. Hardy Arnold to Edith Boecker, 2 October 1933. BHA Coll. 0304.
71. Hardy Arnold to Edith Boecker, 20 October 1933. BHA Coll. 0304.

realised that in English there was no word for Gemeinde, which described a church which was a true 'fellowship'. For Hardy that kind of fellowship was 'the central point of Christianity'.[72] He now appreciated the Quakers' 'great love and readiness to help', and in turn he was taking a humbler approach. His aim was to speak to those 'who are seeking and who are very much gripped by the witness of the Gemeinde, so far as I in weakness was able to represent it'. Hardy was also challenged by the desperate conditions in the slums of Birmingham, despite all the endeavours by the Salvation Army, Quakers, and Socialists, with their 'persistent and touching devotion'.[73] Eberhard Arnold had always wanted to affirm common ground with other movements, and Hardy was now discovering the importance of that for himself. He told Edith in December 1933 that the Quakers 'have real love for me because they esteem our cause and make our need theirs'. He continued, perhaps with some exaggeration, 'John Stephens, his dear wife, Jack Hoyland, and others. . . have told me that they consider our life basically the only way'. Hardy was glad he had been able to witness to Bruderhof life, 'weak as my witness of it is'.[74]

A crucial contact for Hardy was a large Birmingham church, Carrs Lane Congregational Church. This church had a tradition of commitment to the creation of vibrant civic life in Birmingham.[75] Leyton Richards, the Carrs Lane pastor, had been secretary of FoR.[76] In February 1934 Hardy was invited to speak to a group at Carrs Lane. About two hundred came, among them a married couple in their mid-twenties, Arnold and Gladys Mason, who were among the first people from England to join the Bruderhof. It was Gladys who had encouraged Arnold to attend Carrs Lane, where for the first time he had heard the Christian faith applied to social issues. The Masons were profoundly impressed by Hardy and arranged for him to come and stay with them for three weeks. The Masons decided to visit the Bruderhof in the summer.[77] One of Gladys' friends,

72. Hardy Arnold to Edith Boecker, 7 November 1933. BHA Coll. 0304.

73. Hardy Arnold to Edith Boecker, 27 November 1933. BHA Coll. 0304. For Birmingham's industrial history see Schill, *Workshop of the World.*

74. Hardy Arnold to Edith Boecker, 2 December 1933. BHA Coll. 0304.

75. The church had influential ministers in the nineteenth century, notably R.W. Dale. For wider background see Hunt, *Building Jerusalem.* The name of the church can be found as Carr's Lane and Carrs Lane.

76. Richards, *Private View of a Public Man,* 71. Leyton Richards had Congregational ministries and one Baptist ministry.

77. Arnold Mason, 'Arnold Mason tells about his life'. BHA Coll. 0006.

Winifred (Freda) Bridgwater, arranged for Hardy to come to London and speak. On that evening Freda realised she would find what she was seeking in the Bruderhof.[78]

As well as making these contacts, Hardy was invited to Edinburgh. The contact here was Kathleen Hamilton, a teacher who had studied at Edinburgh University and was a member of the (Presbyterian) United Free Church of Scotland.[79] She was strongly committed to the SCM and FoR, and heard from her sister Maureen, who was living in England, about Hardy and the Bruderhof. With her characteristic energy, and utilising her many connections, Kathleen spent her 1934 Easter holidays arranging for Hardy to address various groups in Edinburgh. He spoke at churches and to students, and raised money for a new Bruderhof community, the Alm (Alpine) Bruderhof, in Liechtenstein.[80] The reason for the new community was that the Nazis were intent on seizing control of children's education at the Rhön, and the Bruderhof sought a home beyond Germany's borders.[81] Kathleen became convinced she should join the Bruderhof, although she questioned Hardy about the ways the Bruderhof was begging for money. Hardy replied that it was something he found very hard, but he took comfort from the fact that 'St. Francis [of Assisi] felt it his duty as a follower of Christ to go begging as the most humiliating thing to do!'[82]

Hardy's final few months in England were spent in completing his course of study and also, when possible, cementing some of the relationships he had made. Emmy Arnold wrote to John Stephens in April 1934, as Hardy was starting his third term, to say 'thank you once more from my heart for all the love and help you offered Hardy during his stay in England'. She acknowledged that there were 'differences in our perception of things', but she saw Hardy's period in England as a 'rich time'.[83]

In June and also in July 1934 Hardy met the Lutheran pastor and future Confessing Church leader and martyr Dietrich Bonhoeffer, who was then a minister in German-speaking congregations in London.[84] The

78. Winifred Dyroff, 'Recollections of my early years'. BHA Coll. 0066.

79. Oved, *Witness of the Brothers*, 79, offers no evidence for his statement that she was a Quaker.

80. Kathleen Hasenberg (formerly Hamilton), 'My story'. BHA Coll. 0115.

81. Barth, *An Embassy Besieged*, 157–164.

82. Hardy Arnold to Kathleen Hamilton, 14 July 1934. BHA Coll. 0115.

83. Emmy Arnold to John Stephens, 21 April 1934. BHA Coll. 0288_02.

84. See Clements, *London, 1933–1935*, 158–63; Marsh, *Strange Glory*, 219.

contact—made at Bonhoeffer's request—appears to have made Hardy
and Bonhoeffer aware that, although they had differences, 'essentially
they were allies in a common endeavour to rediscover community in
Christ the peacemaker as the reality of the Church'.[85] Hardy told Eberhard and Edith that in his conversation with Bonhoeffer and two of his
friends, Herbert Jehle and Rudolf Weckerling, they spoke about plans 'to
found a brotherhood with some of [Bonhoeffer's] students, solely on the
basis of the Sermon on the Mount'. This vision later took shape in the
underground seminary in Finkenwalde. Hardy reported that he had an
extended conversation in Hyde Park, London, with Herbert Jehle, who
was a physicist spending a postdoctoral year at Cambridge University.
Hardy found Jehle 'the one I get along with best'. In his usual forthright
way, Hardy considered that Bonhoeffer, despite the theological leadership he was giving, had 'not yet grasped the church as the circle led by the
Spirit of God', with a missing experiential element being 'the pouring out
of the Spirit'. Hardy gave Bonhoeffer Eberhard's work on the Holy Spirit,
later incorporated in *Innerland*.[86]

By now Eberhard Arnold was excited about all that had happened
during Hardy's time in England. On 26 June 1934, he wrote to Hardy to
affirm the 'wonderful leading of God's Spirit that He opened the hearts of
a number of individuals and small circles and even a larger circle around
you'. He hoped that Bruderhof literature translated into English could
'intensify the wish that a community associated with our Bruderhofs and
the Brothers in America be founded in England'. However, Eberhard told
Hardy to pass on a message that for the time being those who felt called
to community life should join either the Hutterites in America or the
Rhön or Alm Bruderhofs. Eberhard believed that 'the united *Gemeinde*
will undoubtedly grasp the right moment, shown by God through His
leading, to arrange a mission journey to England'. In the meantime he
was anticipating that Kathleen Hamilton, Freda Bridgwater, and Arnold
and Gladys Mason would all become part of the Bruderhof and, in the
case of the teachers, would use their gifts with children. 'Your meetings in
Britain', Eberhard told Hardy, 'have already given them a living foretaste

---

85. Clements, *Bonhoeffer and Britain*, 78.

86. Hardy Arnold to Eberhard Arnold, 14 June 1934; Hardy Arnold to Edith Arnold, 15 June 1934. BHA Coll. 0288_02. Bonhoeffer's famous book about community
is *Life Together*, originally *Gemeinsames Leben* (Christian Kaiser Verlag, 1939).

of what it means to entrust oneself completely to the leading of the Spirit in the united *Gemeinde*'.[87]

An 'Inner Leading Brought Us to London'

Eberhard Arnold wrote from the Alm Bruderhof in August 1934 to Hans Zumpe at the Rhön Bruderhof to update the sister community. Hans Zumpe, a bookseller who had married Emi-Margret Arnold, had been appointed to give leadership at the Rhön. Eberhard spoke of evenings at the Alm spent 'joyfully united with the Masons', who were 'very fine people, who have really grasped something of the meaning of the cause'. Eberhard continued: 'As it became necessary for communication with the English people, we installed Hardy in the witness-brother service on Monday. The translating was not always sufficient. Hardy had to be able to talk freely and on the spot with them in English!'[88] Eberhard's 'warm-hearted' approach helped considerably.[89] Emmy Arnold was more prosaic in her description of the language issue: 'Most of us had more or less forgotten our school English, but Hardy was a good interpreter, and we got on very well in spite of the language'.[90] A report in September spoke of the 'inner liveliness' of the four from Britain, with their many questions.[91] Crucially, whatever the language dynamics, the need to consolidate what Hardy had started in Britain was becoming ever more apparent.

By February 1935 Eberhard, writing from the Rhön to Hardy, at the Alm, said that a journey to England, a 'joint undertaking of the Eberhards, father and son, will very soon have to be launched'. Eberhard had 'some anxiety whether I am suitable for this task, as I am lacking in the necessary knowledge of the language and also in other ways'. Although he did not mention it, Eberhard had broken his leg in 1933, and his mobility had not returned. He was in constant pain. It seems he was genuinely hesitant about going to England but took comfort 'in the confidence and faith of the church' about the visit. Eberhard was looking to Hardy to 'do

87. Eberhard Arnold to Hardy Arnold, 26 June 1934. BHA Coll. 0288_02.

88. Eberhard Arnold to Hans Zumpe, 9 August 1934. BHA Coll. 0288_02.

89. Baum, *Against the Wind*, 236–237.

90. Emmy Arnold, *Joyful Pilgrimage*, 139.

91. Eberhard Arnold from the Alm Bruderhof to the Rhön Bruderhof, September 1934. BHA Coll. 0288_02.

most of the work, having been authorized through God's Spirit for this task in England'. Eberhard did make a point of telling him to 'balance your youthful tempestuousness with the gradually growing sedateness fitting to my age, although in the deepest sense I also often lack calmness'. He concluded the letter: 'The need and urgency for this journey together is absolutely clear.'[92]

On 16 March 1935, Germany introduced compulsory military service, which meant that the young men of conscription age at the Rhön left immediately for the Alm. For Eberhard there was deep anxiety about events in Germany, coupled with demanding meetings in England. For Hardy, this was an intense time of translating. They went first to the Netherlands, where leading Mennonites pledged support for the Bruderhof. (This would later prove invaluable when the Bruderhof was ultimately forced to leave Germany.[93]) On 6 April 1935, Eberhard Arnold wrote from London to the Bruderhof communities to say that he and Hardy were enjoying 'the friendliest hospitality of the Quakers'. He was able to confirm that 'as the Brotherhood foresaw, an inner leading brought us to London'. They had met with a number of key Quakers, including John Fletcher, who had been in prison for three years during WWI for his pacifist stance; Joan Mary Fry; and Carl Heath, a significant Quaker writer. Discussions covered finance and the future.[94]

On 11 April Eberhard and Hardy spoke to the Executive Committee of FoR, whose members 'warmly welcomed' this opportunity to hear first-hand about the two Bruderhof communities. There was particular interest in the 'educational and hospitality work' of the Bruderhof, and the FoR minutes recorded the vision expressed by Eberhard and Hardy: 'In spite of the introduction of conscription they wished to maintain the witness in Germany where sixty members remained and they asked for the sympathetic support of the Fellowship in England.' Conversations continued with the Quakers, especially about financial help to build up the Alm Bruderhof, which at that point Joan Mary Fry felt was a more realistic option than moving to England because of the difficulty of finding land in England for farming. She offered to find the substantial sum of £600 for the Alm.[95]

92. Eberhard Arnold to Hardy Arnold, 8 February 1935. BHA Coll. 0288_02.

93. Barth, *An Embassy Besieged*, 220–228.

94. Eberhard Arnold, to the Bruderhof, 6 April 1935. BHA Coll. 0288_02. Carl was the son of Richard Heath.

95. Eberhard Arnold, community meeting, Rhön Bruderhof, 8/9 May 1935. BHA EA 356.

After spending time with London Quakers, the Arnolds moved to the East End of the city, to Kingsley Hall, a centre of work among the poor led by two sisters, Muriel and Doris Lester, whose church background was Baptist.[96] As Hardy reported, Muriel and Doris, who were from a wealthy family, had committed themselves to social and educational work in East London. Eberhard was asked to give a talk in Kingsley Hall, which was 'quite full with about 130 people, mostly workers and their wives'. Eberhard spoke about 'social justice, mammon, murder, lying, and impurity, how everything is connected and how no one who serves these can be a disciple of Jesus'. Hardy commented that Eberhard 'feels very much at home here in the social-educational work of Doris Lester, it reminds him in many respects of the Berlin time'.[97] Eberhard wrote to the Bruderhof on 16 April to say he believed through meetings with groups in London 'the truth makes an impression that goes very deep'. Several meetings generated support for the Bruderhof. Eberhard spoke to some Christian Socialists and through them met a well-known doctor who insisted that the Bruderhof should be supported: 'We must help! We must do something'.[98]

From London, Eberhard and Hardy went to Edinburgh. Writing from there, Hardy told Edith that London had been 'good beyond all expectations'. He was excited about encounters with those in the Scottish art world, such as John Duncan.[99] Eberhard was promised an introduction to Nina Douglas-Hamilton, the Duchess of Hamilton.[100] This would prove valuable, as the Duchess later co-operated with Joan Mary Fry in an appeal for help for the Alm Bruderhof.[101] Drawing-room meetings were arranged in Edinburgh. Two of those who came were shocked that the Bruderhof were not Sabbatarians. Another, Nancy Heard, showed interest in visiting the Bruderhof. Nancy's mother met Eberhard and Hardy

96. Lester, *It Occurred to Me*, 61–62; cf. Wallis, *Mother of World Peace*. See also Dekar, 'Muriel Lester, 1883–1968: Baptist Saint?', 337–45. See more on Kingsley Hall in chapter 6.

97. Hardy Arnold to Edith Boecker, 14 April 1935. From Kingsley Hall, East London. BHA Coll. 0304.

98. Eberhard Arnold to the Bruderhof, 16 April 1935. BHA Coll. 0288_02.

99. For Duncan see Kemplay, *The Paintings of John Duncan*.

100. Hardy Arnold to Edith Boecker, 22 April 1935. BHA Coll. 0304.

101. Joan Mary Fry, *An Appeal to Help the Members of the Alm Bruderhof* (London: privately printed, 1935). Donations were to go to the Duchess of Hamilton.

in a restaurant, explaining that she could not invite them to her house as her husband was a military General and would not welcome pacifists.[102]

Eberhard and Hardy then travelled to Birmingham, where they attended a Quaker meeting with John Stephens. Eberhard reported: 'We sat in silence. It was true silent worship.' He then quoted what Stephens had said to the meeting: 'We have here two friends from Germany, from the Bruderhof. Joan Mary Fry is arranging a collection for them and I want to ask whether we don't also want to send help. I would like to ask Hardy to speak about the needs of the Brotherhood.'[103] Jack Hoyland invited Eberhard and Hardy to speak at Woodbrooke.[104] At a subsequent meeting they had with Leyton Richards, minister at Carrs Lane, there was agreement about the necessity of a contemporary peace witness. Richards, preaching to a Carrs Lane congregation reported as numbering sixteen hundred, said that the decisive thing was 'community of goods, of faith and of life'. He spoke of the Bruderhof, saying that he did not agree with them in everything, but they were an example. At the time there was no clarity in Eberhard's mind about a Bruderhof community starting in Britain, but several people, including Doris Lester and Leyton Richards, decided to make a visit to experience Bruderhof life in mainland Europe.[105]

'To Hear of a Bruderhof in Britain'

The momentum generated within the Bruderhof by the visit to Britain continued throughout the summer and autumn of 1935. Difficulties and challenges of all kinds were evident, not least because of the political situation in Germany. There were communal prayers for 'God himself to intervene'.[106] Among the Bruderhof's guests in this period was Jack Hoyland, who brought several students. On 22 October, at a community meeting at the Alm, Arnold and Gladys Mason, and Freda Bridgwater, were encouraged to journey to England. Arnold Mason stressed that the community was 'in a time of expectation, and we are undertaking this

102. Hardy Arnold, community meeting, Alm Bruderhof, 1 May 1935. BHA EA 349.

103. Eberhard Arnold community meeting, 8 May 1935. BHA EA 353.

104. Hardy Arnold to Edith Boecker, 26 April 1935. BHA Coll. 0304.

105. Hardy Arnold, community meeting, Alm Bruderhof, 1 May 1935. BHA EA 349.

106. Eberhard Arnold, community meeting, 22 July 1935. BHA EA 415, in Barth, *An Embassy Besieged*, 231.

journey very strongly in this feeling'. Gladys said she felt that 'something great has entered into my life, that I must go to England, quite apart from my own wishes'. She wanted to be open so that 'the Spirit of God can work through us'. Freda spoke of the church community as a 'place of light, the lantern in which is the light. Only because we belong to this light can we go forth, otherwise we are nothing'. Eberhard, in response, referred to early Hutterite thinking: 'As Peter Riedemann said, and as we have just been reminded, the Church is comparable to a lantern, and in this lantern burns and shines the light; the light rays which go through the lantern glass reach all the world. And the brothers and sisters who are sent out are the light rays, messengers of God'. He saw the whole community involved, as they prayed together for those who would go, and he concluded: 'This is the hour of mission.'[107]

The three travelled to Birmingham and reported in a letter of 30 October 1935 that they had spoken to a 'class of workers', had been to Carrs Lane, and had shared in an event at which Jack Hoyland spoke about his new book on Francis of Assisi. They had spent time with Hoyland; with Leyton Richards and his wife, Edith; and with Godfrey Pain, a lay leader at Carrs Lane. Not all the meetings appeared to have been a success: the atmosphere of one visit suffered considerably 'from the cake and coffee, the flash-bulb photography and the incessant ringing of the telephone'. They were pleased that Richards, despite having reservations about the economic basis of the Bruderhof, was willing to offer support and had spoken to various people about the Bruderhof's needs, including the possible emigration of members to England. They reported that Godfrey Pain was quite depressed about efforts to set up a community in Birmingham, and they commented: 'It is evident that at times the Spirit has worked strongly among them but it is also very clear that most of the members of this [Birmingham] group had something in their lives that was an obstacle to final dedication and that explains the fact that until now there is no actual material fulfilment after all the really earnest seeking.'[108]

There was great interest in the Bruderhof about developments in England. Kathleen Hamilton wrote to her mother on 4 November 1935 to say, 'Do you know Gladys, Arnold and Freda are in England, sent out on the *Aussendung* [mission] by the *Gemeinde*. I am, oh! so happy about

---

107. Eberhard Arnold, community meeting, 22 October 1935. BHA EA 494.

108. Arnold and Gladys Mason to the Bruderhof, 30 October 1935. BHA Coll. 0288_02.

it. That is the answer to those who say help those at home [in Britain] first. The life must come first, and then the way opens to carry the Good News to those at home.' Kathleen spoke of a possible community in England, alerting her mother to the fact that, 'you may wake up one morning to hear of a Bruderhof in Britain'. For Kathleen, it was 'in God's hands', and if it was God's will then 'all difficulties will be overcome; on the other hand, if it is not His will, its collapse is neither here nor there'.[109] From Birmingham, Jack Hoyland was enthusiastic, telling Eberhard in a letter of 11 November that it was 'really very fine to have Arnold, Gladys, and Freda with us'. On the question of possible emigration from Germany, he believed that approaches Leyton Richards was making to the British government about refuge for the community in England were promising. Hoyland asked Eberhard to tell the community that in his Quaker circles in Birmingham 'we talk about them and think of them daily'.[110] A few days later Hoyland wrote to the Quaker publication, *The Friend*, encouraging more English Quakers to find out about the Bruderhof way of life.[111]

On 12 November 1935 Arnold and Gladys Mason reported back to the community in enthusiastic terms: 'Last Thursday we had a talk with Leyton Richards. Never before had he taken such a friendly attitude, and he seems to have a real understanding for the significance of our life and witness. It was quite a wonderful experience because we felt that he was really moved by the Spirit of God and responded to the truth for which we live and work. And this took place completely without our saying or doing anything.' They added that they had found this happening a number of times in England and believed that 'in this time so critical for both Bruderhofs God is showing us that he moved men's hearts so that the impossible becomes possible'.[112]

On the same day on which this letter was written, Eberhard travelled to Darmstadt to see Professor Paul Zander about the long-term effect of the injury to his leg. Zander, a surgeon and a long-term friend, offered to examine the leg, which had not healed. Emmy described how Eberhard, in great pain, limped along and was taken by taxi to a train to Darmstadt. 'Little did we know that this was his last farewell', she recalled, 'that

109. Kathleen Hamilton to her mother, 4 November 1935. BHA Coll. 0115.

110. Jack Hoyland to Eberhard Arnold, 11 November 1935. BHA Coll. 0288_02.

111. J. S. Hoyland to the editor, *The Friend*, 22 November 1935.

112. Arnold and Gladys Mason, to the Bruderhof, 12 November 1935. BHA Coll. 0288_02.

Eberhard would never see his beloved Bruderhof again'.[113] The operation, on 15 November, was not a success. A second one was scheduled for 22 November, and in the meantime Eberhard spoke to visitors and other patients about their relationship with God. He was insistent: 'I have to go on witnessing till the last moment'. Dr Zander decided that Eberhard's leg would have to be amputated, but there were multiple medical complications, and on 22 November Eberhard died.[114] The witness would have to be carried on by others.

Eberhard Arnold's death was an enormous blow to the Bruderhof. Against the background of tragedy, Freda Bridgwater expressed her own confidence that Eberhard 'had prepared this young brotherhood for the future—consciously, purposefully, and in every conceivable way'.[115] However, the immediate impact was considerable. Many members of the community felt that in the period before Eberhard died they had not retained, as Eberhard himself had, 'the spontaneous love and joy they had experienced in the earlier days of their first love'. The result had been that a 'heavy cloud hung over them'.[116] Emmy Arnold moved with her youngest daughter, Monika, to the Alm, so that they could be closer to her three sons, who were then in Zürich. Georg Barth, whose wife, Moni, was Emmy Arnold's sister, was given responsibility for the Rhön. Hans Zumpe, at the Alm, was overseeing both communities.

In his last letter to Hans and Emy-Margret Zumpe, Eberhard spoke of keeping the Rhön community in Germany, in order 'to give a powerful witness by its life'.[117] But in mid-February 1936 the future became even more precarious as word was received that Germans living abroad would be mobilised for military service alongside those in Germany. The young men living at the Alm would therefore be conscripted, and the authorities in Liechtenstein said they could not prevent this happening.[118] By this time several more British people had either joined or shown interest in joining the Bruderhof. In January 1936 Kathleen Hamilton reported

113. Emmy Arnold, *Joyful Pilgrimage*, 147.

114. Baum, *Against the Wind*, 252.

115. Baum, *Against the Wind*, quoting Winifred Dyroff, 253.

116. Barth, *An Embassy Besieged*, 246.

117. Eberhard Arnold to Hans and Emy-Margret Zumpe, 14 November 1935. BHA Coll. 0288_02.

118. Barth, *An Embassy Besieged*, 248.

to her mother that no fewer than twelve 'Englanders' were living in the community.[119]

Arnold and Gladys Mason and Freda Bridgwater had been preparing the way in England, without knowing all that would transpire in the Bruderhof communities. They were told about Eberhard's death by telegram when they were staying with Doris Lester at Kingsley Hall, and they returned for Eberhard's funeral.[120] Arnold and Gladys were then sent to England again, in January 1936. By late February there was a firm community intention to set up a Bruderhof in England.[121] The Masons were given the task of finding suitable property for a community, and Hans Zumpe and Freda Bridgwater came over to join them in this task. Arnold Mason later recalled: 'We were excited and happy about this decision. It opened up a new future—freedom to live in community away from Nazi oppression—and we began our task with great joy. As I knew the Cotswold country, we set out in that direction.'[122] The fruits of their search would mark a radically new phase in the life of the Bruderhof.

119. Kathleen Hamilton to her mother, January 1936. BHA Coll. 0115.

120. Arnold and Gladys Mason 'Memories'. BHA Coll. 0006.

121. Hardy Arnold to Edith Arnold, 21 February 1936. BHA Coll. 0304.

122. Barth, *An Embassy Besieged*, 249.

3

Putting Down Roots

The Cotswold Bruderhof began in a very small way in March 1936. Early growth was slow and steady. After just over a year, in June 1937, the community comprised forty-seven committed adult members, nine members of the novitiate (those exploring membership), thirty-two children, and five others—young people, guests and helpers. There were also thirteen Bruderhof members, with their children, who at that stage were waiting in the Netherlands to be given permission to come to Britain.

As the Cotswold community put down roots, there were concerted efforts to make and sustain wider contacts. The first circular letter sent out from the Cotswold Bruderhof, on 1 September 1936, spoke of the importance the community attached to visitors. Guests 'keep us in contact with the movements and problems of our time', something that the community believed helped it 'not to become narrow-minded and sectarian'. The community valued a 'broad outlook on life'. Against the background of increasing pressure being exerted by the Nazis against the Bruderhof in Germany, the Cotswold Bruderhof hoped to host events where people could discuss the pressing issues of the day in 'an atmosphere of real openness'.[1] England, Bruderhof members believed, would allow their movement to grow and flourish.

---

1. Prospectus, 'First Bruderhof Letter: The Founding of the Cotswold Bruderhof', 1 September 1936, 11. BHA Coll. 0301_004.

'Many Possibilities for Building Up'

The search for a place to begin a new community in England was a short one. Freda Bridgwater, Arnold Mason, and Hans Zumpe met in Birmingham, where Freda borrowed her father's car and drove Arnold and Hans around various towns in the Cotswolds, a part of England which Arnold knew. It was an area where crafts of all kinds flourished.[2] This resonated with Bruderhof interests. They went to estate agents' offices and were given addresses of places for sale, with permission to view them. On the second day of travelling, and praying for guidance, they found themselves in Cirencester, an old country town, and went to the office of Jackson Stops, a well-known firm of estate agents, auctioneers, and architects, and met one of the directors, Terence McHugh.[3] Jackson Stops had an advertisement for renting or buying Ashton Fields farm, Ashton Keynes, about four and a half miles from Cirencester, described as a 'desirable farm of about 200 acres, half pasture and remainder good working arable land with good road frontage'. The description noted that the 'house is in a poor state of decorative repair, but the property lends itself admirably for conversion into a Gentleman's house'. It was significant for the Bruderhof, however, that the farm lands had been 'highly cultivated'. The land area of about 200 acres was similar to the Rhön. As well as the farmhouse there were farm buildings, two cottages, and a bungalow. There was a local railway station. What was of less interest was that the area was 'convenient for hunting, polo and golf'.[4] The social composition of the area would have an impact later, but at the time it did not seem relevant.

Having made arrangements with the estate agent to view the property the following day, Freda, Arnold, and Hans were in a joyful mood on their way back to Birmingham. When they actually saw the property, however, they realized that the advertisement did not do justice to the poor state of the buildings. But Freda Bridgwater had what she described as 'one of those hunches of mine' and said to the other two, 'This is it'. The owner of the farm was known in the neighbourhood, in part because his father, Colonel Reginald Dyer, was responsible in 1919 for the massacre of unarmed protestors at Amritsar, India.[5] His son needed to sell

2. Bingham, *The Cotswolds*, xx–xxi.

3. Arnold Mason, 'Early Memories'. BHA Coll. 0006.

4. Jackson Stops (Real Estate Agent) Advertisement. marked 'Mrs Chapman', March 1936. BHA Coll. 0334.

5. See Furneaux, *Massacre at Amritsar*.

the farm and could not afford the necessary repairs. Arnold Mason, who took the lead in the business negotiations, spoke to Dyer about renting part of the land and all farm buildings, with a first option to buy the whole property in September 1936. This was provisionally accepted. The conversation with Dyer was a friendly one, and as Freda later recalled: 'Naively we said we needed the place immediately.' Before any documents had been signed they asked permission to move into the Grey Cottage, as it was later named. Dyer agreed, and a truck was hired in Birmingham and loaded with items Freda's parents could spare from their own small household—two camp beds, an old armchair, some silverware, crockery, and a few staple foods.[6] The community had begun.

Not surprisingly, Terence McHugh, the agent, did not find this procedure professionally acceptable. Dyer came to the cottage and explained apologetically that he would need details of the Bruderhof's bank and solicitor, and in the case of those who were going to be party to an agreement but who were not British citizens there would need to be authorisation from the Home Office. The group at Ashton Fields was already expanding to include Gladys Mason, together with the Masons' baby, Jonny, and Alfred Gneiting. In the light of their immediate need for accommodation the group arranged to go and see McHugh, to investigate what arrangements might be possible. He was sympathetic to refugees from German hostility, because he had lost his brother in the First World War, and he gave them permission to stay in the cottage temporarily. That night Arnold and Gladys sat up all night translating and typing out a Bruderhof constitution which would be needed for the Home Office and the lawyers. They urgently needed to find a place to which German Bruderhof members of military service age could come. A deposit of £200 was required.[7] This was a considerable challenge, as the community had virtually no money.

Their needs were immediately made known within the Bruderhof communities. Hardy Arnold came over to England and went with Hans Zumpe and Arnold Mason to the London law firm of Strong & Co., a firm with Quaker roots. Hardy told Edith in a letter on 21 March that he had found Mr Strong 'extraordinarily ready to help'.[8] Arnold and Gladys had

6. Arnold Mason, 'Early Memories'. BHA Coll. 0006; Winifred Dyroff, 'Recollections of my Early Years'. BHA Coll. 0066.

7. Arnold and Gladys Mason, 'Memories'; Arnold Mason, 'Early Memories'. BHA Coll. 0006.

8. Hardy Arnold to Edith Arnold, 21 March 1936. BHA Coll. 0304.

already prepared the way by visiting the firm and explaining the probable establishment of the Bruderhof in England. Strong & Co. had offered, free of charge, to act for the community and to draw up a constitution so that the Bruderhof in England could be recognised as a 'Friendly Society'.[9] Money was also coming in, with a significant part of the needed £200 being offered by a journalist in Bristol, Vincent Evans, who had visited the Rhön and whose brother would later join the Cotswold Bruderhof.[10]

Hardy Arnold also reported on contact made with Dr and Mrs Muir in London. They were friends of Kathleen Hamilton's family. Hardy explained to Edith on 21 March 1936 how after seeing the lawyers they had met Mrs Muir 'the wife of the leprosy doctor' on a street corner, having arranged it by telephone, 'and accepted £85 from her'.[11] Although Hardy referred to Muir as 'the leprosy doctor', this does not convey his full significance. Ernest Muir was a world authority on leprosy. In 1936 he had returned to Britain from India, where he had been engaged for some years in medical mission and most recently had been professor of Tropical Medicine in Calcutta. In 1938 he was secretary-general of the Congress of the International Leprosy Association in Cairo.[12] Muir became a long-term supporter of the Bruderhof.

With initial funding secured, Hardy travelled to Cirencester, which he described as 'a charming little old city like our Schlüchtern', and to the office of Jackson Stops. Writing to Edith on 22 March, Hardy described his fascination with Ashton Fields. 'The buildings are ancient', he said, with the main building being 'like the main portion of a Middle-Ages castle, if one forgets about a tower'. There were 'many old trees, mostly elms and covered with ivy close to the house, and beautiful flowers'. However, he contrasted this pleasing exterior setting with the dilapidated interior of the house, 'full of rubble and there is much junk lying about everywhere'. Also, cooking was 'like in the Middle Ages, in a pot hanging by a chain over the fire!' Nonetheless, he believed there was a good foundation for a community and 'many possibilities for building up and extending'.[13]

9. Such societies were voluntary bodies for mutual benefit and social purposes. See Finlayson, 'A Moving Frontier, 183–206.

10. Arnold and Gladys Mason, 'Memories'; Arnold Mason, 'Early Memories'. BHA Coll. 0006.

11. Hardy Arnold to Edith Arnold, 21 March 1936. BHA Coll. 0304.

12. S.G. Browne, Obituary: Ernest Muir, 1880–1974. *International Journal of Leprosy*, http://ila.ilsl.br/pdfs/v42n4a14.pdf, accessed 24 January 2016.

13. Hardy Arnold to Edith Arnold, 22 March 1936. BHA Coll. 0304.

Fostering Friendships

One of the friends of the Bruderhof who proved crucial for the Cotswold community before they settled in England and whose interest developed during their early months in the country was Leyton Richards, at Carrs Lane, Birmingham. His practical help continued, and when friends of the community made known its needs in the *Manchester Guardian* newspaper in April 1937—when the community was described as 'nearly penniless'—those who could assist were invited to communicate directly with Richards.[14] Additionally, Richards introduced the Bruderhof to Ernest Cooper, Assistant Secretary in the Aliens Department of the Home Office.

Cooper, whose small staff was dealing with increasing numbers of refugee applications from Germany, was known for his efficiency and also for the astute way in which he conducted his operations. It appears that he co-operated discreetly with non-Nazi elements in the German embassy in order to help refugees, many of whom were Jewish.[15] Cooper advised Arnold Mason to invite Bruderhof members individually as 'visitors' to Ashton Fields. If there were difficulties with entry permissions at the ports, Cooper suggested that Arnold could telephone him at the Aliens Department. In due course the many visitors invited by 'Mr and Mrs Arnold Mason' to 'our farm at Ashton Fields' were granted permission to enter Britain.[16]

Despite receiving help of various kinds from a variety of people, it seemed at times as if the Bruderhof counted as their true friends only those who gave them the full support they wanted. On 2 April 1936, Hardy wrote to Edith to say that he and Arnold Mason were meeting people in Birmingham and had come to the conclusion that Jack Hoyland, at Woodbrooke, the Quaker centre, was 'the only real friend whom we have here'. Certainly Hoyland's advocacy was enthusiastic. In November 1935 he told fellow Quakers through the medium of *The Friend* that understanding the Bruderhof way of life was 'very desirable'.[17] Hardy considered that in recent discussions about the life of the Bruderhof, Leyton and Edith Richards and Godfrey and Gertrude Pain (at

14. *Manchester Guardian*, 30 April 1937.

15. For this see London, *Whitehall and the Jews*, 22, 64. London's book covers Cooper's work in detail.

16. Arnold and Gladys Mason, 'Memories'. BHA Coll. 0006.

17. Jack S. Hoyland to the editor, *The Friend*, 22 November 1935.

Carrs Lane) 'swing constantly this way and that, and consequently are extremely unreliable.'[18] However, the reality was that rather than being 'extremely unreliable' these parties and others who had contact with the community were sympathetic but did not necessarily affirm all aspects of the Bruderhof vision.

Hardy planned to travel to the north of England to meet Quakers and others and to make further appeals for help, not least financial assistance. Contact had been made, for example, with 'a rich Quaker lady in Yorkshire', Miss Ellis.[19] Hardy had a specific 'wish list' at this point: the community needed, he noted, 'about another £100 for the Woodturning set-up, and some more cattle'. Several cows were already being purchased by the community at a good price, and it was anticipated that two would have calves by the autumn. The hope was that Miss Ellis, who had 'several estates', might offer the community some cows as a gift. Hardy was well aware of the pressing needs and also of the difficulties, but he was optimistic. 'Things here are going forward on the whole', he told Edith, in line with what the community had been 'inspired to plan' as a result of the situation in Germany. He saw the opportunity in England in spiritual terms as a 'mighty miracle'.[20]

The Cotswold community sought to establish friendly relationships with various professionals, both locally and elsewhere, and these individuals often came to respect the way the community undertook its business. In August 1936 the Bruderhof had the opportunity to buy Ashton Fields rather than continue renting. The whole two-hundred-acre farm was offered to them at £23 per acre.[21] At this point there were only eighteen fully committed members living there.[22] The first Cotswold circular letter, in September 1936, spoke about the option to buy, mentioning that as well as the purchase price there would be a need for funds to convert sections of the property. The money required was an enormous sum for the community—£5,350.[23] Arnold Mason visited the Cheltenham & Gloucester Building Society, and the manager agreed to a

---

18. Hardy Arnold to Edith Arnold, 2 April 1936. BHA Coll. 0304.

19. The Ellis family were long-standing, well-known Yorkshire Quakers. See Backhouse, *The Life and Correspondence of William and Alice Ellis of Airton*.

20. Hardy Arnold to Edith Arnold, 2 April 1936. BHA Coll. 0304.

21. Multiplying by 500 gives approximate amounts in 2017.

22. Household list, 19 August 1936, Cotswold Bruderhof. BHA Coll. 0076.

23. Prospectus, 'First Bruderhof Letter: The Founding of the Cotswold Bruderhof', 1 September 1936, 11. BHA Coll. 0301_004.

mortgage of about two-thirds of the value of the property, with monthly repayments to be spread over twenty years.[24] Discussions also took place in London with the legal advisors, Strong & Co., about other sources of funding, such as the Agriculture Mortgage Corporation. In addition, Mr Strong promised to write a letter to a few wealthy friends to make known the community's financial needs. Among these was Roger Clark, whom Hardy Arnold understood was 'a rather rich Quaker in Street, Somerset'. Clark, who responded to the appeal and contributed to the Cotswold venture, was a director of the Quaker family firm, C. & J. Clark, well known for their high-quality shoes.[25]

Ashton Fields was purchased, and alterations, renovations, and building work commenced. R. A. Berkeley, an architect and builder in Cirencester, helped with plans and obtaining planning permissions. The local district council insisted that all new building should be in the traditional Cotswold style.[26] Berkeley coordinated the employment of local masons and other workmen. They were directed by someone in the Bruderhof with considerable skill in building, Fritz Kleiner, who had left Germany when the Rhön community received a letter in September 1936 stating that the age range for military conscription in Germany was to be extended.[27] After becoming involved in the construction work at the Cotswold Bruderhof, Fritz promised the workmen that he would play his violin for them when a phase of the building project was finished. They were sceptical. However, this was exactly what Fritz did, to the surprise and enjoyment of the men.[28]

Not all the attempts to gain support for the community proved fruitful. Hans-Hermann Arnold, then aged twenty, wrote rather disconsolately in March 1936, having very recently arrived in England, that a visit to London with Freda Bridgwater had proved 'fruitless; the distances from one address to another are huge, the dirtiness discouraging,

24. Arnold Mason, 'Early Memories'. BHA Coll. 0006.

25. See Hudson, *Towards Precision Shoemaking*.

26. Jane Bingham talks about planning restrictions to prevent the use of inappropriate building styles in the Cotswolds being put in place by the 1950s: Bingham, *The Cotswolds*, 48. The Bruderhof experience shows that restrictions were in force in the 1930s.

27. Arnold Mason, 'Early Memories'. BHA Coll. 0006; Barth, *An Embassy Besieged*, 261.

28. Arnold Mason, 'Early Memories'; Arnold and Gladys Mason 'Memories'. BHA Coll. 0006.

the teas or other gatherings in which we found ourselves mostly very superficial'.[29] Hardy Arnold, too, despite his considerable experience in England and his optimism, had set-backs. In September 1936 he wrote to Edith to say that he had gone to visit a 'noble barrister', who a few weeks earlier had promised help, but Hardy discovered that the gentleman had in the meantime died. Hardy also undertook a 'longish car journey' so that he could talk to 'Mr. Lemare, brother-in-law of our Doris Lester'. Lemare was 'extremely wealthy but unfortunately all the more unsympathetic. He asks for an estimated balance since March of this year, before he will actively help.' It is not surprising that business people being asked to help wanted financial accounts, and the Bruderhof began to publish them. However, some contacts offered help without these conditions. In Cambridge, Hardy was welcomed by Dorothea Elliot, who had contacted the community. She was 'extremely warm-hearted', offered £500, and expressed interest in coming to Ashton Fields for one year—living in a caravan.[30]

'Stimulation in Spiritual and Practical Matters'

At the Bruderhof, there was a strong emphasis on welcoming visitors. The first Cotswold circular letter, in September 1936, emphasised that within the community 'stimulation in spiritual and practical matters will always be welcome' and explained that members wanted to hear about the experiences of others. The letter noted that over five months three hundred guests had come to visit, with many living as part of the community for some days or weeks. Jack Hoyland, now known as a firm friend of the community, had brought with him students from Woodbrooke. Students had also come from Oxford, as had over fifty participants in a Fellowship of Reconciliation Youth Conference held in Oxford. By contrast with student visitors, a working-class group had come from Kingsley Hall. Varied Christian traditions were represented among the visitors. Brother Douglas and several Franciscan brothers from Dorset had found their way to the Cotswold community. Given this variety, the letter emphasised a core conviction of the community: 'The Spirit of God never separates but always unites. . . Our task therefore is not to cut ourselves off from the

---

29. Hans-Hermann Arnold to Gertrud Löffler, 27 March 1936. BHA Coll. 0190. Hans-Hermann Arnold and Gertrud Löffler were married in June 1938.

30. Hardy Arnold to Edith Arnold, 3 September 1936. BHA Coll. 0304.

world but to live within the world as a group of simple people who are devoted to a life of practical brotherly love.'[31]

The expression 'simple people' could be misleading. as there was no lack of creativity and intellectual activity within the community. Hans-Hermann Arnold was excited by a communal day on a Sunday in early June, with guests present from London and Oxford. He told his mother: 'The dancing was really nice here for the first time. The guests were enthusiastic, and really experienced the community while dancing.' There were also intense discussions, and 'all felt deeply moved and spoken to', guests and community alike.[32] A few days after the first Cotswold circular letter was issued, Hardy Arnold described to Edith conversations that had been taking place about 'whether it is truly Christ and only Christ who stands at the centre of our life, or whether it is the so-called "cause" and the outer forms of the "orders."' Hardy could see no value in 'order in the church, true discipline, a discerning of the spirits, yes, even unity, if love does not penetrate us completely'.[33]

'Orders' referred to the Hutterite rules for community life.[34] In Hardy's view such rules 'must and shall only be the outward expression of a full and all-embracing love, in and for themselves they are nothing'. He continued: 'Unity without love is compulsion, discipline without love will become law, order without love will be moralistic. In all these things we have indeed failed so badly in the past, and it is my constant prayer to God that the love which glows though everything, which is dedicated and which purifies everything, will be granted to us more and more. Then alone is joy and true surrender possible. Then alone all those qualities of community life which we emphasize so often will have meaning. Then alone is there any purpose in our further building up.'[35]

In this period Hardy and Arnold Mason continued to travel on behalf of the community, seeking to generate support. Edith Arnold wrote to Emmy Arnold in September 1936 to say that Hardy had left for Bristol.

---

31. Prospectus, 'First Bruderhof Letter: The Founding of the Cotswold Bruderhof', 1 September 1936, 5, 11. BHA Coll. 0301_004. The Society of St. Francis was formed in England in 1937 when two communities amalgamated and established their headquarters in Dorset, at Cerne Abbas. The communities were the Brotherhood of St Francis of Assisi and the Brotherhood of the Love of Christ.

32. Hans-Hermann Arnold to Emmy Arnold, 10 June 1936. BHA Coll. 0190.

33. Hardy Arnold to Edith Arnold, 15 September 1936. BHA Coll. 0304.

34. See chapter 6.

35. Hardy Arnold to Edith Arnold, 15 September 1936. BHA Coll. 0304.

Edith reported that '£200 came as a gift from two Quakers whom Arnold and Hardy had visited for half an hour'. As a result of recent fund-raising, £1,800 in total had been received and 'we cannot be thankful enough'.[36] Hardy had also visited Oxford and stayed with Arthur Gillett, a Quaker who was a director of Barclay's Bank. Hardy especially enjoyed meetings in London in which people were 'really going more to the depths'. Among those participating, he told Edith, were 'very fine and lively people' from the Oxford Group and from the Quakers. Several said they intended to visit the Cotswold Bruderhof for a weekend.[37] The Oxford Group, an interdenominational movement led by an American Lutheran, Frank Buchman, had a significant impact on the spiritual experience of many individuals and churches in Britain in the 1920s and 1930s through its emphasis on life changing, building relationships, surrendering to God, confession, or 'sharing', and receiving immediate divine guidance.[38] In their encounters with those influenced by the Oxford Group's approach to spiritual experience, the Bruderhof found the Group's emphases too individualistic. In a typical comment on the Group, Hans-Hermann, now travelling with Hardy, reported that at one meeting, in Barnet, north London, 'the decisive witness of unity' became a crucial issue.[39]

A second Cotswold circular letter, issued for Christmas 1936, referred to some of these meetings in the London area and in particular to the arrival at the community of Cyril and Bessie Harries and their two children, from St Albans, about twenty miles north of London. The letter described how they had given up their home 'in order to devote themselves to the cause of peace and unity' through the community, and how their decision had caused great interest in the London area. The Bruderhof had been invited to about 'ten small informal meetings' around London, attended by an average of twenty to twenty-five people. One development was highlighted: a group of about fifteen people was meeting every week, and was seeking a 'new and radical' response to the issues of modern life. Nearly all of them had visited the Cotswold Bruderhof, and some were asking themselves 'whether it is not the challenge of the hour to leave behind their old life, based on the selfishness of this

36. Edith Arnold to Emmy Arnold, 28 September 1936. BHA Coll. 0304.

37. Hardy Arnold to Edith Arnold, 15 September 1936. BHA Coll. 0304.

38. Randall, *Evangelical Experiences*, 238–61. For Buchman see Boobbyer, *The Spiritual Vision of Frank Buchman*.

39. Hans-Hermann Arnold to Gertrud Löffler, 15 September 1936. BHA Coll. 0190.

materialistic age, in order to seek communally with us for a way which meets the demands of Christ for a new order of life based on love and justice'.[40] Julius Rubin talks about the Cotswold Bruderhof 'aggressively recruiting converts from European refugees, Quakers, and pacifists'.[41] Rubin cites Donald Durnbaugh, who actually describes, in very different terms, Bruderhof 'outreach to sympathizers, especially among the Society of Friends', and the community 'giving shelter to fellow refugees from Austria and Germany, especially children'.[42] There was no aggression.

One new member in this period was Tom (Tommy) Paul. He had been a miner in the Durham area, but after the mines were closed down he was unemployed. After spending some time at college, he became part of a farming settlement in the North Pennines called Fairfield Acres. Over the course of three years living and working in the settlement, Tom met a number of people associated with the British SCM and also its Auxiliary, which catered for former students and had over three thousand members.[43] He was impressed by an article in the SCM magazine by Mary Osborn about the Rhön Bruderhof, which she had visited.[44] In March 1936, Tom heard about the Cotswold community but did not realise it was the same movement as the Rhön. He wrote to the Cotswold address, and Hardy Arnold replied. It was now evident to Tom that the Rhön and the Cotswold Bruderhof were part of the same movement, and he decided to visit. At a subsequent SCM Auxiliary conference, he spoke about the Bruderhof and was told about two young women who had visited and reported that the community 'didn't eat anything but cabbage', but nonetheless members 'looked the picture of health'. Tom, who was in good health himself, cycled three hundred miles to Ashton Fields and arrived as the community was celebrating the purchase of the farm. He met some of the British members, including Freda Bridgwater and Edna Percival, who were teaching the children. They suggested he get started picking potatoes. Tom was fascinated by the community's life and by the

40. Prospectus, 'Second Bruderhof Letter', Christmas 1936, 14. BHA Coll. 0301_004.

41. Rubin, *The Other Side of Joy*, 79.

42. Durnbaugh, 'Relocation of the German Bruderhof to England, South America, and North America', 71.

43. Boyd, *The Witness of the Student Christian Movement*, 34.

44. The Bruderhof continued to keep in touch with Mary Osborn: *The Plough* 1, no. 2 (July 1938), 68.

many guests. Although he had intended to come only for a few weeks, in late 1936 he decided he wanted to stay.[45]

Another person who joined the Cotswold community at about the same time was Sydney Hindley, a poultry farmer from Lancashire. He had strong convictions that war was wrong, and he was in touch with the Peace Pledge Union.[46] He was a Methodist preacher who drew his sermons largely from the Sermon on the Mount, and he was also influenced by reading about the Indian Christian sadhu (holy man) Sundar Singh.[47] Sydney came into contact with Jack Hoyland and through him made a visit to the Rhön. Later, when it was known that Sydney was going to become part of the Cotswold Bruderhof, there was additional excitement that he was bringing his poultry. In a letter to a friend, Robert Headland, Sydney reflected on his experiences at Ashton Fields. Far from being cut off from the 'outside world', Sydney had met 'far more people from all classes and sects and movements and from many different nationalities than I ever did before'. Sydney spoke of the large number of visitors to the Cotswold Bruderhof in the course of a year. For Sydney, the goal of the community was not 'to build up a place merely where we can be comfortable and secure', but rather to 'live in this way as a witness that a life based only on love is possible here and now, and to call people to such a life'.[48]

As Sydney Hindley noted after a year in the community, some members spent extended periods elsewhere. One of those living at a distance was Hans-Hermann Arnold, who was engaged in studies towards a degree at Manchester University and lived in Lancashire Independent College, Whalley Range, a Congregational theological college. Hans-Hermann was grateful for the welcome he received from the theological students there, although he found it hard to see them as 'future proclaimers of the gospel of Jesus'.[49] Hermann Arnold, a cousin of Hans-Hermann, was in a similar position as a 'dispersed' member of the community. He was working in London in publishing, first for Penguin Books, and then for

45. Tommy Paul, 'Life Story of Tommy Paul'. BHA Coll. 0219.

46. See chapter 4.

47. Heini Arnold, when he was young, was also influenced by hearing about Sundar Singh. See Mommsen, *Homage to a Broken Man*, 39–40.

48. Sydney Hindley to Robert Headland, 3 July 1937. BHA Coll. 0324. Sydney Hindley spoke of 3,000 visitors, but the first circular letter (in September 1936) spoke of 300 in five months, so 3,000 a year later is probably an over-estimate.

49. Hans-Hermann Arnold to Emmy Arnold, 16 January 1937; Gertrud Löffler to Emmy Arnold, 3 February 1937. BHA Coll. 0190.

another publisher, James Clark. These dispersed members made valuable contacts, but always valued being back in the community.[50]

Germany: 'To Dissolve the Bruderhof'

As soon as the Cotswold Bruderhof was established, plans were made for Bruderhof members at the Alm who were due to be conscripted into the German military to travel to England. On 25 March 1936, Emmy Arnold wrote to Hans-Hermann to say 'how wonderful it is that you and Hermann were able to land [in England] after all. It seemed to me similar to the story of Peter when he was able to walk on the water as long as he believed, or the people of Israel who were able to pass through the Red Sea because of their faith.'[51] Heini (Heinrich) Arnold, having been a student at the Strickhof Agricultural College in Zürich, had recently married Annemarie Wächter, a young teacher who had joined the community in 1932.[52] Heini and Annemarie planned to leave for England by train, via France, as a honeymoon couple. There were problems at Zürich, because Heini's passport was about to expire, but Annemarie persuaded the consular official to stamp it. It was against his rules, but she was such an *echt deutsche Grete*—a genuine German sweetheart.[53] Another member at the Alm, however, Werner Friedemann, was turned back after flying to England and had to return to Zürich the next day.[54] Emmy Arnold interpreted Werner's failure spiritually, believing 'he had doubts whether the decision for him to go by plane was right, and so because of his doubts he could not land'.[55] The disappointment, however, had a 'worldly' explanation: when Werner Friedemann arrived in England, a telephone call to the Cotswold Bruderhof, to confirm that he had an invitation into the country, was not picked up: the telephone rang in the main Ashton Keynes house while community members were in the nearby cottage and did not hear it.[56]

50. Hermann Arnold, 'Almbruderhof 1935–Cotswold 1936'. BHA Coll. 0015.

51. Emmy Arnold to Hans-Hermann Arnold, 25 March 1936. BHA Coll. 0288_02.

52. Emmy Arnold, *Joyful Pilgrimage*, 127.

53. Mommsen, *Homage to a Broken Man*, 139.

54. Kurt Zimmermann, 'Survey of our Life Together'. BHA Coll. 0319.

55. Emmy Arnold to Hans-Hermann Arnold, 25 March 1936. BHA Coll. 0288_02.

56. Arnold and Gladys Mason, 'Memories'. BHA Coll. 0006.

A plan to transport other members from the Alm to the Cotswold Bruderhof was devised and implemented under the leadership of Hans Meier, a Swiss engineer and a leader of the community in Germany. Hans and Margrit Meier had joined the Bruderhof after being involved in a communal settlement, the *Werkhof* (Work Farm).[57] As part of the attempt by the Bruderhof to seek a united witness against the Nazi regime, Hans Meier had met the German Lutheran pastor and key figure in the Confessing Church, Martin Niemöller—who had told Dietrich Bonhoeffer about the Bruderhof.[58] Hans wrote to the Cotswold Bruderhof from the Alm on 24 March to explain that his group would be travelling with identification papers issued in Switzerland as 'a youth group with a guide [Meier] from the Swiss Youth Hostel Association'.[59] They presented themselves as *Wandervögel*, or wandering minstrels, taking musical instruments with them to add authenticity. Emmy Arnold reported that as they left the Alm they 'seemed to be very awkward, carrying instruments and wearing shorts'. One of the group, she added, 'created a very helpless impression'.[60] It proved easy to cross the Swiss-French border, as the guard only looked at Meier's Swiss passport, and the group found its way to the English Channel.[61]

Arnold Mason was with Godfrey Pain, from Birmingham, when they received news that the group had arrived in Southampton. Mason borrowed a pair of shorts from Pain, to give the impression of being in keeping with his 'minstrel' friends, and he and Pain drove to the Southampton cross-channel ferry dock. A message came from Immigration for Mr Mason to present himself. He met with the newly arrived 'youth group' in the Passport Office. As was evident from his passport, Werner Friedemann had already been refused admission to Britain. Arnold Mason suggested that the issue might be referred to the Home Office. After a tense wait, the Immigration Officer came back and with a knowing smile—having presumably spoken to Ernest Cooper's office—wished the group 'a nice holiday'.[62]

57. See Adam, 'The Practical, Visible Witness of Discipleship' , in Jones and Randall, eds., *Counter-Cultural Communities*.

58. Barth, *An Embassy Besieged*, 124.

59. Hans Meier to the Cotswold Bruderhof, 24 March 1936. BHA Coll. 0007.

60. Emmy Arnold to Hans-Hermann Arnold, 25 March 1936. BHA Coll. 0288_02.

61. Emmy Arnold, *Joyful Pilgrimage*, 156–157.

62. Arnold Mason, 'Early Memories'; Arnold and Gladys Mason, 'Memories'. BHA Coll. 0006.

The German Gestapo was well aware of the Bruderhof communities, as indicated by a Gestapo report on 19 June 1936 which listed the precise number of Bruderhof members, together with their nationalities, at the Alm as well as the Rhön. Among the foreigners were listed Swiss, English, Swedish, Latvian, Italian, Turkish, and Czech nationals. The Gestapo report drew attention to 'the marked increase in the number of English members since the year 1935, all of them young people at that', and specifically highlighted the 'Mason couple' as being 'particularly active in making propaganda for the Bruderhof in England'. The report concluded that there was an urgent need 'to dissolve the Bruderhof'.[63] The Bruderhof was unaware at the time of this conclusion, although the Rhön community had experienced increasing Nazi harassment, which would become even more severe in the autumn of 1936. In view of the deteriorating situation, Arnold Mason and Hans Zumpe travelled from England to Berlin and to the Rhön to try to discover if the Nazis were formulating plans to close down the Rhön and to inquire if the community could expect any help from the British embassy in view of the British members there. They visited the Gestapo headquarters in Wilhelmstrasse in Berlin, where they learned nothing. Arnold Mason also called at the British embassy and was strongly advised that British people living at the Rhön should leave Germany. He was told they could not expect protection from the British authorities.[64]

An indication of what was to come was seen in the autumn of 1936 when mortgages on the Rhön Bruderhof were foreclosed. This was the last of the attempts by the German authorities to exert economic pressure on the Bruderhof. When the news reached the Cotswold community, they contacted a well-known pacifist, Herbert Runham Brown. He was prominent in the War Resisters' International, an organisation which had been involved in the release of conscientious objectors from prisons in Europe.[65] Runham Brown had told the Bruderhof that if they were ever in a real emergency they should talk to John Forrester Paton, of the firm Patons and Baldwins, in Alloa, Scotland, which manufactured spinning yarn. It was decided that Hardy Arnold and Arnold Mason should do this. Hardy reported to the Bruderhof from Scotland on 20 November that their trip had been successful.[66] The Forrester Paton family, who

63. Barth, *An Embassy Besieged*, 253–56.
64. Arnold and Gladys Mason, 'Memories'. BHA Coll. 0006.
65. Prasad, *War is a Crime against Humanity*.
66. Hardy Arnold to the Bruderhof, 20 November 1936. BHA Coll. 0304.

were involved in United Free Church medical work in India, gave the Bruderhof a very large gift, of £1,200, and were to offer further help later. The money to pay off mortgages on the Rhön was taken into Germany by Arnold Mason. As part of this transaction, the Rhön printing machines, the printed sheets of Eberhard Arnold's *Innerland*, and the community's extensive library and archives were all moved out of Germany to the Cotswold Bruderhof.[67]

There were varied responses within Bruderhof circles in the last few weeks of 1936 to its situation in Germany, 'as slowly and inexorably its life was being strangled'.[68] Kathleen Hamilton, who was at the Rhön and who was a prolific correspondent, told her mother in a letter of 13 November 1936 that there was so much she would like to explain, 'but I am debarred from doing so'. She could say 'little of outward events'. This was a clear reference to the fact that the secret police were examining mail coming in and going out of the Rhön. Yet Kathleen was hopeful. Even though the Bruderhof was small and vulnerable, it was an opening 'through which the Spirit of God, Love, can flow, and through this help the whole world'.[69]

On 25 November Hans-Hermann wrote to his mother to say that he was 'completely overwhelmed' by the news that Hardy had been able to secure such a significant amount of money for the community's needs through his visit to Scotland: it was 'like a sign from heaven'.[70] On the last day of the year, however, Edith Arnold wrote very frankly to Emmy Arnold to say that although the Christmas period at the Cotswold community had been 'wonderful', there was an awareness that 1936 had been 'infinitely difficult' for the movement as a whole and that trying to sustain 'the situation with the three Bruderhofs is actually unbearable'. Edith acknowledged in her letter that no one wanted to close the Rhön Bruderhof. But as she put it, the Rhön was 'gradually diminishing more and more, until nothing will be left of the true picture of a Bruderhof'. It seemed better to her for members to be together in Britain where, as she saw it, 'they can represent the witness more powerfully'.[71]

---

67. Arnold and Gladys Mason, 'Memories'. BHA Coll. 0006.

68. Barth, *An Embassy Besieged*, 265.

69. Kathleen Hamilton to her mother, 13 November 1936. BHA Coll. 0015.

70. Hans-Hermann Arnold to Emmy Arnold, 25 November 1936. BHA Coll. 0190.

71. Edith Arnold to Emmy Arnold, 31 December 1936. BHA Coll. 0304.

Areas of Development

Although the Bruderhof members were well aware of the apparently hopeless future in Germany, this did not feature in the first two circular letters from the Cotswold Bruderhof. Instead the emphasis was on the positive, international 'witness of peace and brotherhood'.[72] This was primary. Although witness often took place among those already interested, members wanted to reach out further. This was brought home to Heini Arnold in February 1937 when he visited the famous Quaker school, Sidcot School, south of Bristol. He was by now joining Hardy and others in travelling and seeking to foster support. Heini was warmly received at the school and found the 'whole school committee, consisting entirely of rich Quakers' meeting that day. He was introduced to several of them and received gifts from some for the Cotswold community. But he was given unexpected advice by one of those he met at Sidcot, Hubert Peet, editor of *The Friend*, to take his message beyond the Quaker community. Peet told Heini: 'You have my full sympathy, friend Heinrich Arnold, I wish you much luck and blessing; but don't go to Quakers; they already do a great deal, they won't help much. Break new ground, bring your message to new circles, then your journey will have great blessing and the financial success will be greater.' Heini affirmed this advice. He did not feel that asking for money was a talent he had, but his vision for the future was to 'be led to new circles, into circles of people who perhaps have no inkling at all of all the peace societies, etc., and for whom the communal life can then be a much more important challenge than for those who think they are doing everything'.[73]

The first two Cotswold circular letters emphasized the need to develop the farm: 'A Hutterian Bruderhof is, and always will be founded on an agricultural basis.'[74] Both letters paid tribute to advice being received from the assistant Agricultural Organiser for Wiltshire, L. D. C. McLees, who 'expressed his appreciation for our well-thought-out plans'. Heini Arnold was responsible for the farming and garden work, drawing from his training at the Strickhof Agricultural College. Though the first circular letter noted that Heini was adjusting 'quite well' to the different

72. Prospectus, 'First Bruderhof Letter: The Founding of the Cotswold Bruderhof', 1 September 1936, 3. BHA Coll. 0301_004.

73. Heini Arnold to Annemarie Arnold, 28 February 1937. BHA Coll. 0005.

74. Prospectus, 'Second Bruderhof Letter', Christmas 1936, 10. BHA Coll. 0301_004.

farming conditions in England,[75] a letter on 3 October 1936 from Heini's wife Annemarie to her brother in Germany, Reinhold, painted a slightly different picture. Heini was 'at a loss how to get through all the autumn field work'.[76] Heini himself told Reinhold in December that there had been times in the previous three months when 'I almost felt I couldn't cope with everything'. However, the farm produce was now selling well, and the various branches—arable farming, a dairy herd, a market garden, cattle, pigs, and poultry farming—were progressing; indeed Heini was confident enough to venture 'as a side-line' into horse breeding, and had bought 'two beautiful black mares'.[77]

Apart from the farm work, 'art and craft work' was very important in the community. Georg Barth, whose background in Germany had been in architecture, was in charge of this aspect as 'architect and designer'. In this period Georg had general leadership in the Cotswold community and was commended as someone 'with a great deal of experience in all aspects of community life'. He was preparing for Cotswold's development, including extensions to the Ashton Fields buildings.[78] In December 1936 the community joined the Guild of Gloucestershire Craftsmen.[79] Bruderhof-made bowls, platters, and boxes sold well, including to some of the big furniture shops in London, Bristol, Birmingham, and Leicester. Prior to the Cotswold community, products from the Alm workshop were sold to Heal & Son in Tottenham Court Road, London.[80] There had been some large orders. However, the community hoped to deal in a more personal way with individuals and smaller enterprises interested in quality products. They wanted to respond to 'the wishes of our English friends that we should produce more practical objects which are indispensable in a household'. For those who were interested, there was a price list with photographs, and a number of friends of the community received a specially designed butter dish as a gift.[81]

75. Prospectus, 'First Bruderhof Letter: The Founding of the Cotswold Bruderhof', 1 September 1936, 10. BHA Coll. 0301_004.

76. Annemarie Arnold to Reinhold Wächter, 3 October 1936. BHA Coll. 0005.

77. Heini Arnold to Reinhold Wächter, 19 December 1936. BHA Coll. 0005.

78. Prospectus, 'First Bruderhof Letter: The Founding of the Cotswold Bruderhof', 1 September 1936, 9. BHA Coll. 0301_004.

79. For the Guild see Robinson, *Fertile Field*.

80. For Heal see Heal, *Sir Ambrose Heal and the Heal Cabinet Factory*.

81. Prospectus, 'Second Bruderhof Letter', Christmas 1936, 11. BHA Coll. 0301_004.

The education of children was seen by the community as 'our special concern', and at the end of 1936 the second circular letter reported that the community had five qualified teachers trained in the British educational system, as well as those trained in the German and Swiss systems.[82] In February 1937, Annemarie Arnold wrote: 'Altogether there are now twenty-eight children at the Cotswold Bruderhof: two babies plus a new baby girl (English) born ten days ago and still at home with her mother; five delightful toddlers a year and a half old; nine kindergarten children, and eleven schoolchildren.' Annemarie said that in the mornings she had the kindergarten to look after, and in the afternoons she was with the schoolchildren. For her it was a great joy to see the children's work beginning to flourish.[83] In part because of her family connections with the German educator Friedrich Fröbel, Annemarie was keen on educational methods that involved the children to the full in their own learning. By June 1937 Annemarie could report to her mother and brother that with new arrivals at the Cotswold Bruderhof the total number in the community was 122, including forty-five children. The children's house was a very lively setting, and she was determined that 'as soon as possible we must have another'.[84]

With these various departments of work developing in the community, there was a need for overall coordination. Arnold Mason was at this stage in charge of business and accounting. The second circular letter spoke about it being 'very important, contrary to the ways of many "idealists" and Utopians, to keep exact accounts so that we are able to see in clear figures the results of our communal way of life'.[85] Dennis Hardy, in *Utopian England*, notes, quite incorrectly, that Cotswold Bruderhof financial accounts 'were not published'. He is correct, however, in stating that it is unlikely that the community's activities ever provided sufficient income to make the community financially viable and that outside help was needed.[86] The second circular letter set out a 'Balance Sheet and Profit and Loss Account' and there was a detailed, indeed sophisticated

82. Prospectus, 'First Bruderhof Letter: The Founding of the Cotswold Bruderhof', 1 September 1936, 6; Prospectus, 'Second Bruderhof Letter', Christmas 1936, 12. BHA Coll. 0301_004.

83. Annemarie Arnold to her mother, 26 February 1937. BHA Coll. 0005.

84. Annemarie Arnold to her mother and brother, 24 June 1937. BHA Coll. 0005.

85. Prospectus, 'Second Bruderhof Letter', Christmas 1936, 5. BHA Coll. 0301_004.

86. Hardy, *Utopian England*, 188.

commentary on the figures, covering several pages. Donations were also listed. There was no attempt to hide the need for assistance from friends, especially during a time of rapid expansion, renovation, and the building of new dwelling houses, school facilities, and workshops. Each project was carefully calculated, and independent contractors were used for estimates. All building work was done in accordance with the traditional Cotswold style.[87]

A Changed Centre of Gravity

From 1937, the centre of Bruderhof life was shifting from Germany to England. One result of this change was the use of the English language in Bruderhof communication. Inevitably there were difficulties. Hardy was annoyed that English members were not translating what they were saying into German. This was 'very impolite'.[88] However, as time went on there was a realisation that in an international setting translation was essential. Sometimes if speakers were so absorbed in what they were saying that they forgot about this, there were shouts of 'Translation!'[89] Gerd Wegner was one of those from Germany who took advantage of conversations at mealtimes to learn English.[90] When Arnold Mason and Heini Arnold went to local markets to buy cattle, farm machines, or furniture, they made an unusual duo, bargaining with sellers in German as well as English.[91] The blending of cultures and languages was seen in work with the children. Annemarie Arnold described to her mother the first Christmas Eve at the Cotswold Bruderhof: 'When it grew dark, we all gathered in front of the big house. We walked singing in a long procession to the stable at the back of the *hof* where the manger scene had been set up with a young ox and little calves. The Christmas story was read out in two languages; we sang many Christmas songs, and everybody was given a small red candle lit from the candle at the manger.'[92] The experience of shared Christmas joy in this international community was profound.

---

87. Prospectus, 'Second Bruderhof Letter', Christmas 1936, 5–8, 15–20. BHA Coll. 0301_004.

88. Hardy Arnold to Edith Arnold, 21 March 1936. BHA Coll. 0304.

89. Arnold Mason, 'Early Memories'. BHA Coll. 0006.

90. Gerd Wegner, 'Memories'. BHA Coll. 0475.

91. Arnold Mason, 'Early Memories'. BHA Coll. 0006.

92. Annemarie Arnold to her mother, 4 January 1937. BHA Coll. 0005.

At the Rhön Bruderhof, however, Nazi pressure was intensifying. In early 1937, male members at the Rhön who became liable for military service under further German government regulations made their way by whatever means possible to England. For example, August and Gertrud Dyroff, with their baby, boarded a train dressed in Hutterian costume—Gertrud with a head scarf and long skirt and August with a substantial beard. Their luggage was in bundles. At the border with Holland they pretended to be asleep and the German official saw what he described as 'dirty Poles' and let them through.[93]

On 14 April 1937, the Gestapo arrived at the Rhön Bruderhof, lined everyone up against the wall, and announced that the community was shut down. David Hofer and Michael Waldner, two Canadian Hutterian elders, were present at the time, having been asked by the community to come to the Rhön, and it seems likely that their presence was significant in restraining the Gestapo. Three community leaders, Hans Meier (Swiss), Hannes Boller (Swiss), and Karl Keiderling (German), were, however, singled out and imprisoned in nearby Fulda. Two days later, on 16 April, buses arrived to take community members to the train station. Some went to the Alm, some to Holland, and some on to England. David Hofer, Michael Waldner, and Hella Römer, the community bookkeeper, returned to the forsaken compound.[94] Hella Römer remained under house arrest until 12 May. Emmy Arnold spoke later of the 'divine blessing to have the two Hutterian brothers with us at just this hour'. She recalled how Eberhard had said shortly before his death that 'if an hour of direst need should come upon you in the community, the Hutterian brothers will come to the rescue'.[95]

British community members at the Rhön were able to travel to England without further delay. On 21 April, Kathleen Hamilton and Stanley Fletcher arrived at the Cotswold community and Kathleen described first-hand the sad events of the week before. Gertrud Löffler conveyed Kathleen's report to Hans-Hermann Arnold. Kathleen described how 'a crowd of about sixty men (Gestapo, SS, and others) came on the *hof* in the morning, settled down in the dining room with typewriters and rummaged through all the houses, broke furniture in some rooms, and altogether behaved very crudely and contemptuously. They took possession

93. Barth, *An Embassy Besieged*, 270.

94. Barth, *An Embassy Besieged*, 277.

95. Emmy Arnold to Hans Zumpe, 2 May 1937, cited by Barth, *An Embassy Besieged*, 277.

of the money and passports right away.' It was evident to Kathleen that the presence of Americans, British, and other foreigners at the Rhön had made the police uncomfortable, and they were concerned about getting the foreigners out of the way as quickly as possible. Kathleen was able to offer some reassurance to the Cotswold members about the situation of Hans Meier, Hannes Boller, and Karl Keiderling. David Hofer had visited Fulda prison and had brought back a report that the three prisoners were 'very courageous and joyful'. Kathleen was also able to tell the Cotswold community that all those who were going to apply for entry to Britain were at the Brotherhood House in Bilthoven, Holland, founded by Kees and Betty Boeke.[96]

As well as reporting first hand to the Cotswold community, Kathleen Hamilton wrote to her mother on 22 April to tell her that 'the Rhön Bruderhof is no more and three of our brothers are in prison in Germany'. Freed from German censorship, Kathleen was now forthright about Nazi intentions regarding the community: 'They wanted to scatter us and break us up, to drive the men to obey the State rather than God, to send the women to their nearest relatives, to get the foreigners out of Germany, to get the children to be brought up in the Hitler *Jugend*, in short, to root out a life of love and brotherhood, which recognises God as King in the whole of life, and the State as recognised by God or rather, allowed by God, because men having turned from God need law and force to prevent chaos.' She told her mother, whom she knew would pass on the news to her circle of friends, about the three who had been taken 'by treachery'. Kathleen was determined that 'we shall not rest till our brothers also are free'. The community needed, she said, to raise money: 'We need money—a terrific amount—to get our brothers and sisters to England, to build here that we may have room for them, to buy land to be able to feed them: in short, we stand firm in the faith that God will do great things.' With her customary energy, Kathleen was already making plans to go out and raise funds.[97]

The Cotswold Bruderhof issued a special newsletter in May 1937 entitled, 'A Christian Community: With a short account of its suppression in Germany'. Through this and other means, especially in the way the community was able to connect with the press, efforts were made to

96. Gertrud Löffler to Hans-Hermann Arnold, 22/23 April 1937. BHA Coll. 0190.

97. Kathleen Hamilton to her mother, 22 April 1937. BHA Coll. 0015. Although Kathleen said that all others were out of Germany, Hella Römer was held under house arrest at the Rhön until 12 May.

bring to the attention of the British public the situation of the refugees now in the Netherlands. The newsletter stated that the Cotswold community had to find funds for them—a group 'mostly of women and children'—since the Home Office would only give them permission to come to Britain if their financial maintenance could be guaranteed for twelve months.[98] The Bruderhof was in touch with Sir Wyndham Deedes at the National Council of Social Service, and he had published an appeal in the *Manchester Guardian*. Under the heading 'German Pacifist Community', Sir Wyndham wrote what was a pointed political letter to the newspaper: 'During the time that Mr George Lansbury [by then the former leader of the Labour Party] discussed peace with Hitler the German Secret Police suppressed what is perhaps the last body to make an open stand for peace in Germany'. He described how the Bruderhof had been 'forcibly expelled'. He then explained about the financial needs of the community. Help was 'urgently required'.[99] Other appeals of a similar nature had appeared in denominational newspapers such as the *Methodist Recorder*, indicating the way the cause of the Bruderhof had been taken up in Britain.

An interview with Hardy Arnold was featured in the *Baptist Times*, in which Hardy explained that the Bruderhof shared with many in England a desire 'to get rid of the war-madness and the cruel competition characterising what is called civilisation'.[100] J. H. Rushbrooke, who had been at the Constance conference in 1914 and who knew Friedrich Siegmund-Schultze and Henry Hodgkin, wrote a letter, 'Pacifists Needing Help'. Rushbrooke was secretary of the Baptist World Alliance and was the most influential European Baptist of his time. He wrote about the community in the Cotswolds having received 'a severe shock': 'The entire property of their community, near Fulda in Germany, has been confiscated'. Rushbrooke, who knew Germany well, spoke of expulsions and the imprisonment of those whose only offence was 'pacifism'. He stated that the British government required a total sum of approximately £2,000 in respect of members entering Britain, but that 'members of the Brotherhood are without resources'. Rushbrooke referred to Anabaptist tradition and considered that 'all Baptists would unite in admiration of the fine spirit of the members of the Cotswold Bruderhof and recognise

98. Prospectus, 'A Christian Community: With a short account of its suppression in Germany' (May 1937), 4. BHA Coll. 0301_004.

99. Deedes, 'German Pacifist Community', *Manchester Guardian*, 24 April 1937.

100. 'An Experiment in Christian Communism', *Baptist Times*, 22 April 1937.

them as true brothers in Christ'. He urged *Baptist Times* readers to help.[101] Through these appeals, and with help from Mennonites, they raised the necessary funds.

On 26 June 1937, thanks to the efforts of several supporters of the community—a number of Quakers; the Bruderhof's lawyer, Dr Eisenberg; and Frank Gheel van Gildemeester in Holland—Hans Meier, Karl Keiderling and Hannes Boller were all released from Fulda prison. They arrived at the Cotswold Bruderhof on 2 July.[102] That evening Hannes Boller related how in prison they had faced the possibility of death, and had found that 'love, complete love, casts out all fear'.[103] Writing five days later, Hardy Arnold was convinced that something remarkable was happening: 'One could hardly grasp it at first, seeing the many together, especially being aware that it is a real miracle the way everyone has been led out of Germany as a united people, under no leadership but God's.'[104] The stage was now set for a new momentum in mission in Britain.

---

101. *Baptist Times*,13 May 1937.

102. Barth, *An Embassy Besieged*, 278–80. It was while in Holland that Bruderhof members met van Gildemeester. He had worked as part of the Quaker team feeding children in Germany and became involved in helping to free prisoners of conscience.

103. Hannes Boller, community meeting, 2 July 1937. BHA Coll. 0055.

104. Hardy Arnold, to Emmy Arnold, 7 July 1937,. BHA Coll. 0304.

4

Sharing in Witness

In August 1937 the Cotswold Bruderhof began to plan for *The Plough* as a periodical publication linked to a wider vision for mission. A third Bruderhof letter stated that the 'gathering and building up of a true community life' was impossible without 'mission work', but equally 'there can be no true mission without a centre which endeavours to give a true picture of the life to which people must be called'.[1] There was also a desire to cooperate with others. The 'very good reception' afforded to Bruderhof letters and 'the fact that so many people in this country are deeply interested in the work of the Bruderhof' had led to the idea of a regular publication, 'to keep in contact with everybody who is concerned about life in community'.[2] *The Plough* was launched in March 1938 (along with a German version, *Der Pflug*), with Hardy Arnold as editor. It proved to be popular, and the fact that Hardy drew in a wide range of authors from outside the Bruderhof helped it to make a significant contribution to wider thinking about pacifist Christian communities. Introducing the first issue, Hardy spoke of 'some who feel more and more strongly the need of a spiritual revolution which will change the whole fabric of life'.[3] The Bruderhof wished to be identified with and to contribute to this movement. Through *The Plough*, and through the varied activities of the

1. Prospectus, 'Third Bruderhof Letter', August 1937, 3. BHA Coll. 0301_004.

2. Prospectus, 'Cotswold Bruderhof to Dear Friends', August 1937. BHA Coll. 0334.

3. The Editor, 'The Task of the Plough', *The Plough* 1, no. 1 (March 1938), 1.

Cotswold community, there was a desire to share in witness in Britain, addressing areas such as peace, community, social involvement, church renewal, and a Christ-centred faith.

From the Old to the New

The hope expressed in the first issue of *The Plough* was that it could be instrumental in 'uniting more closely' wider movements in society with people 'trying to establish in a small way' a new kind of communal living, thus 'ploughing the field' (a reference to the periodical's name) for the seeds of a new humanity to be planted. This could not be done through human effort. It was 'the living Christ' who was at the heart of the movement 'from the old to the new', and who was 'the centre of the message of THE PLOUGH'.[4] As a signal that the publication would draw from a broad constituency, one of the articles in the first issue was by J. B. Rusch, a Swiss Roman Catholic who was committed to applying Christian principles to social and political life. He published in *National-Zeitung*, a Basel German-language daily newspaper. His comments on the European situation were translated and reproduced elsewhere, for example in the international weekly *The Living Age: The World in Review*.[5] Hardy Arnold was pleased to feature Rusch's treatment of 'salvation and liberation', which Hardy noted 'shows such vision and imagination'.[6] The next *Plough* was similarly wide-ranging. It included a paper that had emerged from the influential Conference on Christian Politics, Economics and Citizenship (COPEC), held in 1924 in Birmingham, which had brought together fifteen hundred leaders to discuss a Christian social vision. The link with the Bruderhof may have been FoR, since Charles Raven, the chairman of FoR, was a central organiser of COPEC. Writing in 1922, Raven spoke of COPEC as 'unique in religious history. Our quest is a cooperative effort in which every Christian communion in the country has pledged to take its share'.[7] Raven had been a WWI chaplain and later became a pacifist. He and other former WWI chaplains had a 'high

---

4. The Editor, 'The Task of the Plough', *The Plough* 1, no. 1 (March 1938), 2.

5. For example Rusch, 'Swiss Forebodings', in *The Living Age: The World in Review*, 202–203.

6. 'Editorial Notes', *The Plough* 1, no. 1 (March 1938), 38.

7. *The Challenge*, 17 November 1922, 328.

profile in social issues in the 1920s'.[8] The COPEC paper in *The Plough* was international in outlook, arguing that full realisation of Christian community would only happen when, for example, 'Christians of India and China converse with those of Britain and France'.[9]

However, the vision conveyed in *The Plough* concerned local community life as well as global Christian thinking. The issue containing the COPEC article also featured a contemporary item from Birmingham. This was from 'the Birmingham Community Group', whose members had spent Easter 1938 at the Cotswold Bruderhof. This Birmingham community's house (Bruderhof House was later adopted as the name), had members of the Cotswold Bruderhof staying in it for varying lengths of time during 1938. In July, Heini Arnold spoke of 'very lively' discussions there.[10] The members of the Birmingham group, who were part of Carrs Lane, Birmingham, spoke of their Easter experiences at Ashton Keynes: taking community meals together in silence on Good Friday, working in the community on Saturday, and beginning Easter Sunday with the singing of Easter carols and hymns from five o'clock in the morning. After an Easter breakfast, 'which like all the meals at the Bruderhof was a sacrament in itself', time was spent with the children. Following the evening meal there was a reading from the book of Daniel about being in the 'fiery furnace'. The final challenge on this Easter Sunday was 'to make way for the new order of Brotherhood upon the earth'.[11] This was indicative of the aspiration of the Cotswold community. Along with what might be seen as unrealistic ideals there were practical steps. As an example of the kind of efforts being made, later in 1938 a single 'work evening', which went on into the night, saw *Plough* pamphlets printed and packed for despatch: 10,000 in English, 5,000 in German, and 3,000 in Dutch.[12]

A number of features in *The Plough* related to the theme of arts and crafts. Georg Barth wrote on 'Work and Handicraft in the Spiritual Culture of the Church', arguing that the work of human hands in moulding material acted as 'the interpreter of the soul'.[13] Eric Gill, one of the

8. Parker, 'Shell-Shocked Prophets', 192.

9. 'The Holy Nation', *The Plough* 1, no. 2 (July 1938), 51–57. The author of this COPEC paper was not named.

10. Heini Arnold to Annemarie Arnold, 9 July 1938. BHA Coll. 0005.

11. 'Easter at the Bruderhof', *The Plough* 1, no. 2 (July 1938), 60–61.

12. Annemarie Arnold to Heini Arnold, 23 September 1938. BHA Coll. 0005.

13. Georg Barth, 'Work and Handicraft in the Spiritual Culture of the Church', *The Plough* 1, no. 2 (July 1938), 57–60, esp. 57.

leading figures in the Arts and Crafts movement, addressed the much-debated subject of politics in relation to the Gospel in *The Plough*. Gill had been involved in setting up small communities and was a member of the PPU and also supportive of FoR.[14] In his *Plough* article Gill argued against capitalism, which he said was based on 'the notion that those who have money have the duty to get more', while others were exploited. He rejected the power-seeking of fascism and also Communism's agenda that 'the poor may become rich'. The alternative, for Gill, was the teaching of Jesus, which he argued was not an unattainable 'counsel of perfection'; instead, it called people to a demonstrable life of peace, voluntary poverty, and love.[15] Another leading Arts and Crafts figure featured in *The Plough* was Laurence Housman, a prolific author, playwright, and illustrator who, with his sister Clemence, had founded an arts and crafts society that worked closely with the Women's Social and Political Union.[16] Housman had a deep interest in Francis of Assisi, and in *The Plough* he presented Francis as a creative, artistic evangelist, who revelled 'in the glorious liberty of an evangelism based on a few of the simplest sayings of Christ'.[17]

The autumn 1939 issue of *Plough* focussed on education. A number of topics were dealt with under the heading 'Child Life at the Bruderhof'. Among the authors, Gertrud (Trudi) Hüssy had taught Bruderhof children since 1921.[18] Others who had been involved with children's education when the community was in Germany, such as Monika Trümpi, Annemarie Arnold and Emi-Margret Zumpe, wrote about their experiences at the Cotswold Bruderhof. There were contributions about education from some of the British teachers who had joined the community, with Gertrude Vigar writing on the toddlers, Bessie Harries on the nursery school, and Kathleen Hasenberg (previously Hamilton, but now married to Erich Hasenberg) on how children in an international setting learned English. Children themselves also wrote, under the heading 'The Children Speak'. They contributed songs and drawings. An article by Eberhard Arnold summarized the Bruderhof approach to educa-

14. Ceadel, *Pacifism in Britain, 1914–1945*, 281, 289–91, 295, 321.

15. Eric Gill, 'Religion is Politics: Politics is Brotherhood: Brotherhood is Poverty', *The Plough* 2, no. 1 (Spring 1939), 10–12.

16. See Housman's autobiography *The Unexpected Years*.

17. Laurence Housman, 'St. Francis the Man', *The Plough* 3, no. 1 (Spring 1940), 15–18, esp. 17.

18. Baum, *Against the Wind*, 152.

tion. The philosophy was that in the life of a child 'coercive power and supervision are replaced by trust in the awakening guidance of the Spirit'. The article went on to say that 'all corporal punishment is a declaration of educational bankruptcy'. Education was to be geared to the individual young person and his or her gifts. Teaching, play and the enjoyment of the natural world were all emphasised. The Bible was used in the teaching of children, but instead of concentrating on 'dogmatics and religious practice', the belief—and the experience—of the community was that Christ 'comes close to the child'.[19]

The 1940 issues of *The Plough* were the last to be produced from the Cotswold Bruderhof. They reflected the background of war. One of the articles, on the witness of the Christian churches in a time of hatred and cruelty, was by Stanley Fletcher, who had been a member of the Tramp Preachers (also known as the Brotherhood of the Way) before joining the Bruderhof. The Tramp Preachers were a group of about a dozen itinerant (hence 'tramping') preachers who tried to apply Christian beliefs to the issues of society. They were often involved in large open-air meetings. On one occasion, for example, in Merthyr Tydfil, a centre of mining in Wales, they found themselves part of a large Communist gathering, and Charlie Jory, who like Stanley Fletcher joined the Bruderhof, started to debate with Communist leaders about atheism, socialism, and other topics. Soon the crowd abandoned the Communist speakers to hear the Tramp Preachers.[20]

In the spring 1940 issue of *Plough*, Stanley reflected on dark and depressing periods in history and suggested that there had always been those preachers—he instanced the Waldensians in Lombardy and the Lollards in England—who 'spoke of the humility and love of Christ'. Above all he pointed to the sixteenth century as a time when, especially through the Anabaptist movement, the 'faith of the waiting and expectant Church of Jesus was again bright and living in the blackness of the world'. For him Anabaptism represented a 'great spiritual movement'. Although it seemed to Stanley Fletcher, from his experience of meeting a wide range of people, that many were 'helpless, hopeless and without faith', living in the 'crumbling edifices of this modern, man-made world', nonetheless authentic Christian witness still continued. Through a time of great darkness, the message of the final victory of God's love and the

19. Eberhard Arnold, 'Our Approach to Education', *The Plough* 2, no. 3 (Autumn 1939), 67–72.

20. Stanley Fletcher, 'Tramp Preachers'. BHA Coll. 0067.

return of the 'cast-out and crucified Jesus' was still, he believed, a reality that brought light and hope.[21]

Pledged to Peace

In 1934 Dick Sheppard, an inspirational clergyman who was vicar of St Martin-in-the-Fields, Trafalgar Square, London wrote a letter which appeared in the *Manchester Guardian* and elsewhere inviting people who wished to 'renounce war' to get in touch. He picked up on a statement made in the previous year at an Armistice service in the USA by Harry Emerson Fosdick, the outstanding Baptist minister of Riverside Church, New York. Fosdick had declared: 'I renounce war and never again, directly or indirectly, will I sanction or support another.' The response to Sheppard's call in Britain was enormous. Out of this the Peace Pledge Union was formed.[22] By summer 1936 there were around a hundred thousand members.[23] Among those who joined were some leading writers, such as Aldous Huxley, Max Plowman, Vera Brittain, Rose Macaulay, Margaret Storm Jameson, Siegfried Sassoon, and John Middleton Murry. Most of them had been involved in some way in WWI, and part of their response to Sheppard was due to their revulsion against the horrors of modern war.[24] Rose Macaulay noted that Sheppard was able to draw together pacifists who brought different perspectives.[25] The PPU was not an explicitly Christian organisation, although many of those involved saw their pacifism as springing from their Christian faith. Two prominent Church of England figures who became members of the PPU executive committee and contributed radical thinking about Christian faith within modern society were E. W. Barnes, bishop of Birmingham, and Hewlett Johnson, dean of Canterbury, known as the 'Red Dean' because of his left-wing views.[26]

As well as these leaders, the PPU attracted many who felt it offered the chance to be heard. A PPU rally in the Albert Hall in July 1935

---

21. Stanley Fletcher, 'But of that day and hour knoweth no man . . .', *The Plough* 3, no. 1 (Spring 1940), 8–14.

22. Morrison, *I Renounce War*, 8.

23. Huxley and Sheppard, *100,000 Say No!*, 3.

24. Brock and Young, *Pacifism in the Twentieth Century*, 122.

25. Quoted in Roberts, *H. R. L. Sheppard*, 277.

26. Pugh, *Liberal Internationalism*, 95.

attracted seven thousand people. This took place a month after the completion of a year-long campaign in Britain, the 'Peace Ballot', in which the vast majority of the eleven million people who responded showed their desire for a resolution of international conflicts through peaceful means, not war. This did not mean that specifically pacifist convictions held sway, but it signalled a significant coming together of those who resisted war.[27] At the same time as hope was being expressed, there was a degree of disillusionment about failures in disarmament.[28] Over 800 local PPU groups were formed, and for a time it seemed as if the PPU might become a mass movement.[29] Alan Stevenson, a salesman, was one of the PPU members who later joined the Bruderhof. Richard Gregg's 1934 book *The Power of Non-Violence* provided Alan with 'a completely new way of thinking', and his pacifism was reinforced by Dick Sheppard's call.[30] Arthur Woolston, who heard about the Bruderhof through Alan Stevenson, was another example of the PPU's impact. Arthur moved in 1937 to London, where he worked for Boots, the well-known chemist. He contacted the PPU head office, received some literature, and signed the pledge. He stated: 'I could in no circumstances take part in prosecution of war in any way.'[31]

A young Quaker, Humphrey Moore, reported on Bruderhof developments in a PPU publication, *Peace News*, in the later 1930s. In May 1937, *Peace News* covered the end of the Rhön and the way the Cotswold community had developed. The article described the basis of the community's life as 'an absolute communism of property and work and a total rejection of all forms of coercion'. From the beginning, it continued, 'the venture was made in faith', and it explained that Bruderhof life in England had been possible only through the help of friends, with donations spent on building up the farm, creating and running workshops, and providing 'apartments capable of housing a large number of people as well as guests and relatives'. With more community members from

27. Brock and Young, *Pacifism in the Twentieth Century*, 132. Ceadel, *Semi-Detached Idealists*, 280.

28. Lynch, *Beyond Appeasement*, 108. When the World Alliance for International Friendship through the Churches asked its member bodies in 1934 for their views of Disarmament, not a single reply expressed hope for success.

29. Steiner, *The Triumph of the Dark*, 168–169.

30. Alan Stevenson, 'Something of My Life'. BHA Coll. 0314. Richard Gregg's book influenced, among others, Aldous Huxley and Martin Luther King Jr.

31. Arthur Woolston, 'Arthur Woolston's Story'. BHA Coll. 0316.

mainland Europe now needing to be housed, the situation was described as 'highly critical'.[32] *Peace News* took up the story again in June 1937, when it spoke of the Bruderhof as 'a brotherhood of do-ers of the word as written in the Sermon on the Mount'. The community was 'no longer an experiment'. Members were described as 'amazingly practical idealists'.[33] The October 1939 issue commended an article, 'The Call of the Hour', by Hardy Arnold. *Peace News* noted it had been written before war was declared, and was 'more, rather than less, topical both in its content and its title'.[34] The Bruderhof was seen in wider 'peace' circles as offering a prophetic witness.

This did not mean that all those supporting the PPU saw their commitment in the same terms. Fred Goodwin, a student at Cambridge University from 1932 to 1936, became involved in the SCM and also became a pacifist, but he did not believe in signing a pledge. In February 1933 the Oxford Union famously debated the motion that 'this House will in no circumstances fight for its King and country' and voted 275 to 153 in favour. The vote was symptomatic of radical opinions, especially among younger people.[35] In Cambridge University, Charles Raven, the Regius Professor of Divinity, was an influential pacifist voice.[36] Margaret Taylor, who sang in the same Church of England choir as Fred, was also a pacifist, and she and Fred began to have conversations about basing their lives on the Sermon on the Mount. Margaret was keen on the PPU and went to the local railway station on Saturday evenings to sell copies of *Peace News*. Fred, however, did not agree with advocacy being conducted in that way. Nonetheless, they agreed that they wanted to live in a Christian community. They subsequently married and joined the Bruderhof.[37]

Although the PPU supported the Bruderhof's witness, there were PPU members who felt community living carried the danger of being cut off from the world. Heini Arnold was therefore pleased to report that at one 'lively' meeting in Lancaster at which he and Stanley Fletcher spoke—and which, Heini noted, took place in a very historic house where

32. 'Pacifism in Communal Life', *Peace News*, 1 May 1937.

33. 'Idealism in Practice', *Peace News*, 5 June 1937.

34. *Peace News*, 6 October 1939.

35. Pugh, *Liberal Internationalism*, 104.

36. For more on Raven see Randall, 'Evangelical Spirituality, Science, and Mission', in *Anglican and Episcopal History*, 20–48.

37. Margret Goodwin, 'Margaret Goodwin tells of Fred Goodwin'. BHA Coll. 0102.

the Quaker founder, George Fox, spoke in 1675—an experienced PPU member, Thomas Rhodes, suggested that PPU members had been 'negative' in thinking that Bruderhof communities 'cut themselves off from the world'. The Bruderhof representatives who had spoken, Rhodes said, had shown 'that we are the ones who live as isolated individuals'.[38]

As had been the case earlier, Quaker peace witness remained significant for the Bruderhof. The life of the Cotswold community was highlighted in May 1937 in a Quaker publication, *The Friend*, which stated that there was to be a visit to the Bruderhof, organised from Bristol by an adult education centre, Folk House.[39] Heini Arnold visited Folk House in 1937 to speak to a group there, and his description of the Bruderhof led to the idea of a trip from the House to Ashton Keynes. A char-à-banc was hired for the day. One of those who made this visit to the Bruderhof was Marjorie Badham, who was then a factory welfare supervisor in Bristol. At the time she was pondering the meaning of Christianity in the modern world, and was reading the New Testament, especially the Sermon on the Mount. She also began to read Quaker books. Marjorie was deeply affected by her Bruderhof visit, and she later returned to the community for a week. She then spent a university term with the Quakers at Woodbrooke, but for her the experience of the Bruderhof 'transcended anything that modern Quakerism or anything else was saying'. She joined the community and later married Sydney Hindley.[40] Alan Stevenson also explored Quaker spirituality, but considered that many Quakers were removed from the poverty he encountered.[41]

Ruth Cassell, who was studying medicine at the London Royal Free Hospital School of Medicine for Women, joined the FoR and also the Baptist Pacifist Fellowship. She had been baptised at nineteen in a Baptist church, out of 'a desire to belong completely to Jesus'.[42] Among Ruth's friends were Margaret Jess Stern, also a medical student and a Baptist, and Dorothy Cox, who had trained for service in the Baptist Deaconess Order.[43] The Bruderhof had made contact with Baptist ministry among

38. Heini Hardy to Annemarie Hardy, 27 January 1940. BHA Coll. 0005.

39. 'The Bruderhof', *The Friend*, 21 May 1937.

40. Marjorie Hindley, 'Marjorie Hindley's Memories'. BHA Coll. 0324.

41. Alan Stevenson, 'Something of My Life'. BHA Coll. 0314.

42. Ruth Land, 'Ruth Land memory book'. BHA Coll. 0346.

43. Deaconess ministry among Baptists was developing in this period, with some deaconesses taking pastoral leadership in churches: Randall, *The English Baptists of the Twentieth Century*, 190–192.

miners in South Wales who were suffering poverty. This work was led by another Baptist deaconess, Marjorie Parker-Gray. She decided to join the Bruderhof and gave Dorothy Cox peace literature, which then came to Ruth and Margaret, who were nearing the end of their medical studies. Following Ruth's last medical exam, she took a train from London and arrived at the Cotswold Bruderhof later that day. Her impression was of 'a group of very loving people living peacefully together', English and Germans. It was 1939 and everyone she knew expected a war with Germany. These well-qualified Baptist women—Marjorie, Ruth, Margaret and Dorothy—all investigated and subsequently joined the Bruderhof. Ruth later married Ted Land, who came to the Bruderhof having been a member of both the PPU and FoR.[44]

Kingsley Hall, too, constituted a link between the FoR and the Bruderhof. Muriel Lester was deeply involved in FoR, and in 1938 Muriel and Friedrich Siegmund-Schultze were appointed as travelling secretaries of the International FoR.[45] When Kingsley Hall members discussed their vision for 'the salvation of the individual and the creation of a new society', Godfrey Pain, formerly a leader at Carrs Lane, Birmingham, and now at Kingsley Hall, spoke from his experience about the Bruderhof's commitment to a 'propertyless' society and how this linked with their pacifist beliefs.[46] Peace networks existed at multiple levels.

Experiments in Community

In March 1938, Leslie Stubbings, the honorary secretary of the newly formed Community Service Committee, noted the Bruderhof's intention to publish news and announcements from his committee in *The Plough*. In his article Leslie Stubbings wrote about 'courageous experiments in community': some had failed, some had taken a wrong turning, and some had survived, albeit painfully. He believed, however, that there was hope for a new era of communal living. Although not himself a member of the Bruderhof, he was convinced that what had happened at Ashton Keynes

44. Ruth Land, 'Ruth Land memory book'. BHA Coll. 0346.

45. Minutes of the General Committee of FoR, 21 June 1938. COLL MISC 0456/1/6, London School of Economics. British FoR membership was about 8,000 at this point, and still rising.

46. Minutes of a Kingsley Hall Meeting, 28 March 1937, LESTER 1/1/5, Bishopsgate Institute, London.

had 'released a consciousness that was already latent and growing'.[47] The first major gathering of people associated with different community ventures in Britain took place in 1937, at a significant conference in Bath.

Those gathered at Bath were concerned about the failings of society and the threats posed by international competition. In their response to the threat of war, all held to 'Christian Pacifist' convictions. Beyond that, most considered that authentic witness involved community life.[48] Speaking at Bath, Hardy Arnold described community life as 'hard and strenuous', and also as 'pioneering but happy and joyous'.[49] The Quakers were well represented at Bath, as were a variety of other groups that had links to the PPU, such as John Middleton Murry's Adelphi Centre, which was a community in Essex. The PPU's *Peace News*, in April 1938, spoke of *The Plough* as fulfilling an important role in this renewal of wider interest in community. It was a 'most attractively produced' publication, described as emanating from what was by then the 'famous Cotswold community'. *Peace News* declared, 'No-one who is interested in the development of contact and coordination between the various communities in existence should fail to see *The Plough*'.[50]

As a result of the Bath conference, an index of names of those interested in community life was produced. There were 350 people on the list.[51] A substantial volume of papers based on material from the conference, *Community in Britain*, was also compiled, produced by the Community Service Committee and published at the Cotswold Bruderhof Press. The first four papers looked at 'Colonies and Settlements'. Here Hardy Arnold wrote on Bruderhof life; Brinsley Nixon described Hugh's Settlement, formed in 1928 in Hampshire; Nellie Shaw traced the story of the Whiteway Colony, which dated back to the 1890s and was in the Cotswolds; and Alfred Higgins wrote on the Stapleton Colony, established in the 1920s in Yorkshire.[52] Other chapters in *Community in Britain* looked at camps, at provision of services, at various centres, at opportunities for service overseas, and at community principles. Several contributors were well known to the Bruderhof, such as Marjorie Parker-Gray, Mary Os-

47. Leslie Stubbings, 'In England Now', *The Plough* 1, no. 1 (March 1938), 12–19, esp. 12, 14.

48. Hardy, *Utopian England*, 194.

49. *Bath and Wilts Chronicle and Herald*, 26 April 1937.

50. *Peace News*, 9 April 1938.

51. 'Community Service', *The Plough* 1, no. 1 (March 1938), 36.

52. *Community in Britain* (1938).

born, Godfrey Pain, and Jack Hoyland, who with his long-term interest in community was one of those arguing strongly within Quaker circles that pacifism had to take a communal vision seriously.[53]

The Bath conference and the subsequent volume of papers represented a landmark. Various community groups were able to see that they were not working in isolation but were 'battling together against the rising tide of war, unemployment and lost values'.[54] Following the Bath conference and another in Bow, East London, in the following year, further community ventures began. One was the Elmsett farm settlement in Suffolk, co-started in January 1939 by Edmund Cocksedge, who had been a Tramp Preacher. He was twenty-six and recently married when Elmsett began. Having been to the Rhön Bruderhof and to the *kibbutzim* in Israel, he became committed to community living. Through a PPU group, Arthur Woolston heard about the Cotswold Bruderhof and about Elmsett. One member of the PPU group, Percy Levin, was Jewish, and he questioned whether he could join the Bruderhof since it had a Christian basis. Arthur Woolston wrote to the Bruderhof about this. Arnold Mason replied saying the Bruderhof was absolutely certain that a communal life had to be centred on Christ.[55]

At the time, Arnold Mason's answer was too dogmatic for Arthur. He was open to the religious views of a range of people. Arthur decided, therefore, to try Elmsett, which seemed to be in tune with his thinking in this area, although by the time he arrived there Edmund and Amy Cocksedge had already moved to the Cotswold Bruderhof. Towards the end of February 1941, Paul Cavanna, who had been at the Cotswold Bruderhof, arrived at Elmsett, having been encouraged by the Cotswold community to spend time discerning what he was seeking. Paul gave a talk at Elmsett on the Bruderhof, comparing the approaches of the two communities.[56] When Paul returned to the Cotswold community, Arthur felt inwardly drawn to go with him.[57]

The Plough, in line with its commitment, often shared news about the development of communities in England, Scotland and Wales, and sometimes elsewhere. These included the Community of the Way in Bow,

53. J. S. Hoyland, 'The New Tasks of Pacifism', *The Friend*, 9 October 1936.

54. Hardy, *Utopian England*, 196. See also Rigby, 'Pacifist Communities in Britain in the Second World War', 107–122.

55. Arthur Woolston, 'Arthur Woolston's Story'. BHA Coll. 0316.

56. Arthur Woolston to his mother, March 1941. BHA Coll. 0316.

57. Arthur Woolston, 'Arthur Woolston's Story'. BHA Coll. 0316.

East London; a St Hilda's community group at Micklepage Farm, near Horsham, Sussex; and a Community House in Cambridge. *The Plough* also highlighted the Iona Community in Glasgow, which was led by George MacLeod, a Church of Scotland minister who had been decorated in WWI and who had become a pacifist; a community workshop in Edinburgh; and—in Wales—a small home-crofting scheme initiated by Cardiff Peace Groups.[58]

Hardy Arnold spoke at events that drew together people interested in community. In December 1938, for example, he spoke at the Dick Sheppard Peace Centre in London's Bayswater. Sheppard had died in the previous year, which was a major blow to the PPU. Nonetheless, his work continued. Hardy's topic was 'Community in Action', and a 'record attendance' was reported.[59] In 1940, after the Bow conference, a second, enlarged edition of *Community in Britain* was published. This contained information about 'community productions', listing what was available from which community. Out of all the varied communities, the Cotswold Bruderhof appeared most frequently: under bakery, bookbinding, dairy produce, eggs, honey, printing, vegetables and wooden products.[60] Partly in the light of this, in the 'Community Notes and News' column in *The Plough* it was suggested that a training centre might be set up to foster practical skills. Hardy Arnold, as editor, commented that the idea was good, but he insisted that something much deeper was required: 'We need the dedication of our whole lives, head and hand, for true brotherhood—NOW.'[61] It was this radical spirit which the Bruderhof community sought to foster.

There were, however, those who felt an initial sense of calling to the Bruderhof but did not remain with the community. H. J. Soan, the minister of Broad Street Baptist Church, Foleshill, Coventry, resigned from the ministry there in the summer of 1939 and stated publicly that he and his wife Edith, with their children, were intending to join the Bruderhof. He had become convinced about the validity of the communal way of living. He paid tribute to the 'patient and generous spirit' of the Baptist congregation where he had been pastor and said that it was due to the

58. Reports of these communities appeared in the column in *The Plough*, 'Community Notes and News'. See *The Plough* 1, no. 2 (July 1938), 68–69; 1, no. 3 (September 1938), 100–101; 1, no. 4 (December 1938), 132–133; 2, no. 1 (Spring 1939), 28–29.

59. *The Plough* 2, no. 1 (Spring 1939), 28.

60. *Community in Britain* (1940), 181–2.

61. *The Plough* 3, no. 1 (Spring 1940), 28, 32.

'truly Christian behaviour' of the members and leaders that he and the church were 'parting, as Christian people should, in terms of unbroken friendship and good will'.[62] The Soans stayed for a time at the Cotswold Bruderhof, but their enthusiasm for life there waned and they went to Leamington Spa, Warwickshire, to form a new community. A number of the guests at Ashton Keynes went with them.[63]

Others began with very little enthusiasm about the Bruderhof, but that gave way to commitment. Peter Cavanna, a brother of Paul and a law student, was initially cautious about explicitly religious communities. He had been influenced by the thinking of C. E. M. Joad, especially Joad's publication *'Defence' That Is No Defence: A Message to Every Citizen* (1937).[64] Peter looked in a Peace Service handbook for guidance and found reference to the Bruderhof and also Elmsett. He wrote to the Community Service Committee explaining his position and seeking advice. The reply he received was that Elmsett was probably best for someone who was agnostic about religion, as Peter was (he had left the Roman Catholic Church), but if he wanted to see an established community, he should visit the Bruderhof. Peter did so. While he was there, his brother Paul was accepted into the novitiate. As Peter witnessed this, it seemed to him to involve an unacceptable degree of surrender to the community. Soon, however, he felt called to make the same commitment.[65]

Social Engagement

As the Cotswold Bruderhof developed, so did people's curiosity about it. In June 1937, Hardy Arnold wrote to the *Manchester Guardian Weekly* to explain the witness of the Bruderhof in relation to the social and political oppression they had experienced under the Nazis. In his letter, published on 11 June 1937, he spoke of the desire within the Bruderhof for unity among people. This was 'the unity of the spirit and not of race or blood'. Its character was 'absolutely voluntary', not forced. Yet it was not community divorced from belief. Hardy argued for the community's unity to be centred 'in Christ', and added that the Bruderhof had found 'a deep

---

62. *Coventry Herald*, 5 August 1939.

63. Charles Headland, 'Charles Headland remembers Cotswold and Oaksey'. BHA Coll. 0118.

64. Joad, *'Defence' That Is No Defence*.

65. Peter Cavanna, 'Peter Cavanna's Memories'. BHA Coll. 0341.

source of inspiration in spiritual movements of the past, like those of the early Christian Church, the early Franciscan friars, the sixteenth-century Anabaptists, and the first Quakers'. He emphasised that the Bruderhof's stance in relation to society precluded the use of force or 'the exclusion of other nationalities and races'. Such a community, it was evident, 'could not be tolerated in Germany'.[66]

On the same day, *The Spectator*, the oldest continuously published magazine in the English language, published an article in which Hardy took up similar themes. Hardy's article spoke of Bruderhof members as 'simple Christians', who 'could not, in loyalty to their Master, give either the Hitler greeting or salute, or fly a Swastika flag, but in all that was good, winter-relief work for example, they willingly co-operated'. When the 'Aryan racial theory was ordered to be taught in all schools', including the Bruderhof's own school, the community refused. Hardy made a direct appeal 'to all who value such a work of peace and brotherhood', to help the Bruderhof community in England 'to build up within these more hospitable shores the work destroyed in Germany'.[67]

Further comment on the Bruderhof in relation to social engagement continued throughout 1937 and 1938. *The British Weekly*, a respected and widely-read Free Church newspaper, featured the Bruderhof in September 1937. It highlighted a meeting at which a community member had stated: 'We do not withdraw ourselves from the world: we seek to make contact with it at all points—to know all sorts of people, to understand all sorts of problems. We welcome all who come, we keep an Open door ... We try to show the world the way of Love.'[68] Such comments helped to foster interest in the activities of the community within the religious world.

The growing awareness of the Bruderhof among those who could affect public—including religious—opinion led *The Times* to publish an extended, illustrated article on features of the Cotswold Bruderhof's communal life.[69] Meanwhile *The Plough* was determined to give social issues significant coverage. Hardy Arnold was delighted to announce in

66. E. C. H. Arnold, 'The Cotswold Bruderhof', *Supplement to The Manchester Guardian Weekly*, 11 June 1937.

67. E. C. H. Arnold, 'The Fate of a Christian Experiment', *The Spectator*, 11 June 1937.

68. C. E. Roberts, 'A Visit to the Bruderhof in Ashton Keynes', *British Weekly*, 8 September 1937.

69. *The Times*, 6 September 1938.

the July 1938 *Plough* that Middleton Murry would be contributing an article. Hardy requested a report from John Stephens, whom he knew well from his Birmingham days, on the situation in Vienna. Stephens, who had been spending time with the city's large Jewish population, said he had 'never been confronted with so vast a problem of human suffering' as he had in Vienna. Another Quaker, Thomas Dent, well known for his work for the Friends Committee on War and the Social Order, wrote to *The Plough* encouraging varied social endeavour, 'in the direct Bruderhof way' or 'in the whirlpool of politics'.[70] Quakers were deeply involved at this stage in the plight of refugees and had joined with Jewish organisations to negotiate with the Home Office. The Quakers had centres for Emergency Committee work in Paris and Prague.[71]

Middleton Murry's article in *The Plough*, entitled 'The Way to Community?', which was featured in September 1938, proved provocative, as was not unusual with Murry. He began by saying that he believed the Bruderhof's work was 'of vital importance for the victory of the Christian spirit'. However, he went on to argue for a different model of community, stating: 'The natural centre of the Christian community in England, I believe, is the rural parish church, and its natural leader the parish priest'. He admitted this sounded 'more like a dream than a reality'. While he saw the Bruderhof approach as valuable, he could not 'accept it as a pattern for our endeavour in England', although he also acknowledged that ultimately this kind of 'separated and unique community' might be the only option. As well as making broader points about social change, Murry stated that he was unhappy about *Plough* book reviews which had, in his opinion, shown 'dogmatic absolutism'. Books by two friends of his, Jack Hoyland and Charles Raven, had been subject to critique.[72] *The Plough* reviewer, Kathleen Hamilton, was especially condemnatory of Raven's book, *War and the Christian*, in which Raven looked at questions from different standpoints. Hamilton rejected this approach, arguing: 'What is needed is not friendly discussion, a trying to see the good in both sides resulting in making black and white an indeterminate grey'. Rather, for her the call was to follow Jesus 'on the way of unconditional love'.[73]

70. 'Notes, Comments and Announcements', *The Plough* 1, no. 2 (July 1938), 66–69.

71. Sherman, *Island Refuge*, 26.

72. J. Middleton Murry, 'The Way to Community?', *The Plough* 1, no. 3 (September 1938), 95–97.

73. Kathleen Hamilton, 'Books', *The Plough* 1, no. 2 (July 1938), 72.

Middleton Murry found the reviewer's implication that she knew this way and had taken it 'a very, very great claim to make'.[74]

In December 1938 *The Plough* published desperate cries for help in letters it had received from Jewish refugees in Germany and Austria. The Cotswold Bruderhof had by that time taken in twenty such refugees and reported that the community's 'houses, cottages and temporary buildings are absolutely full'.[75] Their attempt to provide a place of refuge had only limited success, as they realised that a number of the refugees were used to a middle-class way of life and therefore tended to find the ethos of the Bruderhof somewhat uncongenial.[76] In spring 1939 *The Plough* printed an appeal for donations to help bring a small group of refugees to Birmingham. The plight of these individuals was powerfully set out.[77] In the summer of 1939 another group, comprising thirty young men and women from *Hashomer Hatsa'ir*, a Jewish youth organisation, came to stay at the Cotswold Bruderhof. Arthur Ben-Ysrael, the emissary for the organisation in London, visited the Cotswold community and fell in love with the way of life. It seemed like a kibbutz. Arrangements were made for the Jewish young people, who had escaped from Germany, to come and live as a homogenous group. Yaacov Oved later gathered memories of that time. One of those who had been in the group, Yael Gilad, spoke about how the Jewish young people observed the Bruderhof and 'learned to admire their modest way of life'. It was noted that as they developed relationships with *Hashomer Hatsa'ir*, the Bruderhof 'abstained from anything that might be considered missionary activity'.[78]

In 1939 Henri Lasserre, a Swiss Canadian who had visited the Cotswold Bruderhof in the previous year and had been deeply impressed,[79] wrote to Hardy Arnold asking whether the Bruderhof would be likely to disapprove of community members who took personal initiatives in seeking social progress.[80] In reply, Hardy Arnold insisted that in community

74. J. Middleton Murry, 'The Way to Community?', *The Plough* 1, no. 3 (September 1938), 97.

75. 'Cries for Help from Germany and Austria'; and 'The Need of Refugees', *The Plough* 1, no. 4 (December 1938), 123–125, 134–135.

76. Stanley Fletcher, 'Stanley Fletcher's Life Story'. BHA Coll. 0067.

77. 'A Further Cry for Help for Refugees', *The Plough* 2, no. 1 (Spring 1939), 32.

78. Oved, *Witness of the Brothers*, 101–102. For the experiences of Jewish refugees in the 1930s see Berghahn, *Continental Britons*.

79. Watson, *Pioneer in Community*.

80. Watson, *Pioneer in Community*, 75–76; *The Plough* 2, no. 2 (Summer 1939), 54–56.

'individual characteristics come to expression more fully than perhaps anywhere else'. In terms of Christian action in society, Hardy suggested to Lasserre that the starting point was community life 'growing from *within*, and thus changing life *without*'. This, he argued, was 'impossible without a deep spiritual life', which he saw as needing to be present in individuals and a group as a whole. Hardy saw the Bruderhof as drawing from a particular tradition of spiritual and theological thinkers, all of whom gave attention to the church's role in society. As representatives of this tradition, which he believed was little known at that time in England, he mentioned Kierkegaard, Johann Blumhardt, Leonhard Ragaz, Karl Barth ('to a certain extent'), Reinhold Niebuhr and Eberhard Arnold. There was variation among these thinkers, but for Hardy they constituted a 'prophetic school', which was 'neither entirely mystical nor fundamentalist nor liberal', and he argued that it was this prophetic witness which offered hope for the future.[81] Aspects of this tradition's thinking about Christian mission and engagement with society would grow in importance in the coming decades.

Denominational Dialogues

Considering the Bruderhof's position regarding authentic Christian witness, there was bound to be dialogue with those representing other denominations. In England, it was natural for groups with roots in seventeenth-century Dissent—Congregationalists, Baptists, and Quakers—to show interest in the Bruderhof. Carrs Lane, Birmingham, had one of the strongest peace movements of any Free Church congregation in Britain; in 1937 Carrs Lane's Pacifist Group had over two hundred members.[82] Several members joined the Bruderhof, as announced in the *Carrs Lane Journal* of September 1938.[83] These included Guy Johnson, Eleanor Dutton, Francis Beels, Lloyd Jones, and Nancy Watkins.[84] Leyton Richards, the Carrs Lane minister, spoke in a personal way, with 'regret and good will', about the contribution these members had made to Carrs Lane.

---

81. *The Plough* 2, no. 2 (Summer 1939), 56–57.

82. Minutes of the General Committee of the FoR, 14 and 15 June 1937. COLL MISC 0456/1/6, London School of Economics.

83. *Carrs Lane Journal*, September 1938, 4–6.

84. Guy Johnson's lengthy resignation letter was published in *The Plough* 1, no. 3 (September 1938), 97–99.

Guy Johnson, for example, had been brought up in the church, went to university, trained to be a lawyer, and returned to be 'one of our most devoted and useful members'. He was 'universally loved'. From his own experience of the Bruderhof, Leyton Richards said the communal way had 'much to teach us', and he wanted to keep 'in the closest possible touch' with the community. He welcomed their 'obedience to what they feel to be the call of Christ to them'. At the same time, he wanted to affirm people who, rather than leaving their calling and employment, brought 'a Christian outlook and a Christian spirit to bear from the inside, upon the problems of the social and economic order'. He wished to avoid 'harsh and uncharitable judgment' being passed on those taking differing paths. The Christian witness, he argued, allowed room for diversity.[85]

In the case of Baptists, a Baptist Pacifist Fellowship was formed in 1934 with a covenant to 'renounce war in all its works and ways; and to do all in our power, God helping us, to make the teaching of Jesus Christ effective in all human relations'.[86] The Bruderhof's commitment to the early church movement was highlighted in the *Baptist Times* in April 1937.[87] A month later Hugh Martin, a Baptist who had participated in FoR's international work and was the main force behind the SCM's publications, spoke at the Baptist Assembly and urged Christians to take no part in war.[88] Some younger Baptists were asking more fundamental questions about the relationship between war and social injustice. One group from Manchester expressed the opinion that for war to be abolished it was necessary to have 'social revolution involving the end of Capitalism and the establishment of Socialism'.[89] Although this group did not mention the Bruderhof, their argument that a new type of society was needed resonated with Bruderhof thinking. When Eberhard Arnold's introduction to Early Christian writings was published in English in 1939, the *Baptist Times'* review could not have been more affirmative: 'It is in every sense scholarly and complete and is a translation from the work of the learned and saintly Eberhard Arnold.'[90]

85. *Carrs Lane Journal*, September 1938, 4–6.

86. Minutes of the Baptist Pacifist Fellowship, 12 December 1934. D/BPF, Box 1, Angus Library Regent's Park College, Oxford.

87. 'An Experiment in Christian Communism', *Baptist Times*, 22 April 1937.

88. 'Baptist Assembly', *Baptist Times*, 13 May 1937.

89. 'The Denomination and War', *Baptist Times*, 20 January 1938.

90. *Baptist Times*, 11 January 1940. Eberhard Arnold, *The Early Christians* after the Death of the Apostles.

Among Quakers there were ongoing discussions in 1939 and 1940 in *The Friend* about the possibility of a Quaker Bruderhof.[91] Cyril Harries, from the Cotswold community, responded that he welcomed 'the concern felt by many Friends to find a way of life which is the expression of Christ's spirit in a world which does not recognise him in its daily life.'[92] A few months later, Kathleen Streatfeild, a Quaker (and former Anglican) from Yorkshire, enquired about coming to Ashton Keynes as a guest. Hans-Hermann Arnold invited her to describe 'why you are interested in community living.'[93] She explained that she was twenty-eight, was Housing Manager of the Sowerby Bridge Urban District Council, and was 'a member of the Society of Friends and therefore also a pacifist and a socialist.'[94] Kathleen (Kate) joined the Bruderhof and later married Peter Cavanna.

Within Methodism, with its roots in the evangelical revival of the eighteenth century, there was considerable interest in peace and in community living. The FoR reported in March 1937 that Methodist Peace Fellowship groups were more numerous than any other similar (denominational) groups.[95] Through the influence of significant Methodist figures such as Donald Soper and Henry Carter, a Methodist Peace Fellowship had been formed in 1933.[96] Both Alan Stevenson and Arthur Woolston were inspired by hearing Donald Soper preaching at Kingsway Hall in London.[97] In the summer of 1937 an article appeared in *The Methodist Church Record*, from South Wales, reporting on a visit some Methodists had made to the Cotswold Bruderhof. 'It was', for this group, 'a thrilling adventure to visit this international settlement'. The article suggested that thought should be given to 'the deeper spiritual significance of communities such as this', separate from 'the world of capitalism and war and

91. *The Friend*, 5 April 1940, contained a commentary on the discussions.

92. *The Friend*, 12 April 1940.

93. Hans-Hermann Arnold to Kathleen Streatfeild, 5 September 1940. BHA Coll. 0055.

94. Kathleen Streatfeild to Hans-Hermann Arnold, 9 September 1940. BHA Coll. 0055.

95. Minutes of the General Committee of the FoR, 15 and 16 March 1937. COLL MISC 0456/1/6, London School of Economics.

96. For Soper see Mark Peel, *The Last Wesleyan: A Life of Donald Soper* (Lancaster: Scotforth Books, 2008).

97. Alan Stevenson, 'Something of My Life'. BHA Coll. 0314; Arthur Woolston, 'Arthur Woolston's Story'. BHA Coll. 0316.

immorality', yet welcoming all. There was a personal link between the Cotswold Bruderhof and Methodism in south Wales through Cyril Harries, who had served in a Methodist Sunday School in Swansea.[98]

In early 1940, Heini Arnold and Stanley Fletcher spoke in various Methodist churches. Writing from Manchester, Heini described meetings for young people hosted by Alfred Lidster, a young Methodist minister who hoped to start a community within Methodism.[99] Around this same time, the Oxford Group, with its stress on individual guidance and personal leading from God, was also influential in Methodism. At one Methodist church, Heini Arnold debated with members of the Group, insisting that it was 'not the leading of the individual that is important; the only important thing is the will of God, and that it happens. God leads! And He leads on one way'. This meant, for Heini, embracing both inner community life and communal engagement in social justice.[100]

Heini's interest in social justice in the British context could be traced, in part, to his relationship with the Salvation Army.[101] While living for a time in Birmingham in September 1938, Heini Arnold was drawn to the organization, as Eberhard Arnold had been.[102] The Army, like the Bruderhof, emphasised spiritual experience and social commitment. The spirituality of the Salvation Army meetings Heini attended left him 'deeply impressed' and evoked in him 'a strong personal love' to God. At one event, although the Army hall was packed with people, special note was taken of the Bruderhof members, and 'one Salvation Army officer after another came up and thanked us for coming'. Heini continued: 'After the opening song, "All for Jesus," one of the choir band stepped out, greeted the people, greeted us especially and expressed the wish that we really draw close to each other'. For Heini the high point of the evening was a solo, 'More Like Jesus'. The Salvation Army differed from the Bruderhof in significant ways, but Heini valued the shared desire to be 'more like Jesus', in the whole of life. He concluded that perhaps no one would be brought to the Bruderhof through this contact with Salvationists, but

---

98. *The Methodist Church Record: The Organ of the Swansea and Gower Circuits*, August 1937.

99. Heini Arnold to Annemarie Arnold, 11 February 1940. BHA Coll. 0005.

100. Heini Arnold to Annemarie Arnold, 6 February 1940. BHA Coll. 0005.

101. Lamb, *The Social Work of the Salvation Army*.

102. Heini Arnold to Annemarie Arnold, 11 July 1938. BHA Coll. 0005.

'I have the feeling that it will be a contact that will mean something for both sides.'[103]

Many in the Church of England were cautious about radical religious movements that challenged the status quo. Dick Sheppard commented in 1936 that a number of Free Church ministers had joined the PPU but not many of his fellow-Anglican clergy.[104] The FoR was, however, pleased to report in 1938 on the development of an Anglican Pacifist Fellowship.[105] Anglican figures involved included Sheppard himself; George Lansbury, who had led the Labour Party; Maude Royden; Charles Raven, and Vera Brittain.[106] The Bruderhof's main Anglican contacts were the Tramp Preachers, or the Brotherhood of the Way, led by Charles Stimson, an Anglican clergyman who was committed to pacifism and brotherhood. Stimson had founded the Brotherhood in 1927, with Franciscan tradition as its model.[107]

In September 1936 a Brotherhood of the Way conference, with about twelve preachers, took place at the Cotswold Bruderhof.[108] There Stimson raised the possibility of the Bruderhof becoming part of the Church of England.[109] By this time, however, some of the Brotherhood, most prominently Stanley Fletcher and Bruce Sumner, realized that their future was with the Bruderhof's community life. Heini Arnold was convinced that 'the best of the Tramp Preachers' had made that choice.[110] In late 1937 Stimson sadly agreed, reporting on 'some of our best and most beloved preachers' joining the community. Although Stimson had at first been delighted to discover a group (the Bruderhof) which came 'so near all we had been teaching', his hopes for working together had been dashed as several preachers—he mentioned Stanley Fletcher, Charlie Jory and George Vigar—had left the Brotherhood, having in Stimson's view been 'swallowed whole' by the Bruderhof. The positive result, for Stimson, was

---

103. Heini Arnold to Annemarie Arnold, 25 September 1938. BHA Coll. 0005.

104. Huxley and Sheppard, *100,000 say No!*, 4.

105. Minutes of the General Committee of the FoR, 14 and 15 March 1938. COLL MISC 0456/1/6, London School of Economics.

106. Barrett, *Subversive Peacemakers*, 225.

107. Barrett, *Subversive Peacemakers*, 212–13. See also 83–84.

108. Hardy Arnold to Edith Arnold, 29 August 1936. BHA Coll. 0304.

109. Hans-Hermann Arnold to Emmy Arnold, 28 September 1936. BHA Coll. 0190.

110. Edith Arnold to Emmy Arnold, 28 September 1936. BHA Coll. 0304.

that the Brotherhood had renounced a 'separatist spirit' and was now confirmed 'as a society within the Church of England'.[111]

Christocentric Witness

The fact that the Bruderhof stressed community could imply that witness to the need for communal living overshadowed witness to the centrality of Christ. However, the experience of many of those joining the Bruderhof was that they learned more about Christ within the community. Hardy Arnold was clear that Christ was the centre of his faith. In March 1938, he wrote to his brother, Hans-Hermann: 'There is a hard battle in front of us still. Often courage sinks. But—Christ will win the victory! Of that we are confident. Let us grow in humility! In love! In faith!'[112] Later in the month he wrote: 'The present situation in the world lies heavily on my soul. . . How irrefutably necessary it seems to be that Christ, the Lord, is proclaimed in word, life and deed. We can never hinder the catastrophe. But we should carry Christ into the need and sin.' Hardy saw a great danger 'that we think too much of ourselves'—within the community—while forgetting human need 'and its solution and redemption in Christ'. He concluded, 'We need a deep movement of heart, but only God can give it.[113] In September 1938, responding to Middleton Murry's article in *The Plough*, Hardy expressed disappointment at the 'rather narrow nationalistic' and 'churchy' outlook in Murry's article, with its advocacy of the central role of the Church of England. In place of this, Hardy proposed a Christ-centred focus. 'Not the Bruderhof', he insisted, 'but *Christ* is the way, the only way.'[114]

Alan Stevenson, whose journey had taken him into the PPU and Quaker life, was an example of how the Bruderhof's Christocentrism had an impact on the experience of individuals. He spoke of his first year at the Cotswold Bruderhof as 'a real time of learning'. He had a strong aversion to war and violence and, with this, a powerful sense of social justice. But in coming into the community he saw that his beliefs needed much more depth. By 1938, after his initial year, he felt he was 'being awakened

111. C. C. Stimson, 'Where we stand', *The Brotherhood of the Way Magazine*, November-December 1937, 1-2.

112. Hardy Arnold to Hans-Hermann Arnold, 2 March 1938. BHA Coll. 0304.

113. Hardy Arnold to Hans-Hermann Arnold, 18 March 1938. BHA Coll. 0304.

114. 'Editorial Notes and Comments', *The Plough* 1, no. 3 (September 1938), 102-3.

to the very deepest meaning of the life at the Bruderhof and above all the meaning and significance of the life of Jesus'. He was becoming 'more and more aware of what the life meant and of the necessity of giving up everything to follow Jesus'. During the subsequent months of 1938 Alan began to understand more of how God had created the world, that it was God's world, and that God had sent Jesus for the purpose of bringing a new way of love to all humanity. He was baptised in November 1938.[115]

Although peace was integral to the Bruderhof, it, too, was secondary to Christ for members of the community. John Hinde, who worked in London, was a pacifist—in touch with the PPU and FoR—but did not have a positive first impression of the Bruderhof. The community sounded 'old-fashioned and fundamentalist'. However, when a friend and he began to feel the need 'to get back to the real roots of our pacifist beliefs', they realised that 'the message of Jesus had a lot to do with it'. In 1940, John heard Hardy Arnold speak at the Dick Sheppard Club, and his conception of the Bruderhof changed. The person he encountered was not 'a rustic farmer type', as he had expected, but a young, well-educated man who spoke in a very lively way and 'with a certain indefinable peace about him that captivated me'. John Hinde was struck by the fact that Hardy spoke about the early Christians in the time of the New Testament, and did not mention the Bruderhof until the audience asked about it. After visiting the Bruderhof and reading *The Plough*, John felt drawn to the community. Following a time of observing, he became part of the novitiate, and he was baptised in October 1940. During the months in the novitiate he was especially concerned with the promise of the kingdom of God on earth, and the church as an embassy of that kingdom. It was very clear, as he put it, 'that I was giving my life completely to Jesus and to the way I had experienced at the Bruderhof'.[116] The source of the way of peace was to be found in the way of Jesus.

One of those outside the Bruderhof who understood its ethos was Jack Hoyland. He had a deep respect for Eberhard Arnold and was involved in translating Eberhard's work on the Early Christians. Hoyland affirmed the importance of this work for contemporary Christianity. Writing in *Peace News* about Eberhard Arnold's thinking regarding the early church, Hoyland took the opportunity to pay tribute to what he saw as at the heart of the movement that had taken shape in Sannerz. He

115. Alan Stevenson, 'Something of My Life'; 'Bruderhof Memories'. BHA Coll. 0314.

116. John Hinde, 'John Hinde's Life Story'. BHA Coll. 0395.

said many readers of *Peace News* were acquainted with the Bruderhof and had been to the Cotswold community and had 'admired the courage and resource of this company of three hundred men, women and children who, not content with talking about peace and a new Christian social order, have given up everything in order to build these things in concrete fact before our eyes'. He continued: 'Eberhard Arnold, as those of us who remember him personally can well testify, was above all a great Christian', and it was because he followed Christ so closely that 'he realized that Christ's will was that His teaching should be put once more into operation in a community which included every side of life.' For Hoyland there was such a community, 'witnessing to Christ in our own Wiltshire'.[117] The witness to Christ was central.

In the summer of 1940, in the last issue of *The Plough* to be published from the Cotswold Bruderhof, the introductory article spoke of how the Bruderhof had been formed in the aftermath of war in Europe, and now, twenty years later, another war was raging. The cause of peace was under intense pressure. The British government prosecuted the PPU for circulating a poster which stated: 'War will cease when men refuse to fight. What are You going to do about it?' The PPU, feeling it had no option, withdrew the poster.[118] At such a critical time the Bruderhof wished, through *The Plough* and other means, 'to repeat our pledge to the cause of brotherhood'. This was not, the article in *The Plough* stressed, a pledge marked by human endeavour to achieve brotherhood, but was a response to 'the call of Christ, which we have heard'. It was a call 'so clearly expressed by Jesus in the Sermon on the Mount and in all the testimonies of the apostles to Christ, the Church and the Kingdom'. It was the conviction of the Bruderhof that 'community in all spiritual and material things' was at the heart of this call; that communal life was integral to 'the spreading of the good tidings of the coming Kingdom, and the call to repentance throughout the world'.[119] Emmy Arnold recalled Eberhard Arnold's words some twenty years earlier, that 'Jesus was seeking to win our souls, seeking that we might belong utterly to him.' Their worship, work and witness in community had been a response to that seeking. Emmy was adamant that 'the difficulties and struggles we have

117. *Peace News*, 9 February 1940.

118. Brock and Young, *Pacifism in the Twentieth Century*, 152.

119. 'Our Pledge', *The Plough* 3, no. 2 (Summer 1940), 33.

lived through in these past twenty years' meant that all those wanting this kind of life needed 'a real foundation, a basis of faith beneath your feet'.[120]

120. Emy (Emmy) Arnold, 'From the Old to the New', *The Plough* 3, no. 2 (Summer 1940), 54.

Leyton and Edith Richards with Arnold and Gladys Mason at the Alm Bruderhof, Liechtenstein, 1935

Winifred "Freda" Bridgwater, later Dyroff, at the Alm Bruderhof

Plan of the Cotswold Bruderhof, May, 1938

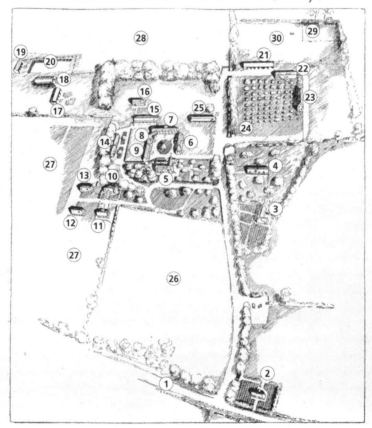

Description

1. Road to Ashton Keynes.
2. and 3. Cottages.
4. Dining-room.
5. Dwelling house and communal kitchen.
6. Stone barn.
7. Former byre, now rebuilt as dwelling house.
8. Former stable, now dwelling house.
9. Turning shop.
10. Baby house.
11. Kindergarten.
12. and 13. School.
14. Railway carriages used as dwelling rooms.
15. Poultry-brooding house and run.
16. Hospital.
17. Shed for making concrete blocks.
18. Dutch barn.
19. Stable.
20. Gravel pit.
21. Smithy, carpenter's shop, cart shed.
22. Laundry, sewing, spinning and weaving rooms small power station.
23. Printing, bookbinding and publishing house, office.
24. Orchard.
25. Open shed.
26. Arable land.
27. Garden.
28. Pasture land.
29. Bee garden.
30. Chicken meadow.

Site plan of Cotswold Bruderhof, published in *The Plough* in 1938

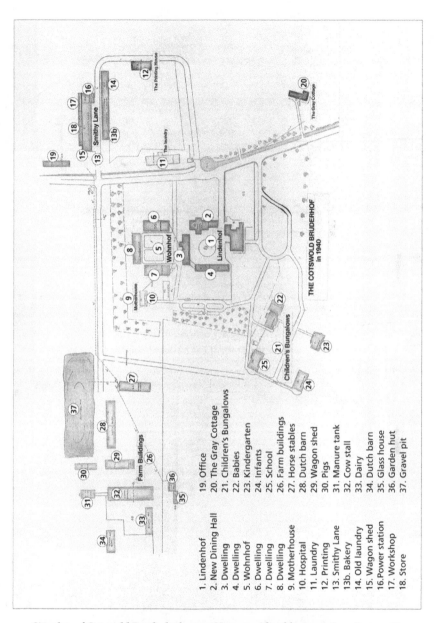

1. Lindenhof
2. New Dining Hall
3. Dwelling
4. Dwelling
5. Wohnhof
6. Dwelling
7. Dwelling
8. Dwelling
9. Motherhouse
10. Hospital
11. Laundry
12. Printing
13. Smithy Lane
13b. Bakery
14. Old laundry
15. Wagon shed
16. Power station
17. Workshop
18. Store
19. Office
20. The Gray Cottage
21. Children's Bungalows
22. Babies
23. Kindergarten
24. Infants
25. School
26. Farm buildings
27. Horse stables
28. Dutch barn
29. Wagon shed
30. Pigs
31. Manure tank
32. Cow stall
33. Dairy
34. Dutch barn
35. Glass house
36. Garden hut
37. Gravel pit

Site plan of Cotswold Bruderhof, 1940. Note considerable expansion since 1938

Emmy Arnold at the Cotswold Bruderhof,
one year after the death of her husband Eberhard

Hardy Arnold

Edith Boecker Arnold

Hella Headland, bookkeeper, twice remained behind to close the financial affairs of the community when they emigrated; in 1937 in Germany, and again in 1941 at the Cotswold Bruderhof

Cotswold Bruderhof dining room

A communal meal

Dancing on the lawn at the Cotswold Bruderhof

Visit of the Salvation Army band to the Cotswold Bruderhof, 1939

Cyril Davies was a recently qualified doctor when he joined the Cotswold Bruderhof. He used his medical knowledge at the community, but acquired new skills as well

Erich Hasenberg making craft items in the workshop

Some of the Jewish children who came to the Cotswold Bruderhof

Departure from the Cotswold Bruderhof for Paraguay

Stanley Fletcher (left), and Charles Headland (right) with guests, 1941

Date	May 1936	November 1936	February 1937	July 1937	October 1937	February 1938	November 1938	June 1939	October 1939	April 1940	November 1940	February 1941	June 1941
German	16	37	47	85	114	99	117	115	119	119	117	17	2
British	14	17	18	22	24	50	64	90	111	116	151	57	1
Swiss		5	7	21	26	19	30	31	30	33	32	2	
Dutch				3	4	4	8	7	7	7	8		
Czech					1	1	6	6	3	3	1		
Austrian	1	1	1	1	1	1	17	3	10	9	1	1	
Italian					1		1	1	1	1	1	1	
French					2	2	2	2	5	6	3		
Turkish				1	1	1	1	1					
Swedish					1	1		2	2	2	2	2	
unidentified		1		10	4		2		22	17			
Total	31	61	73	143	179	178	248	258	310	313	316	80	3

Table showing the population of the Cotswold Bruderhof by nationality over time

5

Communal Life

A s visitors came and went from the Bruderhof and as broader interest grew, the communal life that had been established in the Cotswolds became the subject of many articles in national and local newspapers. In January 1939, for example, Maurice Fagence, who would later become an international war correspondent, wrote a detailed article on the community after visiting it. He was especially struck by the different nationalities and associated languages he found in the community. In the workshop, for example, he discovered that a member from Germany and one from Czechoslovakia had worked together all through the crisis of the German annexation of the Sudetenland. Fagence was also impressed by Kathleen Hasenberg (previously Hamilton), whom he described as a 'pretty girl of about 25', and someone who 'seemed able to render every European language in her own delightful Scotch brogue'.[1] Here was an unusual international community.

Community Spirit

There was a specific community spirit at the Cotswold Bruderhof which many people who encountered it found attractive and which led to the growth of the community. In July 1937 Charles Headland stayed with the community initially for a week, but the impact was such that he

1. M. Fagence, 'A Community Camp of Refugees', *Natal Mercury*, 19 January 1939.

subsequently became a member. His twin brother Robert—who also later joined—had told Charles about it. At the end of his week there, at the midday community meal, Charles was asked if he would like to say something. After he did so, practically everyone in the dining room—about a hundred people—came up to shake his hand, to wish him well, to express the hope that they would see him again, and to say how glad they were he had stayed with them. Charles was deeply moved, and although a reserved person he left the dining room in tears. He was attending a Congregational church in London where people in the congregation were friendly, but by comparison with what he experienced at the Bruderhof his church seemed to lack depth.[2]

For Charles Headland, 'the atmosphere of love' drew him to the Bruderhof. He came to the conclusion that the spirit within the community was because life in its totality was being shared. His life back in Croydon now seemed to him to be 'very disintegrated'. He went to work every day with people he never saw elsewhere. His church was separate from his circle of friends—who were largely connected with the peace movement. By contrast, in the Bruderhof, work, family, and friendship all cohered. Charles was also concerned about how to foster international friendship, and at the Bruderhof he found German, British, Swiss, Dutch, and other nationalities living and cooperating together.[3]

In 1938, Bruce Sumner, a former Tramp Preacher, gave an account in *The Plough* of the community's growth. He spoke of the concentration on 'building up to meet the demands of the large number of people of which the community now consists'. He believed the growth showed the 'strength of attraction and the strength of witness'. Bruce noted that in the previous year no fewer than twenty-six new people had become full members of the Cotswold Bruderhof, more than in any year since the beginning in Sannerz. Most of the new members and those new to the novitiate were British, but a few had come from the Sudeten territory of Czechoslovakia and from the Netherlands. Only one of the new members had been brought up in the community. Bruce was pleased to be able to speak about this particular 'child of the community', who having reached the age of discretion had decided of her own free will to become a committed member. This was an important reminder of 'the great educational task which we have with our own children and with

2. Charles Headland, 'Life Story'. BHA Coll. 0118.
3. Charles Headland, 'Life Story'. BHA Coll. 0118.

children who have been entrusted to us'. Bruce's hope was that the spirit in the community and the example given to children would mean that in time they would make 'a radical decision for denial of self-interest and for the discipleship of Jesus'. Many children brought up in the Bruderhof, he believed, already had a 'longing for a life of service to others'.[4]

One visitor to the community in 1939 observed in an article that there was 'nothing more admirable in the Bruderhof than the way the children are looked after'. The article's author, Claire, writing in the *British Weekly*, commented that although the dress in the community was old-fashioned and 'picturesque', the children she met were 'being brought up on the most modern, healthy lines', with teaching in the school classes taking place in 'very small groups'. All the children learned in both English and German. She was also fascinated by the singing of the Jewish young people she met who were living in the community at the time. All of this spoke to her of 'unity and love'.[5] Asked by the paper to supplement the report, Freda Bridgwater explained that family life was important, but that mothers could turn their attention to various communal enterprises because their children were being looked after. The same was true of fathers. Both men and women were engaged, she said, in 'joyful work for the community'. Freda's emphasis was on the cooperative nature of what went on in the Bruderhof. A worker did not have to 'compete' with others. For her, community was 'more than just living together and working together on a co-operative basis', since that could spring from selfish ends. Rather the spirit of the community was expressed in serving and in 'seeking unity with all the others in discovering what the will of God is'.[6]

When John Hinde first arrived at Ashton Fields, he was shown to a compartment in a railway carriage which had been converted into accommodation. There were a number of other guests there, mostly single men around his own age. During the first few days John found everything rather solemn and heavy. There were interesting—but, for him, overly earnest—discussions at 'guest breakfasts', where a group of fifteen to twenty guests had breakfast together. Different Bruderhof couples led

---

4. Bruce Sumner, 'The Cotswold Bruderhof: A report of the events and activities in 1938', *The Plough* 2, no. 1 (Spring 1939), 17–18.

5. Claire (no surname), 'Living in Community', *The British Weekly*, 24 August 1939.

6. Winifred Bridgwater, 'The Cotswold Bruderhof', *The British Weekly*, 31 August 1939.

discussions. John was used to the stimulus of working for Lloyd's of London, and initially he found the Cotswold tasks 'rather tiring, and tedious'.[7] Then on his first weekend there were several weddings in the community. Among the couples married in this period were August Dyroff and Freda Bridgwater, Charles Headland and Hella Römer, and Sydney Hindley and Marjorie Badham. John witnessed a complete transformation in the atmosphere. The community was filled with joy, singing, and dancing, and 'the serious-looking bearded, Hutterian-costumed brothers actually got up and made fools of themselves'.[8] It was the humanity of the Bruderhof which helped John to decide to continue and later commit himself.

Along with the challenge of building up a community in which so many people were new, went the challenge of having the right people in positions of responsibility. With this in mind, Emmy Arnold wrote to Hans Zumpe in August 1937 about gifts of leadership. At this point Hans had overall responsibility for the Bruderhof as the 'Servant of the Word' (a Hutterian term). Emmy, perhaps presciently, wanted to encourage an attitude of trust in the Holy Spirit 'to provide these gifts among us; that we might have more gifts of the Spirit, shepherds, teachers, apostles, prophets who lead the church by the Spirit and are blessed by God for this'. For her, as for Eberhard, the example of the New Testament church was paramount: 'If one reads through the whole New Testament there are always gifts of the Spirit confirmed by God, both for spiritual leadership and for the practical temporal needs, the latter being a different gift than the first.' It seemed to Emmy that the Holy Spirit's guidance would especially be needed as the community grew. She wrote: 'With the new people constantly coming, we do have to ask God for a gift of the Spirit in our community life.'[9]

The language used by Emmy echoed what she would have heard thirty years earlier from Scandinavian Pentecostals, and the 1930s represented a period of considerable Pentecostal growth in England. George Jeffreys, an influential Pentecostal evangelist, held a ten-week campaign in Birmingham in 1930 and regularly filled the Bingley Hall, which seated over twelve thousand people.[10] There is no evidence, however, of contacts

7. John Hinde, 'Memories of Cotswold'. BHA Coll. 0395. For the history of Lloyd's, the insurers, see Brown, *Hazard Unlimited*.

8. John Hinde, 'Memories of Cotswold'. BHA Coll. 0395.

9. Emmy Arnold to Hans Zumpe, 27 August 1937. BHA Coll. 0288_02.

10. *Elim Evangel*, 20 June 1930; 27 June 1930. George Jeffrey was the leader of the Elim Church, one of the two main Pentecostal denominations in interwar Britain.

between the Bruderhof and Pentecostals in the 1930s. Whereas Emmy spoke of the 'gifts of the Spirit' in leadership, others in the community described leadership without referring to the dimension of the Holy Spirit. Georg Barth's wife, Moni, commented to Emmy that Hardy Arnold was seen as someone with 'considerable discretion and a real oversight in everything'. She also referred to his 'intellectual gifts'.[11] It was not clear to what extent Emmy's desire for 'more gifts of the Spirit' was being fulfilled.

Rhythms of Living

A normal working day at the Cotswold Bruderhof began with the community member designated as 'nightwatchman' waking up all the households. With the community expanding considerably in 1937–38, and with accommodation consequently being reconfigured, the waking-up process each morning was not always straightforward. Arnold Mason noted in the nightwatchman's log-book for July 1937 the fact that the task was 'rather difficult and is sometimes unsuccessful because the nightwatchman does not know where everyone sleeps'.[12] A few weeks later, Cyril Harries noted in the log-book that it was hard to do the job effectively when very tired. The tiredness was due to the fact that little or no previous notice was given about who was nightwatchman, which meant that no prior rest was taken, even 'for an hour or so'.[13] Also, it was impossible to get from one part of the community to another on foot in order to keep to the waking-up time, and Cyril suggested providing a bicycle.[14] On his first shift as nightwatchman, Brian Trapnell, from Birmingham, had no difficulty in keeping awake. On the whole, despite being nervous, he enjoyed what he called his 'first essay at night watching'. He noted that he had seen a hedgehog inspecting the new concrete in the yard. He concluded his diary entry: 'The Community having been duly knocked up, I emulated the well known diarist [Samuel Pepys] and retired to bed.'[15]

11. Moni Barth to Emmy Arnold, 12 May 1937. BHA Coll. 0305.

12. Arnold Mason, 'Nightwatchman's Book', 13/14 July 1937. BHA Coll. 0055.

13. Cyril Harries, 'Nightwatchman's Book', 23–24 August 1937. BHA Coll. 0055.

14. Cyril Harries, 'Nightwatchman's Book', 1–2 September 1937. BHA Coll. 0055.

15. Brian Trapnell, 'Nightwatchman's Book', 23–24 September 1937. BHA Coll. 0055.

The experience continued to be problematic for some, however, due to 'extreme weariness'.[16]

Sleep was an issue for many community members. Meetings often went on late into the evening. George Vigar noted in his nightwatchman log in September 1937, for example, that a meeting with guests had been followed by a meeting of community or 'brotherhood' members which meant that many in the community were not asleep until midnight.[17] Under the 'new order of the day' operational from February 1938, brotherhood meetings were to end by nine-thirty, with all lights out by eleven. The night watchman was then to wake the community at six in the morning.[18]

Work was central to the rhythm of the community. One of the first German words Charles Headland learned was *Arbeit* (work).[19] Meals shared together were also important. The community breakfast, which was adopted as the norm under Hutterian influence, involved not only eating together but also singing. Emmy Arnold was intrigued by the habit which had become common by 1939 of singing lively Salvation Army songs together at this point.[20] No doubt this helped the waking-up process! Work then continued throughout the day, apart from the midday break when lunch was eaten. The food was simple, and at times not to the liking of guests. One visiting medical student from Scotland stated categorically that eating the starchy food—noodles, bread, potatoes, etc., with little protein—was asking for trouble. However, the bread, baked by Josef Stängl, made from rye and wheat, was of much better quality than commercial bread.[21]

Work was divided out by a work distributor, with Fritz Kleiner, drawing from his experience in Germany, recognised as the expert in this role. A report on the Cotswold Bruderhof in April 1939 indicated

16. Cyril Harries, 'Nightwatchman's Book', 14–15 October 1937. BHA Coll. 0055.

17. George Vigar, 'Nightwatchman's Book', 20–21 September. 1937. BHA Coll. 0055.

18. Erich Hasenberg, 'Nightwatchman's Book', 28–29 February, 1938. BHA Coll. 0055.

19. Charles Headland, 'Charles Headland Remembers Cotswold and Oaksey'. BHA Coll. 0118.

20. Emmy Arnold to Hans-Hermann Arnold, 16 March 1939. BHA Coll. 0288_02.

21. Charles Headland, 'Charles Headland Remembers Cotswold and Oaksey'. BHA Coll. 0118.

how much communal work had been and was being done. At that stage the community had four farms, making a total area of eight hundred acres. There was a focus on dairy farming and crops. In addition, the community undertook poultry farming, bee-keeping, pig-breeding, and market-gardening. A tuberculin tested (T.T.) milk licence had been obtained. There were also wood-turning, printing, publishing, and bookbinding departments, and these were all working at capacity. The report stated that during the period of three years of Bruderhof life in Britain much community building work had been done, farm roads and drainage had been improved or provided, workshops had been built, and farm buildings had been erected.[22] The layout of the buildings was intended to be suited to the communal type of life. Dwellings were in two adjacent quadrangles, the first the main house and converted farm buildings, and the second a completely new quadrangle of apartment houses. School, kindergarten and nursery were in a group of four bungalows reached through a little wood. The workshop was separate. All around were the gardens. In 1940 a new dining room came into use—the upper part of the big barn.[23]

In the evenings, community members came together for relaxation and conversation, as well as meetings. In March 1938, Gerd Wegner, preparing for a shift as nightwatchman, was delighted to observe the community, 'grown now to 208 people, standing around in smaller or larger groups on the wonderfully moonlit *Hof* and still conversing for a while'. He was also pleased that everyone went to their rooms punctually and the lights were out across the community houses at 10.30pm, although two members were busy until 11.00pm trying to catch a bull, after it had got loose.[24] A month later, Gerd reported that after supper some of the women in the community had sung a few lullabies to two new mothers, Marianne and Edith. The brotherhood, he added, had then met to come to agreement about people desiring baptism, and baptisms were scheduled for the forthcoming Sunday.[25]

Sometimes in the summer period, aspects of farm work extended on into the evening. On one evening in 1937, the threshing of the rye and the stacking of the straw went through into the later afternoon, and this

22. Prospectus, 'Friends of the Bruderhof Limited', 25 April 1939. BHA Coll. 0055.

23. Winifred Dyroff, 'The Cotswold Bruderhof'. BHA Coll. 0066.

24. Gerd Wegner, 'Nightwatchman's Book', 14–15 March 1938. BHA Coll. 0055.

25. Gerd Wegner, 'Nightwatchman's Book', 29–30 April 1938. BHA Coll. 0055.

work was only finished in the evening. Most of the community members were there to see the completion. When the machine stopped they sang a well-known harvest hymn in German and English, 'Wir pflügen und wir streuen den Samen auf das Land', 'We plough the fields and scatter the good seed on the land'. Being there on that occasion, and seeing the beautiful summer evening and the hedged English fields, evoked in Stanley Fletcher a sense of connection with the sonnets of Wordsworth. He added a self-deprecating note: 'How foolish we are, we English!'[26]

Relaxation in the evenings often included music and dancing.[27] The influence of the German Youth Movement was still felt at the Cotswold Bruderhof, so dancing included German as well as English folk dancing.[28] For Charles Headland, the German dances were hard to pick up. What was particularly good about these events, as he saw it, was that all ages took part.[29] A nightwatchman report in February 1938 noted that after supper the evening was free and described how the young people danced beside the dining room and after that sang songs around the linden tree.[30] Quite a number of community members played the violin. Towards the end of the Cotswold period, the community had a gramophone. The singing included contributions by special groups, such as the schoolchildren. Choral works were performed.[31]

Part of the free time was also given to study and learning. The library was available, with its eleven thousand books. There were English lessons for German speakers, with three different groups—beginners, intermediate, and advanced. Emmy Arnold pronounced the classes to be 'great fun'. The British women who had been trained as schoolteachers took the main responsibility for the classes. Appropriately, one of the set texts was *The Plough*. On Sunday evenings some of the members studied Anabaptist history. Emmy Arnold used her evenings to write the story of the Bruderhof, including her own story and that of Eberhard.[32] She

---

26. Stanley Fletcher, 'Nightwatchman's Book', 7–8 August 1937. BHA Coll. 0055.

27. Gerd Werner, 'Nightwatchman's Book', 18–19 April 1938. BHA Coll. 0055.

28. Nancy Trapnell, 'Memories of Cotswold and Paraguay'. BHA Coll. 0347.

29. Charles Headland, 'Charles Headland Remembers Cotswold and Oaksey'. BHA Coll. 0118.

30. Günther Homann, 'Nightwatchman's Book', 20–21 February 1938. BHA Coll. 0055.

31. Chalres Headland, 'Charles Headland Remembers Cotswold and Oaksey'. BHA Coll. 0118.

32. This memoir would eventually be published as the book Emmy Arnold,

was determined to do this 'because no one else can when one day I am no more'.[33]

'Free Out of Love to Christ'

As a community no longer based in mainland Europe but in Britain, the Bruderhof sought to explore its spiritual identity in a new setting. One insight into this can be found in a letter of March/April 1938 written to friends of the Bruderhof in Switzerland. The letter spoke of the attempt of the Cotswold community to witness to a life under a different order, an order in harmony with the longing for justice, peace, and love: 'This is the order of Christ, passed on to us in the Gospels and the Acts of the Apostles.' For those who had been at the Alm, living in the 'mighty world of the Alps', there had been a fresh realisation of the reality of the words of one of the Psalms: 'I will lift up my eyes to the hills. From whence comes my help? My help comes from the Lord, who made heaven and earth.' (Psalm 121:1–2). In a new context, the letter emphasised, divine help remained an absolute necessity, and it was 'still our hearts' concern that in spite of everything that threatens our present age, we may preserve true freedom'. There was a continuing commitment to freedom from things that were seen as being in opposition to the way of Christ: 'We want to be free from possessions, from inner and outer demands made upon us, free from ourselves, free from the fear of persecution.' This freedom was for the purpose of serving others: 'We must be free for the world around us, for all suffering fellowmen, free out of love to Christ. We want our whole life to be bound to him alone. The only thing that matters is that again and again we fight a decisive battle against all the demons of this age, that we fight for this love alone, which is a reality revealed in Christ.'[34] Aspects of Bruderhof identity are clearly evident in this letter, such as experience of and witness to Christ, nourishment from scripture, struggle against evil, and a sacrificial life of service.

These themes were largely repeated in a message Hardy Arnold delivered during Advent 1938 (on 7 December) at the Cotswold Bruderhof

---

Torches Together, later reissued as Emmy Arnold, *A Joyful Pilgrimage*.

33. Emmy Arnold to Hans-Hermann and Gertrud Arnold, 17 November 1939. BHA Coll. 0288_02.

34. Prospectus, 'Letter to our friends in Switzerland'. March/April 1938. BHA Coll. 0334.

before the baptisms of several new members. He began with the traditional Trinitarian blessing given at such events: 'May the infinite peace that comes from God alone and the love that pours into our hearts from Jesus Christ through the Holy Spirit which alone leads to true community be with us at this time.' Hardy expressed the great joy felt in the community because 'our numbers are being increased by people whom Christ himself has called to go his way'. This was happening, he said, referring to increasing Nazi aggression in Europe, 'at a time when one can feel very clearly that the powers of darkness are taking control'. What was being conveyed was not, however, a defeatist spirituality. Rather, the baptisms, in which people expressed personal faith and through which membership of the community was sealed, strengthened 'the witness and message which we give'. Hardy emphasised mission. He referred to the 'old Hutterian teachings about baptism', arguing that the Hutterites 'repeated again and again, very clearly, that the charge of mission is given to the Church'. He spoke of how Jesus sent out his disciples, 'and he sends them out still today, to win souls for his Kingdom'. Hardy drew from Jesus' teaching in Matthew chapter 10: 'He who receives you, receives me.' Jesus' prayer in John chapter 17, his 'wonderful prayer as High Priest', was also quoted. Jesus, Hardy insisted, prayed 'for those disciples of his and for us'.[35]

Hans-Hermann Arnold was concerned that as the Bruderhof sought to carry out its mission there was no one among the younger generation of Bruderhof leaders who was 'well versed in the Bible'. His perspective, as he put it in February 1937, was that Emmy, his mother, was the only leader who had a depth of biblical knowledge. At the same time, he was aware that knowledge of scripture was not enough. He anticipated that 'mission can come if the Holy Spirit is especially strongly with and among us'.[36] It is possible that members of the community responded in the months that followed to a shared sense that together they needed to engage more deeply with the Bible.

On 22 November 1937, the community remembered the death of Eberhard Arnold two years previously. They sang *'Marter Christi, wer kann Dein vergessen'* (O Christ, who can forget your death?), by Zinzendorf, a hymn sung at Eberhard's funeral. Then a group sang Psalm 22, followed by—as Emmy recounted—'a very good conversation about the understanding of God's kingdom', about the raising up of believers

35. Hardy Arnold, community meeting, Cotswold Bruderhof, 7 December 1938. BHA Coll. 0055.

36. Hans-Hermann Arnold to Emmy Arnold, 6 February 1937. BHA Coll. 0190.

at the second coming of Christ as recorded in 1 Thessalonians 4:13–17, and 'about the last judgment'.[37] It seems that there was a focus on Paul's letter to the Thessalonians in this period. The passage about those who had died in Christ being raised at the Last Day was of great importance, as Eberhard's death was in the minds of community members. Hardy wrote to Hans-Hermann a few weeks later about the experience in the Cotswold community 'becoming freer and more joyful, more brotherly, and more communal', and he linked this with recent communal reading of 1 Thessalonians 5:12–24, with its teaching about community life. For him this constituted 'a simple, but tremendously powerful call' to be a Christ-like community.[38]

At the same time as the community was engaging more fully with passages in the Bible, there was a rediscovery of the writings of Johann Christoph Blumhardt. Eberhard Arnold had been profoundly affected by reading about Blumhardt, a German Lutheran pastor who in his ministry from the 1840s onwards saw Jesus bringing healing and deliverance in powerful ways.[39] In early 1937 Heini Arnold wrote to Emmy to say how appreciative he was of Friedrich Zündel's biography of Blumhardt. Heini regarded Blumhardt as 'of special importance to us now', because of his 'fiery and clear Jesus-love' and his comprehensive witness to the Kingdom of God.[40] Five months later, Heini wrote to Annemarie about what had taken place in the meetings at the Cotswold community on the previous Sunday. There had been a meeting for fellowship and worship (*Gemeindestunde*) in the morning. In the afternoon there was a brotherhood meeting which dealt with buildings. The highlight of the day for Heini, however, was a further *Gemeindestunde* in the evening. It incorporated a 'Blumhardt reading'. Heini's comment was: 'Wonderful meeting!'[41]

Faith in God's power to heal was tested in the following year when Emmy Maria, the three-month-old daughter of Heini and Annemarie, became very ill. They wrote to Annemarie's brother on 20 November

37. Emmy Arnold to Hans-Hermann Arnold, 24 November 1937. BHA Coll. 0288_02.

38. Hardy Arnold to Hans-Hermann, 2 March 1938. BHA Coll. 0304.

39. Baum, *Against the Wind*, 146–148. Karl Barth called Blumhardt 'one of the most remarkable men of the nineteenth century'. Barth, 'Friedrich Naumann and Christoph Blumhardt', 40.

40. Heini Arnold to Emmy Arnold, 5 January 1937. BHA Coll. 0055. For the biography mentioned: Zündel, *Pastor Johann Christoph Blumhardt*.

41. Heini Arnold to Annemarie Arnold, 7 June 1937. BHA Coll. 0005.

1938 to say that little Emmy Maria's kidneys were failing and her heart was affected. No more medical help was to be expected. They continued: 'All the same, we have not given up hope for our child. We know that Jesus Christ can do everything. So we put our faith in him and place the life of our best beloved child in his hand.'[42] Emmy Maria died the next day. With a sense of deep need, Heini turned again to Blumhardt's writings.[43] Speaking later, Heini referred to Blumhardt's commentary on the passage from the book of Revelation (Rev. 20:12–20), with the words of Jesus, 'I am coming', and the response, 'Yes, come, Lord Jesus.'[44]

Given the demanding life of the community, it could be difficult to find space and time to reflect personally on the spiritual journey. This was where the nightwatchmen had something of an advantage. Adolf Braun, an early member of the Bruderhof in Germany, was the nightwatchman on the last evening of 1937 and the morning of 1938. He commented in the diary for his watch: 'Years come and go, bring joys and sorrows. And all the world is an ocean full of moods. What today is peaceful, tomorrow roars and rages. May our trust be in God! All else will not help us.' He went on to write about the human tendency to 'try to force our moment of transitory existence' to take on a significance it did not warrant when compared with 'God's timeless rhythm of creation'. Yet Adolf was also strongly aware of being among those who were 'objects of his [God's] world-encompassing love, yes to a certain extent helpers in His almighty being and working, sons and daughters of God, "brothers" of Jesus Christ, sharers in His future'. As he thought about the 'mystery of the midnight hour between the years', he saw that moment as significant, yet also as 'a flash of light that flits through the shutter of a camera'. He hoped that the 'image' which the camera had captured would be life-giving.[45] Kurt Zimmermann, on the night of 18–19 March, wrote of his own experience of a significant moment: 'It was a bright, star-clear night and the half-moon was shining on this first night watch for me in three years. The last time was in February 1935 at the Rhön Bruderhof. In between lie three long

42. Heini and Annemarie Arnold to Reinhold Wächter, 20 November 1938. BHA Coll. 0005.

43. See Mommsen, *Homage to a Broken Man*, 152–154.

44. Heini Arnold, community meeting, 23 November 1940. BHA Coll. 0055.

45. Adolf Braun, 'Nightwatchman's Book', 31 December 1937/1 January 1938. BHA Coll. 0055.

years of separation and all that accompanied it. Yet now we are united on one Bruderhof. May God be given the honour and thanks for that.'[46]

Festivals and the Christian Year

The celebration of the Christian year was an important aspect of Bruderhof communal life. In 1936 Edith Arnold described for the benefit of the continental European Bruderhof communities the first Advent and Christmas at the Cotswold Bruderhof. Inevitably, she found the celebrations very different from those in Germany. Edith related this period in the community's life to times of great uncertainty in Germany and spoke of the way in which 'all the festivity and joy that was expressed conveyed the special seriousness of this hour'. Those who were seeking to bear witness to Jesus were, she suggested, 'abandoned and treated like Mary, who in all her poverty, forsaken by men, sought shelter'. Yet, on the other hand, she continued, 'in this very celebration of Christmas we realized that God has not forsaken us.'[47]

As a British person with experience of Free Church life, Charles Headland found the Bruderhof celebration of Advent quite a new experience. Much Free Church worship in the 1920s was characterised by 'the supremacy of spirit over form and of spontaneity over tradition'.[48] The Bruderhof sought to combine spontaneity and tradition, and Charles and others learned to appreciate this. As part of the Advent celebrations at the Cotswold Bruderhof, massive Advent garlands hung from the ceiling, combined with much red ribbon, and there were four large red candles. One was lit on the first Sunday in Advent, two were lit on the second Sunday, and so on, until on the last Sunday all four were lit. The message was of divine light in the coming of the Christ Child. The community dining room, workplaces, and family rooms were all well decorated with spruce.[49] During this 1936 Advent season, Crofton Ganes from Bristol, whose business included furniture, brought 'twelve very nice three-legged stools for the Children's House' and Christmas trees, which Edith Arnold

46. Kurt Zimmermann, 'Nightwatchman's Book', 18–19 March 1938. BHA Coll. 0055.

47. Edith Arnold to the Bruderhofs, 28 December 1936. BHA Coll. 0304.

48. J. W. Grant, *Free Churchmanship in England, 1870–1940*, 272; cf. Randall, 'Austere Ritual', 432–46.

49. Charles Headland, 'Charles Headland Remembers Cotswold and Oaksey'. BHA Coll. 0118.

noted were 'very rare here'. His wife had limited movement in her hands but had made Christmas candles and silver stars for the community.[50]

Christmas Eve, in continental European style, was an important time in the community. There was a striking live nativity scene with a cow from the farm, and there were lighted candles on the Christmas tree. Presents were then given. The first Cotswold Christmas included special readings over the course of three days. On Boxing Day, Crofton Ganes came along with friends from Bristol, making thirteen guests. The children presented a Christmas play. Everyone joined in German and English Christmas songs.[51] During the Christmas season *The Oxford Book of Carols*, published in 1928, was often used for community singing. There were few Christmas puddings, which for some English members was a rather controversial issue, but splendid German *Stollen* (sweet bread) and *Plätzchen* (biscuits) were made in the community bakery.[52]

Setting the scene for Christmas 1938, Emmy Arnold wrote in *The Plough* on 'Expectation and Fulfilment'. She contrasted the message of the angels about 'peace on earth' with the situation in Europe, in which powers of darkness were intent on 'bloodshed and the fratricide of nations'. The article set out the sweep of salvation history, from the prophets who were 'in constant expectation of the coming of this Messiah king', to the birth of the child who was 'truly man, and yet was truly God', through the ministry of Jesus until he was 'cast out by the mighty of this world'. Emmy then asked what could now be seen of the activity of 'this Christ who came, and will come again'. She pointed to the coming of the Holy Spirit and to the second advent of Christ. Her call was to carry on the deeds of Jesus 'in quiet and unobtrusive ways', while also, like the Old Testament prophets and like the virgins with oil in their lamps, being prepared for Christ at his coming, 'an *expectant* Church'.[53] Emmy's reflections were theologically informed and thoughtfully applied. They were presented in various ways within the community, for example through a drama of the Ten Virgins.[54]

50. Edith Arnold to the Bruderhofs, 28 December 1936. BHA Coll. 0304.

51. Edith Arnold to the Bruderhofs, 28 December 1936. BHA Coll. 0304.

52. Charles Headland, 'Charles Headland Remembers Cotswold and Oaksey'. BHA Coll. 0118.

53. Emmy (Emy) Arnold, 'Expectation and Fulfilment', *The Plough* 1, no. 4 (December 1938), 106–8.

54. Emmy Arnold to Heini and Annemarie Arnold, 28 November 1938. BHA Coll. 0288_02.

When Kathleen Hamilton described the life of the Bruderhof to her mother, she spoke of Easter as 'the most important time in the year' for the community. It was also an important time for Kathleen, since it was on an Easter Sunday in 1933 that she had been 'stunned with joy' as she had realised in a new way 'the reality of the atonement'. This realisation had led her to the Bruderhof. At Easter, she explained to her mother, the community's intention was for celebrations to involve a 'solemn realisation of what God's love cost Him, and of joy that it is given to us to share in this cost—to share in the event for which the whole creation waits'.[55] Charles Headland found some of the beautiful Easter hymns in German sung in the community quite striking, especially '*Als Jesus von seiner Mutter ging*', which spoke of the parting of Jesus, in his death, from his mother. Among the English Easter hymns was 'Now the Green Blade Riseth'.[56] Good Friday was a quiet day, with silent meals and time to read. On Easter Sunday, and the days following, there was an emphasis on joy and power. At Easter 1937, one of the messages, by Hardy Arnold, was based on Luke chapter 24, about the two disciples on the road to Emmaus. Hardy stressed particularly the reality of Christ as alive. He linked this with the challenge of mission, insisting that only if Christ was alive in the community in the present could mission happen. Resurrection and mission were seen as intimately connected.[57] In his message at the baptisms in December 1938, Hardy again argued for the crucial nature of the resurrection. Talking about the 'new birth', in John chapter 3, he spoke of being 'born again through the resurrection of Christ'.[58]

The other major event in the Christian year at the Bruderhof was Whitsun, or Pentecost. From its early days, Pentecost had been important to the community. It was following the Whitsun 1920 conference that the community was formed in Sannerz. At that Whitsun conference there was a particular concern for 'the movement of the Spirit of Pentecost two thousand years ago and its consequences ever since'.[59] During the Whitsun period at the Cotswold Bruderhof in 1937, the Saturday and Sunday

55. Kathleen Hamilton to her mother, 12 April 1935. BHA Coll. 0115.

56. Charles Headland, 'Charles Headland Remembers Cotswold and Oaksey'. BHA Coll. 0118.

57. Edith Arnold to Hans Zumpe and brothers and sisters, 31 March 1937. BHA Coll. 0304.

58. Hardy Arnold, community meeting, Cotswold Bruderhof, 7 December 1938. BHA Coll. 0055.

59. Emmy Arnold, *Joyful Pilgrimage*, 34–35.

saw more than 120 visitors arriving. One of these was Lilian Stevenson of the FoR, who had been a friend of the Bruderhof since its Sannerz days. For Moni Barth, the 1937 Whitsun *Gemeindestunde* was 'the true experience of Whitsun' and reminded her of Sannerz. It was, from her perspective, 'as if a mighty struggle with the terrible powers of war and lying is taking place on the earth, and God pours out his Holy Spirit on all who want to fight for the other kingdom, his kingdom'. She believed that those who came to the Cotswold Bruderhof were not simply coming to a community, but were 'drawn into this experience of the Spirit'.[60]

As well as the events of Advent, Christmas, Easter, and Whitsun, there were other significant communal occasions, such as baptisms and the celebration of the Eucharist. Preparation for the Lord's Supper, as it was termed in the Bruderhof, was taken with great seriousness.[61] Although the Lord's Supper was seen as very important, it was not celebrated on a regular basis. There were other celebratory occasions. In February 1939 Salvation Army members from Birmingham came to play and speak. The Army band numbered at least forty.[62] They stayed overnight and in the morning one of them announced: 'Brothers and sisters, this is a unique experience not only for me but for all my comrades. It brings to us a sense of responsibility that perhaps some of us have never before realized, that Jesus spoke of the standard he had set for Christians on earth. The manner in which you brothers and sisters have come together irrespective of your professions reminds us of the way Jesus Christ chose fishermen such as Peter and lawyers such as Paul, and blended them together to make them serve one common purpose'. He concluded by speaking of the joy of the celebration and by saying that it would 'be a help in many of our experiences when we go out into the world to help men and women, to know that there are people who gave up everything to follow Jesus'.[63]

Friends of the Bruderhof

Writing in the spring 1939 *Plough*, Bruce Sumner reported that 1938 had been a year within the community 'of great struggle with lack of capital,

60. Moni Barth to Emmy Arnold, 24 May 1937. BHA Coll. 0305.

61. See chapter six.

62. Nancy Trapnell, 'Memories of Cotswold and Paraguay'. BHA Coll. 0347.

63. Unnamed speaker, community meeting, Cotswold Bruderhof, 26 February, 1939. BHA Coll. 0055.

a struggle which was not altogether unsuccessful'. One of the factors that had improved the financial situation towards the end of the year was the formation of a company, The Friends of the Bruderhof Limited. Bruce explained: 'A number of friends have helped us by subscribing for 4% redeemable preference shares'.[64] The prospectus for the company, which was filed with the Registrar of Companies, stated that £15,000 of share capital had been issued. Repayment was to be within twenty years.[65]

Four directors of the company were not members of the Bruderhof. The best known was George P. Gooch, from West London, who had been a Liberal Member of Parliament and was president of the National Peace Council from 1933 to 1936. He was a significant historian whose books had a focus on Europe.[66] H. F. Bing was warden of the Folk House, Bristol. A. P. I. Cotterell, a Quaker from Gerrards Cross, Bucks, had a civil engineering company. H. S. Moore, from North London, was a journalist. The other two directors were Hardy Arnold and Arnold Mason. The function of the company was 'to raise and lend money to the Cotswold Bruderhof Society'. It was explained, by way of background, that it was 'only through the generous help of many friends' that it had been possible for the community to become established in England. The prospectus stated that capital to be loaned to the Bruderhof Society by the company would help to liquidate existing liabilities, would assist in paying off a mortgage with the Cheltenham and Gloucester Building Society, and would provide funds for the building of further buildings, the purchase of equipment and machinery, and the care of those community members in need.[67]

Bruce Sumner also spoke of 'the considerable help of two friends'.[68] At the time these two were not named, but a later report which surveyed the financial position of the Bruderhof in England gave more detail. Gifts came from three main sources, with about one-third coming from

---

64. Bruce Sumner, 'The Cotswold Bruderhof: A report of the events and activities in 1938', *The Plough* 2, no. 1 (Spring 1939), 21.

65. Prospectus, 'Friends of the Bruderhof Limited', 25 April 1939. BHA Coll. 0334.

66. Among his books was *History of Modern Europe, 1878–1919* (New York: H. Holt & Co., 1923).

67. Prospectus, 'Friends of the Bruderhof Limited', 25 April 1939. BHA Coll. 0334.

68. Bruce Sumner, 'The Cotswold Bruderhof: A report of the events and activities in 1938', *The Plough* 2, no. 1 (Spring 1939), 21.

those joining the community, one-third from a range of friends, and a remarkable one-third, amounting to £20,766, from a single individual, a successful businessman, Gerald Vaughan.[69] In 1938 Gerald and his wife Elleline stayed as guests of the community. They were an impressive-looking young couple, but Elleline's moods alternated dramatically between serious morbidity and great joy. They came first to Ashton Keynes on a drive through the area. Elleline said later that she had been looking at a map and had seen a light moving on it. They followed its direction and came to the Cotswold Bruderhof, where they stayed for a brief time.[70]

As unexpectedly as they had arrived, the Vaughans moved on, without leaving any address. However, a search led to the discovery of an address for Elleline's mother, who lived near Bristol. Hardy and Emmy Arnold travelled to the house and met Elleline, who did not seem surprised to see them. The Vaughans then drove back to Ashton Keynes.[71] Gerald's decision to be so generous to the Bruderhof might well have stemmed from his appreciation for their desire to support Elleline. In November 1938 Emmy Arnold wrote to Hans-Hermann and Gertrud Arnold, who were in London, to say that Elleline was again unsettled. Emmy had been 'deeply moved' by Elleline's 'struggle for Christ' and had told her 'she must not stop fighting'.[72] Hans-Hermann and Gertrud then linked up with Gerald and Elleline in London, spending considerable time with them and having 'some really interesting talks'. At that point Elleline was reckoned to be much better, and Gerald was 'very hopeful'.[73] Gerald never joined the Bruderhof; Elleline's struggles continued.[74]

Gifts from Gerald Vaughan and others helped to transform the community's financial situation. It was possible for significant building work to go ahead. Among the projects were family dwellings, school buildings, the printing press, the carpenter's shop and turnery, and a new laundry. Everything was constructed in what Emmy termed 'a simple

---

69. Report 'SOCIETY OF BROTHERS, Cotswold Bruderhof 1936–1942, Oaksey Bruderhof 1939–1940, Wheathill Bruderhof 1942–'. BHA Coll.0334.

70. Winifred Dyroff, 'The Cotswold Bruderhof'. BHA Coll. 0066.

71. Emmy Arnold, 'The Beginning and Early Years of the Bruderhof Communities'. BHA Coll. 0288.

72. Emmy Arnold to Hans-Hermann and Gertrud Arnold, 5 November 1938. BHA Coll. 0288_02.

73. Hans-Hermann Arnold to Emmy Arnold, 20 January 1939. BHA Coll. 0190.

74. Hans-Hermann Arnold to Emmy Arnold, 12 July 1939. BHA Coll. 0190.

and beautiful style'.[75] Although friends were crucial, and self-sufficiency could not be achieved, community members were determined to try to do as much as they could. It became possible to install a generator, which meant independently producing electricity. Hans Meier bought a second-hand control panel, although no one apart from him mastered its workings. All the concrete blocks used for building were made in the community. There was good-quality local gravel, and this mixed with cement made durable blocks and roads. Fritz Kleiner bought a second-hand block-making machine.[76] Expansion in farming to four farms came through the purchase of Tellings Farm, adjoining Ashton Fields, and then Ashdown Downs and Old Manor farms. A significant further step was the purchase of the three-hundred-acre Oaksey Park Farm and manor house.[77] Increased emphasis on farming, especially dairy farming, drew on expertise within the community. Gerrit Fros, who joined from the Netherlands, was a well-qualified veterinary surgeon. He and his wife Cornelia, who was a teacher, had been active in the Peace Movement.[78]

In their thinking about economic viability, the Bruderhof did not see inner resourcing and support from outside friends as being opposing approaches. Rather, both were essential for the work to advance. When Arnold Mason and Heini Arnold tried to buy a second-hand hut for accommodation purposes, they went to Bristol and found a long wooden building they thought would be large enough. They asked the dealer to keep it for them. They then proceeded, rather nervously, to the 'elegant furniture store' owned by Crofton Ganes. He was busy with customers, but when he had a free moment they explained about their hoped-for purchase. He immediately went to his office and wrote out a cheque for the amount needed. Arnold Mason's account captures something of the atmosphere: 'We returned to the dealer, paid for the hut, had a thankful and joyful meal together and caught the next train.'[79] Dr Ernest Muir was another financial supporter of the Bruderhof who valued what com-

---

75. Emmy Arnold, 'The Beginning and Early Years of the Bruderhof Communities'. BHA Coll. 0288.

76. Arnold Mason, 'Early Memories'. BHA Coll. 0006.

77. 'Concerning the Bruderhof Communities', *The Plough* 2, no. 2 (Summer 1939), 58. There was a full report on Oaksey in the same issue of *The Plough*: 'The New Bruderhof Community at Oaksey', 49–52. This development is covered in chapter 7.

78. Their daughter Nellie married Alan Stevenson. See Nellie Stevenson, 'Life Story'. BHA Coll. 0314.

79. Arnold Mason, 'Early Memories'. BHA Coll. 0006.

munity life offered. When Hans-Hermann and Gertrud Arnold needed to stay in London, the Muirs welcomed them.[80] In turn, Muir asked for the community's help with Alec, his son, a very able medical student who had suffered a breakdown. It was agreed that Alec would be accommodated and looked after, and Muir gave the community £2,000.[81]

Although the financial support of friends was important, friendship was valued in its own right. Bruce Sumner wrote of the death in August 1938 of ninety-two-year-old Jabez Watkins and described him as a 'friend who had grown so dear to us'. Jabez and his wife Elizabeth had moved with their daughter Nancy to the Cotswold Bruderhof in the summer of 1938, after being associated with the community group based in Birmingham.[82] Jabez was convinced through reading the New Testament that it must be possible for Christians to live together as brothers and sisters.[83] When the Bruderhof invited Jabez and Elizabeth to join Nancy, who was becoming a member, Jabez was happy to make the move as well, although Elizabeth initially found it a struggle. She was his second wife and was thirty years younger than him. When they did finally move, Elizabeth as well as Jabez found a home in the community.[84] In the short time he lived the communal life, Jabez was recognised as a Christian with a deep faith—a faith that challenged others—and as someone waiting and longing for the breaking in of God's kingdom.[85] He greatly enjoyed the Cotswold countryside, and lived to see the fields harvested. A short while later, on the night of 18 August 1938, he was, as Nancy put it, 'called to his heavenly home in his sleep'.[86]

This 'missionary charge'

The missional aspect of Bruderhof community life was in part embodied in its hospitality. Guests were invited to discuss at mealtimes what was on

80. Hans-Hermann and Gertrud Arnold to Emmy Arnold, 24 October 1938; 3 November 1938. BHA Coll. 0190.

81. Hermann Arnold, 'Almbruderhof 1935–Cotswold 1936'. BHA Coll. 0015.

82. Bruce Sumner, 'The Cotswold Bruderhof: A report of the events and activities in 1938', The Plough 2, no. 1 (Spring 1939), 18–19.

83. Nancy Trapnell, 'Nancy Trapnell tells about her father'. BHA Coll. 0273.

84. Nancy Trapnell, 'Nancy Trapnell tells about her father'. BHA Coll. 0273.

85. Hardy Arnold, 'The History of the Cotswold and Oaksey Bruderhofs, 1936–1941'. BHA Coll. 0304.

86. Nancy Trapnell, 'Nancy Trapnell tells about her father'. BHA Coll. 0273.

their minds or to ask questions. At times the interchange could become heated. However, both guests and community members had the opportunity to speak from their hearts, which could lead to mutually stimulating exchange.[87] On 15 August 1937, Stanley Fletcher, as the nightwatchman, recorded that the community supper 'ran into a long guest meeting'. Varied views of Christianity were discussed.[88] A week later, when George Vigar was nightwatchman, there was again 'a long guest meeting'. George was pleased to record that 'our doctor visitor and his wife declared they wanted to attempt our way of life with us. Our joy was very great.' He added that God had led three new people to join the community in the course of two days.[89] The 'doctor visitor' was Tommy Gibson, who was in general practice on the Isle of Arran in Scotland. The Cotswold guest notes for 19 September commented that Gibson and his wife Mina had read about the community in the *Manchester Guardian*. Both were described as 'very open and seeking and do not confess to Christianity, but believe in a nonviolent communism'. By 25 September it seemed that the Gibsons had decided to come to the Bruderhof.[90] For reasons unknown, this never happened. Indeed, of the sixteen guests on 19 September, only one, Charles Headland, became a community member.

The numbers of Cotswold guests—day visitors and those staying longer—rose steadily during 1937-38 as news about the community spread. October 1937 saw the biggest group of visitors the Cotswold Bruderhof had welcomed to that date. The Workers' Educational Association in Swindon organised a day visit for 160 people.[91] In April 1938 Annemarie Arnold reported to her family that good progress was being made with buildings. There were new houses and apartments, which were bright and spacious. As Easter approached she was concerned, however, about how much accommodation would be needed because of the number of guests coming. Between forty and fifty were known to be planning to stay, and there were always day visitors who arrived unan-

87. Charles Headland, 'Charles Headland Remembers Cotswold and Oaksey'. BHA Coll. 0118.

88. Stanley Fletcher, 'Nightwatchman's Book', 15–16 August 1937. BHA Coll. 0055.

89. George Vigar, 'Nightwatchman's Book', 20–21 September. 1937. BHA Coll. 0055.

90. Household list, 25 September 1937. The reference in the guest notes is to a decision made by the Gibsons on 21 September. BHA Coll. 0055.

91. Gerd Wegner, 'Nightwatchman's Book', 2–3 October 1937. BHA Coll. 0055.

nounced. As part of the community's Easter presentations, a group had been practising the powerful St Matthew Passion by Heinrich Schütz. As well as the music by Schütz and other composers, attendees sang traditional German, English, and Scottish folk-songs, mostly (in the case of the German songs) about wandering through the country.[92]

Throughout 1938 a number of guests who came to the Bruderhof felt the call to become members of the community. Emmy Arnold was delighted that at the Advent breakfast that year Rosemary Warden (later Ivy Stängl), a Scot who had lived in France, asked to become part of the novitiate.[93] Rosemary's aunt had read the article about the Bruderhof in *The Times*, and when Rosemary read it she wrote to the Cotswold community, asking to learn more.[94] In all, twenty-six people joined the community as full members in 1938 and ten people became part of the novitiate.[95]

During his address before the baptisms in Advent 1938, Hardy Arnold spoke about the 'missionary charge' which Jesus gave his disciples after his crucifixion and resurrection. Hardy saw this commission continuing after the Ascension, through the power of the Spirit. He instanced the Spirit speaking to the apostle Philip (Acts chapter 8), telling him to 'go to the chariot of the man from the East to bear witness to Christ'. In the call of the apostle Paul (Acts chapter 9), could be seen 'distinctly and poignantly the intervention of Christ'. As Paul was on his way to Damascus, Christ met him and said, 'Saul, Saul, why persecutest thou Me?' Paul was then sent by God, as Hardy put it, to join 'the mission service of the Church at Damascus'. There Paul was baptised—here Hardy was connecting with the baptisms which were to take place in the community—and became a follower of Jesus. Another example of mission activity offered by Hardy was Cornelius (Acts chapter 10), who 'by means of a vision was told to go to the disciples'. An angel said, 'Go to Joppa, and speak to Simon who is called Peter, and he will show you what the will of God is'. Hardy commented: 'The angel could himself have told him what the will of God was, and proclaimed forgiveness of sins, but he did

92. Charles Headland, 'Charles Headland Remembers Cotswold and Oaksey'. BHA Coll. 0118.

93. Emmy Arnold to Heini and Annemarie Arnold, 28 November 1938. BHA Coll. 0288_02.

94. Rachel Stangl, 'Life of Oma Ivy'. BHA Coll. 0252.

95. Bruce Sumner, 'The Cotswold Bruderhof: A report of the events and activities in 1938', *The Plough* 2, no. 1 (Spring 1939), 17.

not do it.' Human agency was involved. Such examples showed Hardy that 'just as the early Church and the apostles were given the charge of teaching the people, so it is with us'. Having sought to establish his case from Acts, Hardy cited Paul in 2 Corinthians 5: 'Therefore Paul says we are ambassadors, and we bring a message because God has given us this task.' The missionary commission, Hardy argued, remained applicable. Through the church, God was 'carrying on his work in this way, gathering those who are his'.[96]

The view being put forward was that mission involved not only welcoming those who came to the community but also members travelling out from the community to seek ways to communicate the message entrusted to them. Often they took literature with them. *The Plough* in spring 1939 referred to what Hardy Arnold later described as 'vigorous mission work'. In the space of a few months, community members were able to speak at more than fifty meetings in London, Bristol, Oxford, Birmingham, Cambridge, Nottingham, Manchester, and elsewhere. Two members also went to Switzerland and stayed for six weeks, making or renewing contacts with individuals and groups.[97] During early 1940, meetings in the north-east of England were held jointly between the FoR and the Bruderhof. Representatives from the community took part in meetings in churches, halls, and private houses, and at conferences.[98]

Publishing was another important aspect of outreach. The first title to be published by the Cotswold press, in a series entitled 'Eberhard Arnold, Lectures and Writings', was *The Individual and World Need*, translated by Kathleen Hamilton. The book was well received and was followed by Eberhard Arnold's widely acclaimed introduction to the writings of the Early Christians. *The Plough* publishing house was especially seen as 'a means of witness' when fifteen thousand copies of *A Call, the Way to True Peace* were published in 1938, in English, German, and Dutch. The response to this 'call to true peace' was described as 'very encouraging'. It was reprinted in a French paper, *L'Essor*, the Swedish *Idealisten*, and in various Dutch papers.[99] As an example of how literature was used

96. Hardy Arnold, community meeting, Cotswold Bruderhof, 7 December 1938. BHA Coll. 0055.

97. Hardy Arnold, 'The History of the Cotswold and Oaksey Bruderhofs, 1936–1941'. BHA Coll. 0304; Bruce Sumner, 'The Cotswold Bruderhof: A report of the events and activities in 1938', *The Plough* 2, no. 1 (Spring 1939), 19.

98. *The Christian Pacifist*, June 1940.

99. Arnold Mason, 'Early Memories'. BHA Coll. 0006.

with individuals, when Rosemary Warden became interested and wrote to the Bruderhof asking for more information, she was sent a copy of *The Plough*, which convinced her to visit the community.[100]

Under the heading 'Our guests', the summer 1939 issue of *The Plough* reported on 'the great opportunity for the furtherance of the community witness which offers itself through the great number of guests and visitors who come to the Bruderhof'. Between Easter and the summer of that year the community had welcomed about a thousand guests, some of whom came to live and work for a few days or even weeks, while some came for an afternoon or evening visit. Whitsun 1939 saw more than two hundred visitors at the community, when 'deep experiences of the Spirit' were shared.[101] As transport became more of an issue with the expansion of the community's activities, one response was the purchase of a second-hand funeral coach and two horses. The vehicle looked like an old stage-coach. Because it often transported people to and from Tellings Farm, as well as including Ashdown Farm and Old Manor Farm, it became known as the *Telling Kutsche*.[102] The Old Manor farmhouse was not needed by the community and was sold to the Youth Hostels Association (YHA), who converted it into a fine youth hostel, able to accommodate forty people. Those who wanted to visit the Bruderhof and stay overnight could become members of the YHA for a small sum. This meant more guests could come for short periods.[103] The variety of guests was significant, with *The Plough* speaking in 1939 of socialists, Salvationists, PPU members, University students, FoR members, and groups from workmen's clubs.[104]

In addition to guests from various parts of Britain, visitors came from several countries in Europe, from North America, and even from China.[105] In 1939 Dr P. C. Hsu visited from China, where he had taken part in the founding of short-term Christian communities. He came into contact with Christianity in 1913 as a student, and having become a Christian went on to study at Union Theological Seminary, New York. He returned to China to lecture at Yenching University, and in the 1920s

100. Rachel Stangl, 'Life of Oma Ivy'. BHA Coll. 0252.

101. 'Our Guests', *The Plough* 2, no. 2 (Summer 1939), 58–59.

102. Arnold Mason, 'Early Memories'. BHA Coll. 0006.

103. Hardy Arnold, 'The History of the Cotswold and Oaksey Bruderhofs, 1936–1941'. BHA Coll. 0304.

104. 'Our Guests', *The Plough* 2, no. 2 (Summer 1939), 59.

105. Hardy Arnold, 'The History of the Cotswold and Oaksey Bruderhofs, 1936–1941'. BHA Coll. 0304.

was known as a brilliant thinker. He was associated with FoR work in China, having met Henry Hodgkin and later Muriel Lester. Against the background of Japanese conquests in the 1930s, he was part of a group which organised a retreat for Chinese and Japanese Christian leaders.[106] By the later 1930s he was a representative of China at international Christian gatherings, for example at the third International Missionary Council (IMC) conference at Tambaram, India, in 1938. Hsu spoke about Christian work in rural areas.[107] During his visit to the Bruderhof in 1939, Hsu gave a talk about experiments in Christian community, which he called Christian Ashrams, in China. These were stimulated in part by Muriel Lester's influence. Hsu affirmed the Bruderhof emphases on pacifism, family life, a new socio-economic order and work, but also added intellectual involvement. He saw the need for 'an intellectual centre and a training centre' for Christians in China. The report of Hsu's talk which appeared in *The Plough* included responses from Bruderhof members that endorsed the importance for mission of commitment to intellectual engagement and social involvement.[108]

As it continued to grow in the Cotswold setting, a crucial part of the Bruderhof's vision was to support the 'spreading of the message of the life and the calling'. This spread was taking place through varied forms of mission. Hardy Arnold was clear about the priority of 'new birth', since anyone who had not experienced this 'and cannot show it and prove it in actual life, is no disciple of Jesus Christ'. Authentic Christian community, for him, was not connected with denominational labels: whether someone was a Catholic, a Lutheran, a Calvinist or Greek Orthodox, he stated, 'without the new birth all is in vain'.[109] It was new life in Christ that was at the heart of Christian communal life.

106. Brittain, *Rebel Passion*, 150.

107. Sun, 'The Madras Meeting on Rural Work', 125–29.

108. 'A Talk by Professor P. C. Hsu', *The Plough* 2, no. 4 (Winter 1939), 119–25.

109. Hardy Arnold, community meeting, Cotswold Bruderhof, 7 December 1938. BHA Coll. 0055.

6

Cross-Currents

W hen Eberhard and Emmy Arnold began to explore the history of the Anabaptists they did not know that in North America Hutterite communities still existed. Although there have been suggestions that Eberhard Arnold came to know about the American Hutterites in the mid-1920s through the scholar Robert Friedmann, it has been established by Markus Baum that Arnold first became aware of them in 1921, through a letter from J. G. Evert, a Mennonite and philology professor at Tabor College in Kansas.[1] During 1930–31 Eberhard Arnold was on an extended, year-long visit to the Hutterite communities in America, which were mostly by then in Canada, and when he returned he said to the Rhön community: 'I must assert: there is nothing in the whole world, neither in the available books and writings handed down, nor anything in present-day life-communities, which can be compared to the essence, character, and spirit of the Brotherhoods men known as Hutterian; nothing else could bring us forward or deepen us more strongly.'[2] After his death, and with the addition of many British members to the Cotswold community, new currents of thought began to be felt in the Bruderhof. The community was responding to diverse influences.

1. Baum, *Against the Wind*, 134.
2. Irmgard Keiderling to Else von Hollander, 15 May 1931. BHA Coll. 0152. In Baum, *Against the Wind*, 205. Irmgard quotes Eberhard Arnold in this letter. As secretary at the Rhön Bruderhof at the time, she quotes the official minutes from her own shorthand.

Being Hutterite

In early 1926 Robert Friedmann supplied Eberhard Arnold with the address of Elias Walter, a Hutterite elder at the Standoff Colony in Alberta, Canada, and Eberhard began a correspondence with Walter and other Hutterite elders, such as Joseph Waldner. In a letter to Waldner he spoke of 'the joy we have in your Bruderhofs of the Hutterian brothers in America'. Eberhard was 'deeply strengthened' by knowing of communities that 'faithfully continue the way of Jakob Hutter'. The Rhön Bruderhof's principles were reiterated in this letter: 'We reject bearing arms and military service, war taxes and oaths, public office, and taking part in political elections and parties, all private property and all private life, all evil occupations for earning a livelihood, all work for self, all self-will, and sin.' This life was only possible, Eberhard wrote, 'through the love that comes from the faith of the apostles and prophets in the Father through Christ and the Holy Spirit. This faith works in us through the Holy Spirit and through Holy Scripture.' Eberhard paid tribute to Hutterite writings. They were 'the guidelines of faith from which we never want to stray'. Eberhard went on to speak of the activities at the Rhön and to make a plea: 'All this work needs $10,000 as a basis for a sound Hutterian establishment. We ask you from our hearts to send us help before it is too late.'[3]

In 1928 Eberhard began to place more emphasis on adopting 'Hutterian Orders', the guidelines that governed Hutterian communities. During the second half of 1928, in correspondence with Elias Walter, Eberhard expressed the feeling there was in the Rhön Bruderhof of 'resolute certainty' and 'firm irrevocable will' to join the Hutterites. He also asked if two 'Servants of the Word' (Hutterite leaders) could come from North America to Germany.[4] This did not happen at that stage, but in any case plans were emerging for Eberhard to visit American Hutterite communities with the aim of uniting the Rhön Bruderhof with them. The procedure was not straightforward. Elias Walter explained that the American Hutterites were divided into three groups, spread across South Dakota in the United States, and Manitoba and Alberta in Canada.[5]

3. Eberhard Arnold to Joseph Waldner, probably 1928. BHA Coll. 0288_02.

4. Eberhard Arnold to Elias Walter, 6 November 1928, in Eberhard Arnold, *Brothers Unite*, 6–9.

5. The three groups are called the Lehrerleut, the Dariusleut, and the Schmiedeleut. (*Leut* is German for people). There are some cultural as well as geographical differences. See Katz and Lehr, *Inside the Ark*.

During this period Elias Walter donated funds for the Rhön community to publish Hutterite writings. Some members of the Rhön community worked to copy original Hutterite documents, for example a 355-page manuscript with court records concerning the early Hutterite leader Peter Riedemann.[6] Eberhard travelled to Sabatisch (Šoboti and Velké Leváre both in present-day Slovakia), which had been early Hutterite settlements. He met descendants of the Anabaptists and saw various Hutterian sites. Among his finds was a copy of a significant Hutterian document of 1652 in the Moravian Herrnhut archives.[7]

Eberhard's convictions about the Hutterites were recalled in a talk which Hardy Arnold gave to the Cotswold community on 31 March 1939, entitled, 'Review of Our Connection with Hutterians'. Hardy began by noting that it had been almost twenty years since the community began in Sannerz. He emphasised that 'the urge to do this was that we wanted to follow Jesus and do his will. Right from the beginning it was clear to us that the only strength for such a life comes from the free working Spirit of God.' But Hardy did not want to foster a view that the Bruderhof was separatist in its outlook. He continued: 'Right from the beginning, too, it had been the wish of this little circle not to stand alone, but to become completely united with whatever group there might be to whom the Spirit had spoken in the same way, and who were giving the same witness and living the same life.' He explained that there had been 'very close contact' with the Quakers, but that increasingly the community at Sannerz and then at the Rhön was drawn to the Hutterites and read writings and books 'about the Hutterian apostles, and accounts of the deaths of the martyrs'.[8]

Hardy then described how contact was established with Elias Walter. He did not attribute the developments to the initiative of Eberhard alone but to a shared leading of the Spirit. He told those listening to him: 'It became very clear to us now that here in the Hutterian brethren we had found those with whom we were standing on a common basis of faith, and with whom we were identical in our way of life. In all the important

6. Baum, *Against the Wind*, 180.

7. Eberhard Arnold to David Wipf, 31 December 1929, in Eberhard Arnold, *Brothers Unite*, 46–48. This was a letter of 1650 from Andreas Ehrenpreis, the Hutterite bishop, which he drew up with missionary intentions in mind. In 1652 he printed it as a booklet. See Friedmann, 'An Epistle Concerning Communal Life', 249–54.

8. Hardy Arnold, community meeting, Cotswold Bruderhof, 31 March 1939. BHA Coll. 0055 .

questions of faith which had been so radical in the early beginning of Sannerz there was complete agreement.' These convictions included rejection of self-profit and property, and rejection of violence. There had been doubts on the part of some in the Bruderhof about whether there was 'complete agreement' with the North American Hutterites. What Hardy wanted to stress was that in the late 1920s the Hutterites were seen by the Bruderhof as a movement led by the Holy Spirit: 'No contradiction between the Spirit and the [Hutterian] order was felt at that time.' Rather, Bruderhof members were impressed by finding that their feelings were expressed in Hutterian life, which was astonishing 'because historically we had no contact whatsoever with them.'[9]

Although the Rhön Bruderhof members in the late 1920s were intent on unity with the Hutterite communities in North America, John Horsch and his son-in-law Harold Bender, as American Mennonites, also encouraged Eberhard before and during his American trip. Bender made a visit to the Rhön, and Eberhard wrote to him on 20 May 1930 to express gratitude that Bender had been 'given the power and insight' to realize that 'the only single thing of importance for us is representing the true and real gospel.'[10] Bender replied that he hoped those at the Rhön would be 'shining witnesses' to God's love and strength, and told them: 'That is what you have become for me.'[11] Bender's evolving ideas about the 'Anabaptist Vision' and Anabaptist witness would prove crucial for Mennonite self-identity. In an article in *Church History* in 1944, he argued that Anabaptism represented 'consistent evangelical Protestantism.'[12] Eberhard's belief, as he expressed it to Horsch in 1929, was that the Hutterites in North America affirmed 'the gospel of personal conversion through the reconciling blood of Christ.'[13] After Eberhard arrived in America he reported home—in June 1930—that he had attended a Mennonite meeting lasting many hours which was 'astonishingly lively', with 'English revival-

9. Hardy Arnold, community meeting, Cotswold Bruderhof, 31 March 1939. BHA Coll. 0055.

10. Eberhard Arnold to Harold Bender, 20 May 1930, in Eberhard Arnold, *Brothers Unite*, 53.

11. Harold Bender to Eberhard Arnold, 26 May 1930, in Eberhard Arnold, *Brothers Unite*, 54.

12. Bender, 'The Anabaptist Vision', 3–24. This article was published in the *Mennonite Quarterly Review* a month later.

13. Eberhard Arnold to John Horsch, 14 September to 9 October 1929, in Eberhard Arnold, *Brothers Unite*, 42.

ist songs' being sung. He had been able to speak to the congregation for an hour, emphasising 'our special themes'—'Pentecost at Jerusalem', the 'gospel of Christ', and 'love and community, in which everything belongs to God and to the church of the Spirit'.[14]

The journey to form a union with the Hutterites involved Eberhard in a gruelling schedule. He was questioned in detail at each stage of his journey about his communal Anabaptist credentials. The Hutterites seemed at that time to have no understanding of what Eberhard said about their lack of mission, but they finally accepted him and appointed him to 'proclaim the word of God' in Germany.[15] They insisted, however, that he had to be baptised into the Hutterites. He explained that he could not deny his earlier baptism by immersion with its 'sense of incorporation into the body of Christ'. He found it (as he noted in his diary) 'quite hard to submit to the baptism of pouring over', but he saw it as incorporation into the Hutterite Brotherhood.[16]

There was excitement at the Rhön Bruderhof when news came on 20 December 1930 that the Rhön community was now united with the three Hutterite groups. Eberhard's return seemed imminent. However, they soon learned that he planned to revisit all the North American communities to seek funds to support the work in Germany. When he did return in the spring of 1931 there was some disappointment among those at the Rhön, since, as Emmy put it, the Hutterite communities 'had given precious little towards our building up'.[17] Eberhard's own report in May 1931, after his return, showed something of the mixed feelings he had at the time. He told the Rhön community that the intention was not 'to become Hutterian in the sense of 1930–31; but we do want to become Hutterian in the sense of those first sixty years, from 1528–1589'.[18] It was the first period of Hutterite history, marked by adventurous outreach in mission, which the Bruderhof found exemplary and inspirational.

Hardy Arnold's 'Review' in 1939 conveyed the outcome of Eberhard's journey to North America: there was 'a complete uniting with the brothers'. Hardy recalled that 'it was clearly recognized by us [at the

14. Eberhard Arnold to Emmy Arnold, 18 June 1930, in Eberhard Arnold, *Brothers Unite*, 64.

15. Baum, *Against the Wind*, 200–201.

16. Eberhard Arnold to Emmy Arnold, 1 December 1930, in Eberhard Arnold, *Brothers Unite*, 181–82.

17. Emmy Arnold, *Joyful Pilgrimage*, 114.

18. Irmgard Keiderling to Else von Hollander, 15 May 1931. BHA Coll. 0152.

Rhön] how much we had to learn from the brothers in regard to constancy and firmness'. Hardy acknowledged, however, that unity with the Hutterites was a reflection of trust in Eberhard, the only one who had been to America. In Eberhard's heart, Hardy said, there was a strong 'desire for our uniting'.[19] In 1932 Annemarie Wächter, then a recent member of the Rhön community, gave her family an idealistic account of the Hutterites, which reflected Bruderhof thinking: 'The inner life of their communities is still as pure, living and original as it was at the time of their formation'.[20]

Hardy was careful to note, however, that at the time of Eberhard's visit to North America 'certain weaknesses and faults' in the Hutterite communities were 'spoken of quite openly'. Three issues had been seen as of particular importance. Firstly, the Hutterites were in the three groupings. Hardy commented that sadly there was 'not always complete unity between them, but even tension'. Secondly, Eberhard during his visits observed that too much stress was placed upon 'the economic capability and standing and independence of each separate Bruderhof'. Some communities were better off than others. In Hardy's words, 'there was no equalizing of the positions'. The third concern, Hardy reiterated, was that among the Hutterites there was 'so little mission'. Hardy added that there were some 'other points which were noticed'.[21]

Emmy Arnold commented on some of these 'other points'. Although women at the Rhön were willing to accept the Hutterite head covering or *Kopftuch*, since it seemed to convey the idea of simple peasant dress, there was little enthusiasm for the Hutterite black and grey colours for the men, since the brighter colours of the German youth movement were preferred. The community also debated whether they should follow Hutterite customs and should give up pictures, which could 'often say much more than words', photographs, and 'hiking with flutes and guitars . . . and all the beautiful folk songs and songs of religious awakening'. All this, said Emmy, 'belonged to our life'.[22] These elements were not abandoned

19. Hardy Arnold, community meeting, Cotswold Bruderhof, 31 March 1939. BHA Coll. 0055.

20. Annemarie Wächter to her mother and siblings, 28 February 1932, in Annemarie Arnold, *Anni*, 145.

21. Hardy Arnold, community meeting, Cotswold Bruderhof, 31 March 1939. BHA Coll. 0055.

22. Emmy Arnold, *Joyful Pilgrimage*, 113.

in the succeeding years, although some at the Rhön tried to purge the community of pictures.

As Baum puts it, if all that belonged to the Sannerz community's joyful beginnings had been given up, all that would have remained would have been a 'cheerless caricature of the dynamic life of the earliest Hutterites'. However, Baum also notes that to the end of his life Eberhard 'stood unshakeable in his conviction that uniting with the Hutterites in North America came at just the right time, that they provided the German Bruderhof with important guidelines for survival and gave it legitimacy'.[23] As Eberhard saw it, they were uniting with a long spiritual tradition. He commented in August 1931: 'It is important to me that the source of our blessing is with the [Hutterian] brothers and arises from the tremendous witness of the apostolic mission through the centuries. Our blessing comes only in this way, and in no other.'[24] Eberhard was strongly opposed to any narrowness, insisting in May 1935: 'If we are to go along with no one but the old Hutterian brothers and insist on everyone accepting our beliefs. . . then I will have no part in it but will protest against it as long as I live.'[25] At the time when Eberhard made this statement, he and Hardy had just returned from Britain, where they had made many contacts, and perhaps Eberhard saw that Bruderhof witness in Britain could not flourish if narrow Hutterite stances were adopted.

An Anabaptist Congregation in London?

During their visit to Britain in the spring of 1935, Eberhard and Hardy became intrigued by Kingsley Hall, the Christian community in Bow, East London, led by Muriel and Doris Lester. Hardy Arnold later described how Eberhard 'liked it very much' at Kingsley Hall.[26] Muriel Lester, who was widely known as a leading figure in FoR by the 1920s, was born in 1883, the same year as Eberhard, and like him had grown up in comfortable surroundings. Muriel discovered the writings of Tolstoy and sat and passed the Oxford and Cambridge Joint Board with an essay on 'war and

---

23. Baum, *Against the Wind*, 207.

24. Eberhard Arnold, community meeting, 22 August 1931. BHA EA 31/11.

25. Eberhard Arnold, community meeting, 27 May 1935. BHA zu EA 360.

26. Hardy Arnold, community meeting, Cotswold Bruderhof, 31 March 1939. BHA Coll. 0055.

peace'.[27] But instead of going to Cambridge University, she committed herself to work among deprived families in East London. In 1905 she entered a period of intense spiritual experience. She wrote in her diary on 1 January 1905 that she was very happy 'trying to be nearer to Jesus' and was seeking to give him an 'abiding place' in her experience.[28] Later that year she felt she was 'born again' when she was reading John chapter 3.[29]

In 1912 Muriel and Doris rented rooms in East London, and their brother, Kingsley, minister of a small church, lived with them until his early death in 1914. Muriel taught classes of adults about her conviction that people should do Jesus Christ 'the honour of taking Him seriously, of thinking out His teaching in terms of daily life, and then acting on it even if ordered by police, prelates, and princes to do the opposite'. Some who came to her adult school were not convinced, however, about the place of Christianity in everyday life. Muriel wrote: 'They knew that Christianity was my ground of hope, my source of happiness, the spring of my energy'. The group members soon acquired enough New Testaments to start discussing the Sermon on the Mount from Matthew's Gospel.[30] In 1914 the group took over a disused Strict and Particular Baptist Chapel. They proceeded to take out the pews, to put in chairs, and to install a bar counter for a teetotal pub.[31] The opening ceremony at Kingsley Hall, as they called it (after Kingsley Lester), was presided over by Thomas Phillips, minister of Bloomsbury Baptist Church. Muriel had been baptised on profession of faith, in the Baptist tradition, but in her spirituality she drew from Ignatius of Loyola, Brother Lawrence, Francis of Assisi, and a leading contemporary Anglo-Catholic writer who was also a pacifist, Evelyn Underhill.[32] As meetings commenced at Kingsley Hall, speakers of different denominations were welcomed. It was made clear that the

27. Wallis, *Mother of World Peace*, 10.

28. Muriel Lester Diary, 1897–1906. LESTER 1/1/2, Bishopsgate Institute, London.

29. Wallis, *Mother of World Peace*, 20–21. Koven notes the attention given to the Welsh Revival in the newspaper of Loughton Union Church (Baptist-Congregational) where the Lesters were members. See Koven, *The Match Girl and the Heiress*, 153.

30. Muriel Lester, *It Occurred to Me*, 52.

31. Muriel Lester, *It Occurred to Me*, 57.

32. Wallis, *Mother of World Peace*, 35, 41–42. For Underhill see Armstrong, *Evelyn Underhill, 1875–1941*.

teaching would centre on Christ, and it was also emphasised that 'Roman Catholics, Protestants & Atheists are equally welcome'.[33]

There were several reasons why Kingsley Hall appealed so much to Eberhard Arnold. It reminded him, Hardy noted, of the social work in Berlin of his friend Friedrich Siegmund-Schulze. Hardy emphasised the way in which Muriel and Doris had been shocked by 'the great poverty and dirt of this slum area [Bow], the many taverns, and the presence of drunken men and women in the streets'. In particular they were concerned that children were being brought up knowing only that environment, and like the Bruderhof they directed ministry towards caring for and educating children. Eberhard and Hardy also noted the community aspect. Hardy recorded: 'They now have five houses close together there, with centres for children, young people, and adults, and living quarters for themselves and their staff. The Lester sisters are moved by a genuine Christian love for the poor, and their presence in Bow has made a great impact there, both by making the authorities more aware of the need in this and other slum districts so that they do more for these people, and by their own influence on this neighbourhood in Bow'.[34]

Kees and Betty Boeke were part of the Kingsley Hall community for a time, but—as the community reported—a 'jingo press campaign in 1917 succeeded in getting them banished [from Britain] as undesirable aliens'. Probably, Muriel Lester observed about the campaign undertaken in newspapers such as the *Daily Mail*, Holland needed them more than London did, 'and God let the wrath even of the *Daily Mail* serve the cause of the Fellowship of Reconciliation'.[35] Kees Boeke represented an early Kingsley Hall and FoR link with Eberhard and with the Bruderhof's beginnings in Germany.

The multifaceted world of Kingsley Hall, however, was far removed from the restricted one of the Hutterites. When Eberhard and Hardy were at Kingsley Hall in April 1935, Muriel was in India, working with Gandhi under the auspices of FoR, and it was Doris who arranged a number of meetings at which Eberhard spoke. The varied people the Arnolds met showed them that Kingsley Hall was both a vibrant local community, worshipping and serving, and a centre for wider pacifist and ecumenical endeavour. As well as speaking at arranged meetings, they were invited

33. Bruce Road Adult School Minute Book, 1 June 1914. LESTER 1/1/3.

34. Hardy Arnold, community meeting, Cotswold Bruderhof, 31 March 1939. BHA Coll. 0055.

35. Lester, *It Occurred to me*, 79–80.

to a Kingsley Hall evening event which included 'a group of young adults spending the evening dancing together in the usual style'. Eberhard told them about the experience at the Rhön of 'communal circle dances and their deep inner significance, expressing the hope that a similar experience of full community would also be given to them'.[36]

There was an ongoing interest at Kingsley Hall in 'full community'. In 1921 Muriel had written: 'It isn't enough to give away money, we feel we have no right to possess it'.[37] In that year Muriel and some others agreed to share a common life, as 'the Brethren of the Common Table'. They were indebted to the thinking of Bernard Walke, an Anglo-Catholic priest and a member of FoR.[38] Three years later a Church Fellowship and membership was formed at Kingsley Hall. In Baptist and Anabaptist style, the church was 'self-governing', and had a membership 'open to all who love Jesus Christ and delight to worship and work together'.[39] Muriel, who became the pastor, described how a communion service was instituted, a church membership roll formed, and church meetings started. During a mission, she said, several people decided to 'throw in their lot with the little company of followers of Christ, take up their position in the long and often struggling process of the faithful that has stretched across the centuries, and assume their share of responsibility for the witness of the universal Church in every century'.[40] With a committed membership, deep relationships, communal living, mission, a social vision and a peace witness, it could be seen as a community in the Anabaptist tradition.

Doris Lester asked for advice from the experience of the Bruderhof about developing community life further at Kingsley Hall, but Hardy recalled that 'most of the staff were members of the Oxford Group movement', with its emphasis on individual guidance. The problem of accommodating differing viewpoints was illustrated by a dramatic incident that took place when Eberhard was there. A Swiss lecturer visiting England arrived at Kingsley Hall and enquired how Eberhard had managed to attract audiences in London. He said that he himself had made great efforts to find audiences for his particular 'message', but with little success. Eberhard asked the (unnamed) Swiss lecturer what he wanted to speak

36. Hardy Arnold, community meeting, Cotswold Bruderhof, 31 March 1939. BHA Coll. 0055.

37. *The Evening Standard*, 2 April 1921.

38. Barrett, *Subversive Peacemakers*, 84–87, 213–16.

39. Kingsley Hall Constitution. LESTER 7/2/9.

40. Lester, *It Occurred to Me*, 115, 118–119.

about, to which he replied that his topic was 'a Christian method of birth control'. Eberhard expressed his disapproval in 'a thunderous voice', and Doris, 'quite exasperated and distressed', asked Hardy why Eberhard was shouting. She said that this was not done in Kingsley Hall, commenting that Gandhi had stayed there during his extended time in London, and 'had been very quiet and a very honoured guest'. Eberhard insisted that 'he was no saint and did not want to be one, like Gandhi'. He wanted, rather, to be 'a servant of God, and if necessary shout and protest against evil'. Almost a year later, in Zürich, Hardy met the Swiss lecturer again, who told Hardy he was thankful for the way Eberhard had challenged him.[41] In some areas greater diversity of opinion was acceptable at Kingsley Hall than was the case in the Bruderhof.

Hutterite Brothers

Although Eberhard Arnold visited and admired Kingsley Hall, and although Doris Lester and others from Kingsley Hall visited the Bruderhof communities, from the beginnings of the Cotswold Bruderhof a mutual relationship did not deepen in the way that it might have done. Rather, what the Cotswold community hoped for—and this was in line with Eberhard's earlier hopes—was to foster close ties with the Hutterites in North America. It seemed that encouragement from that quarter was on the way in early 1937 when at the request of the Bruderhof in Europe two Hutterian elders (the Brothers) were sent from North America to spend some time with the European communities.

Heini Arnold wrote to Emmy on 5 January 1937 to say that the Cotswold community was 'in great expectation of the two Hutterian Brothers'. He hoped that Emmy, who was at the Alm Bruderhof, could play a full part in the visit since she knew how to respond to the Hutterian teaching on 'outward things'. He added that 'the Brothers lay great stress' on these—the 'Orders'. There was some anticipation of possible tensions to come. On the issue of 'outward things', Heini instanced the use of candles in Cotswold community meetings. He knew that the Hutterites had 'no candles in inner meetings', which was a mark of their historical desire to break away from Catholic Church practices. However, Heini's experience

---

41. Hardy Arnold, community meeting, Cotswold Bruderhof, 31 March 1939. BHA Coll. 0055.

in community, in Germany and in England, was that candles were 'a symbolic expression to us of gathering around the true light of God'.[42]

A month later, David Hofer from the James Valley Hutterite Colony, Manitoba, and Michael Waldner, who was from Bon Homme, South Dakota, arrived in England. David Hofer wrote on 8 February 1937 about their first impressions of England: 'Everything was wonderfully green, and the people live together in villages.'[43] The two Brothers had not informed the Cotswold community about their transatlantic sailing arrangements, and the community followed shipping news to track down liners coming from Canada. By getting in touch with the shipping company in Southampton and by looking at train schedules, Hans Zumpe and Hardy Arnold managed to meet the Brothers in Swindon.[44] For their part, the Brothers were blissfully unaware that they might have communicated in advance about travel times. David Hofer simply recorded: 'With God's help and Fatherly protection we arrived at 3 o'clock in the afternoon at the place where we met Hans Zumpe and Hardy Arnold and were greeted in a very friendly way. Then after 15 minutes came a horse and wagon. It was a two-wheeled buggy. We drove to the Hof of the dear *Gemeinde* and they came and met us friendly with singing and handshakes and received us in a warm hearty way.'[45] The warmth was genuine. Edith Arnold described the scene: 'It was moving to see these two dignified white-bearded men, who undertook such a long journey just out of love. . . A really deep love radiates from them, a love that truly comes from Christ.'[46] The Brothers soon began to involve themselves fully in the Cotswold community, especially in worship and in farm work.[47]

Heini Arnold's anticipation of debate about 'outward things' was, however, very quickly fulfilled. On 10 February, when David Hofer led the Cotswold prayer meeting, the Brothers asked that men sit on one side of the meeting and women on the other. There was no concept of this in meetings at Sannerz, the Rhön, the Alm, or the Cotswold community, and the Brothers offered no justification other than the fact, as David Hofer noted in his diary, that men and women sitting together was

---

42. Heini Arnold to Emmy Arnold, 5 January 1937. BHA Coll. 0055.
43. David Hofer, 'Diary'. BHA Coll. 0484.
44. Arnold Mason, 'Early Memories'. BHA Coll. 0006.
45. David Hofer, 'Diary'. BHA Coll. 0484.
46. Edith Arnold to Emmy Arnold, 9 February 1937. BHA Coll. 0304.
47. Arnold Mason, 'Early Memories'. BHA Coll. 0006.

'not according to the [Hutterian] Orders'. The next day Michael Waldner led the prayer meeting. The topic was the Sermon on the Mount. What was read by way of exposition was from Hutterian writings. David Hofer believed the community had been affected by the readings and wrote: 'It went through their hearts to hear the teachings of our forefathers.'[48]

On 17 February there was a prayer meeting with Hans Zumpe, who had responsibilities across the Bruderhof communities. Hans was about to travel and David Hofer noted: 'All shook hands in the meeting, wishing him God's protection.' Hutterian traditions were emphasised by the Brothers in Hans' absence. On the naming of new-born children, they stated: 'There should be only names given which are in the Bible or which are Hutterian.'[49] When there was some loud laughter in the Cotswold dining room about an amusing incident, the Brothers said they considered such laughter out of place.[50] Hardy Arnold wrote in a letter to Hans Zumpe that there had also been a discussion about pictures and photographs. David Hofer had objected to a visitor to the Cotswold community taking photos and told the guest that the community was 'not yet Hutterian on that point'. Hardy was disappointed that David Hofer had 'stressed the points of difference between us to someone outside, while we had always stressed the basic unity in faith and life'. It was, for Hardy, an incident that was 'very deeply connected with the question of mission' and with 'the conduct of the Brothers to people outside in the world'.[51] These were deeper issues than the 'Orders'.

It was not that the Brothers saw nothing in the Cotswold Bruderhof to affirm. Among David Hofer's early notes were these: 'We are finding much unity and self surrender—they love one another with godly love. There is no enmity. We wished we [in North America] would be in such a unity and complete love.' The Brothers also became interested in how mission work was carried out in the European context. On 18 February David Hofer wrote: 'Mission work also is done towards those who hunger and thirst for God's Word.' The following day the Brothers travelled to London. David Hofer made notes about the experience: 'We went to London, the biggest city in the world, 10 million inhabitants.' He added that they had seen 'a Woolworth store'. On arrival back at Ashton Keynes, 'we

48. David Hofer, 'Diary'. BHA Coll. 0484.

49. David Hofer, 'Diary'. BHA Coll. 0484.

50. Arnold Mason, 'Early Memories'. BHA Coll. 0006.

51. Hardy Arnold 31 March 1937 to Hans Zumpe, 31 March 1937. BHA Coll. 0304.

got a report from those who had been sent out on mission. They found people who want to visit the Bruderhof as guests.'[52] However, it was very difficult for the Brothers to understand a community that was open to the world outside. Emmy Arnold expressed to Hardy her hope that the efforts being made to enable the Brothers to understand 'our organisation as a mission church' would be fruitful.[53]

Language issues hindered attempts at communication. Within the Cotswold community talks and discussions were translated so that German speakers and English speakers could all understand. The Brothers, however, 'were accustomed to read or speak in an uninterrupted flow and found it difficult to make pauses for translation'. English members began to ask to be excused from meetings.[54] Which songs were sung in meetings was also problematic. David Hofer criticised the community's *Sonnenlieder* volume of songs as too worldly.[55] From another perspective, Vollmer suggests that the songs 'manifest most clearly the spiritual productivity of the [Bruderhof] circle'. The collection included folk-songs, hymns from the Reformation and from the Anabaptists, songs of the Moravian Brethren and the revival movements, songs of the youth movement and the workers' movement, and many poems.[56]

The Brothers appeared to be largely unaware of the tensions. They were excited that they were able to baptise five candidates. This was a 'moving celebration'. There was serious preparation for Good Friday, for Easter Sunday, and for the celebration of the Lord's Supper. David Hofer noted that 'everybody wants to take part in the Lord's Remembrance in deep fear of God'.[57] In the week leading up to Easter, Moni Barth reported to Emmy Arnold that 'inner preparation' for taking the Lord's Supper was so intense that meetings were taking place at five o'clock in the morning, before the working day, and in the evenings.[58] Hardy fielded some new community members' struggles 'to understand the Biblically strict and very formal-appearing manner of the Brothers and their proclamation

---

52. David Hofer, 'Diary'. BHA Coll. 0484.

53. Emmy Arnold to Hardy Arnold, 20 March 1937. BHA Coll. 0288_02.

54. Arnold Mason, 'Early Memories'. BHA Coll. 0006.

55. Hardy Arnold to Hans Zumpe, 31 March 1937. BHA Coll. 0304.

56. Vollmer, *Neuwerk*, 75.

57. David Hofer, 'Diary'. BHA Coll. 0484.

58. Moni Barth to Emmy Arnold, 30 March 1937. BHA Coll. 0305.

of the Word'.[59] It was crucial that all should come to the Lord's Supper with the right attitude. Eberhard had spoken of the significance of the Supper as a time when each member 'renews a holy bond' and 'resolves to love and honour the Holy Spirit at work in all the services of the church community'.[60] The teaching brought by the Brothers to the Cotswold community on Good Friday 1937 included a traditional passage for this theme, Isaiah 53.[61] Hardy expressed a widespread view that Michael Waldner's Good Friday teachings were very hard to understand. There were problems 'because of the very singing tone he uses in the Teaching; so probably most of us left this meeting with a rather heavy heart, particularly since in this Teaching little was said about the true, all-embracing significance of the death of Christ.' Michael Waldner stressed, said Hardy, the 'very important cleansing of our individual souls with the blood of Christ' and did this 'very vividly and in great detail'.[62]

Despite some sense in the community that the vision of Christ's work presented on Good Friday was a restricted one, there was a desire to enter into the joy of Easter Day and to come together at the Lord's Table. There were memories of powerful occasions in the past. Writing to her mother in 1935, Kathleen Hamilton said that she had never in her life experienced anything like the Lord's Supper as celebrated in the Bruderhof.[63] On Easter morning 1937, a communal breakfast was followed by readings from the Easter Gospel, and from Blumhardt, and German and English Easter songs were sung. The Brothers found it 'very different' but said they greatly enjoyed it. An Easter egg hunt for the children was organised. In the evening there was the Lord's Supper. David Hofer, whom Hardy described as speaking 'in a very lively, urgent way that goes to the heart', talked for over three hours on 1 Corinthians chapter 11.[64] David Hofer wrote in his diary that the 'Lord's Supper teaching' during this long meeting 'so touched the hearts of the dear brothers and sisters that at the end of the meeting they shook hands with one another and greeted one

---

59. Hardy Arnold to Hans Zumpe, 31 March 1937 BHA Coll. 0304.

60. Eberhard Arnold to the Rhön Bruderhof, September 1934. BHA Coll. 0288_02.

61. David Hofer, 'Diary'. BHA Coll. 0484.

62. Hardy Arnold to Hans Zumpe, 31 March 1937. BHA Coll. 0304.

63. Kathleen Hamilton to her mother, 23 June 1935. BHA Coll. 0115.

64. Hardy Arnold to Hans Zumpe, 31 March 1937. BHA Coll. 0304.

another with peace and unity. . . And still more: the brothers embraced one another and the sisters embraced one another.'[65]

Moni Barth was unwell and unable to be at the Supper, and at 11.00pm, when it finished, she was brought 'half a loaf' and 'an earthen pitcher with wine'. David Hofer, Georg Barth, Hardy and Edith Arnold, and Arnold and Gladys Mason all came to 'receive the Meal' with Moni. At her bedside, David Hofer read 'the sacramental words', as Moni put it, and 'spoke with much emotion about the torment of Jesus that he bore and suffered for the sake of our sins'. Finally, David Hofer said that 'through this Lord's Supper we all were united in a very special way'.[66] Hardy believed something happened during this time 'for which we had longed'. The two months with the Brothers had raised questions about unity, but at the Supper Hardy saw clearly that 'Jesus Christ the crucified and risen one must show his might in us here and now. . . And only through Christ's power can full unity with the Brothers be attained'.[67]

'Movements of the Present Day'

The Brothers moved on from the Cotswold community after Easter, having been requested by the Rhön Bruderhof to travel there as soon as possible, in the hope that their presence might restrain the Nazi authorities. They undoubtedly gave greatly needed support to the Rhön community in their time of crisis and extreme need.[68] Following this, the Brothers visited the Alm and also many historic sites connected with Hutterite history, arriving back in England on 24 August. The Cotswold community met them and expressed friendliness, but the Brothers considered—as David Hofer noted in his diary—that 'love and the trust were not so great any more'.[69] During the time they were at the Alm, Emmy Arnold had tried to read to the Brothers from Eberhard's American letters and to explain his point of view about witness in the modern world. Writing to Hardy and Edith, Emmy did not hide the struggles that had been taking place with the Brothers. She wrote: 'Sometimes one gets the impression that they feel something of it—but then again that they cling firmly to

65. David Hofer, 'Diary'. BHA Coll. 0484.
66. Moni Barth to Emmy Arnold, 30 March 1937. BHA Coll. 0305.
67. Hardy Arnold to Hans Zumpe, 31 March 1937 BHA Coll. 0304.
68. See chapter 3 above.
69. David Hofer, 'Diary'. BHA Coll. 0484.

their traditions and can't take in anything new. We have to remember that these brothers are getting on in age and usually think in terms of centuries, so they are unable to take in such fast flashes of the Spirit as we know them—so we must have much patience.' For her, however, patience could be combined with plain speech. She considered that 'in their standpoint to the world and mission, [the Brothers] simply take up an unbelieving attitude and do not recognize the movements of the present day'. Michael Waldner had asked Emmy what fruit there was from the community's social work in Germany, and in response Emmy listed people who had been reached by this ministry and had joined the community. Michael Waldner, said Emmy, was 'extremely shaken and overcome'.[70]

Emmy was similarly frank in writing with some guidance for Hans Zumpe. The first of two letters to him came after David Hofer told her he was 'very unhappy because we [the Cotswold community] did not want to be completely Hutterian'. Emmy reported to Hans that she had replied that 'we hold the same confession of faith' as early Hutterites confessed. David Hofer then spoke about the Hutterian Orders 'which had originated from the Spirit', to which Emmy responded that the Orders 'would have to come from the Spirit with us too, and we could not simply accept the forms that the Spirit brought about for them'. She urged David Hofer to 'compare us rather with the beginnings of Hutterianism than with present-day Hutterianism. He would find more likeness there. . . For instance, we read yesterday that the Anabaptists with Jacob Hutter celebrated the Lord's Supper with brothers among them who were not yet baptized.' There was some hope, however, since David Hofer had said, 'It is better with you than with us, who are simply born into the church!'[71]

Despite this encouragement, Emmy spoke in her second letter to Hans of continuing difficulties because the Brothers 'regard everything from their point of view; e.g., they consider things that are more usual with them to be better'. Also, while Eberhard believed that the earliest Hutterite teachings were preferable, Emmy spoke of how the North American Hutterites determinedly drew from later teachings. But David Hofer was not open to this debate. He simply stated: 'I cannot understand and acknowledge that your church is more similar to the beginning times of our fathers than ours, at least what we have seen here.' Emmy was worried that even though the Brothers had 'contributed to a certain inner

---

70. Emmy Arnold to Hardy and Edith Arnold, 31 May 1937. BHA Coll. 0288_02.
71. Emmy Arnold to Hans Zumpe, 4 June 1937. BHA Coll. 0288_02.

deepening', their presence also tended to inhibit freedom.[72] Writing to her son, Hans-Hermann, she added ruefully that the Brothers 'take up much time and energy!'[73]

Finding a way forward for the Cotswold community as a Hutterite Bruderhof was not simple. Emmy saw that it was especially difficult in England, when the community was being 'visited so much by modern people', to insist on ancient customs.[74] As an indication of the problems, an argument broke out between Hans Zumpe and the Brothers about Hutterian customs in relation to men's beards. The Brothers told Hans that he kept his beard too short. In reply Hans related a story about some Dutch Mennonites: those who had beards fell away from their faith, but those who had no beards remained steadfast. David Hofer commented in his diary: 'As if he would say that beards have nothing to do with devoutness; and we spent three hours dealing with this question.'[75] Another issue was women being involved in community discussions. David Hofer noted: 'The sisters take part in their deliberations, and it will be hard for them to change this practice, especially because of Emmy [Arnold], who is clever and wise, and has a lot to say.'[76] Before the Brothers left the Cotswold community, Hardy Arnold and Georg Barth were confirmed by them and by the whole community as Servants of the Word. The lead-up to this involved protracted debates. Hans Zumpe had wanted to delay the process. Ultimately, however, his view did not prevail. David Hofer recorded: 'Many spoke about the free and safe leading and guidance of God.'[77]

On 15 September 1937 there were heartfelt farewells to the Brothers from the Cotswold community. Despite evident tensions, the relationship with the Brothers had not broken down. Important questions about leadership had been raised. The community subsequently relieved Hans Zumpe of his leadership responsibilities.[78] Writing to Hans-Hermann on 8 November 1937, Emmy Arnold summed up the situation: 'We are very happy that it is given to Hardy and Georg now to lead the brotherhood

72. Emmy Arnold to Hans Zumpe, 17 June 1937. BHA Coll. 0288_02.

73. Emmy Arnold to Hans-Hermann Arnold, 22 June 1937. BHA Coll. 0288_02.

74. Emmy Arnold to Hardy and Edith Arnold, 31 May 1937. BHA Coll. 0288_02.

75. David Hofer, 'Diary'. BHA Coll. 0484.

76. David Hofer to Joseph Kleinsasser, 28 March 1937. BHA Coll. 0484.

77. David Hofer, 'Diary'. BHA Coll. 0484.

78. Hardy Arnold, 'The History of the Cotswold and Oaksey Bruderhofs, 1936–1941'. BHA Coll. 0304.

forward. In questions of order the community life here still leaves a great deal to be desired. It will still take considerable time until we can make progress... We all wish earnestly that Hans may soon come back into the service of a servant of the Word.'[79]

It became obvious in the early months of 1938 that Georg Barth and Hardy Arnold wanted to offer a vision which would attract others. The launch of *The Plough* in March 1938 was an ideal opportunity to do this. In the first issue Georg and Hardy combined forces to produce a substantial article, 'The Hutterian Communities in Five Centuries'.[80] They noted the growing interest in Hutterite history, highlighting significant books published in the 1930s.[81] They were delighted that the Cotswold Bruderhof was publishing for the first time important Hutterite historical sources. The article took readers through phases of Hutterite life. An important letter from 1811 written by Johannes Waldner, a Hutterite elder in Russia, was reproduced. It gave an account of Hutterite history from 1528 to 1811.[82] Much of the Hutterite story had involved experiences of severe persecution and other kinds of suffering. Pressure continued in the early twentieth century when the government of the USA withdrew promised exemption from military service. Hardy and Georg included in *The Plough* what they rightly termed 'a heart-rending account of the suffering of those who were imprisoned' at that time. Two Hutterite conscientious objectors during the First World War, Josef and Michael Hofer, died in prison—they were in Alcatraz and then Fort Leavenworth—after having been subjected to torture. Their treatment included being kept in freezing conditions and having their hands stuck through an iron grating and chained together so that they had to stand for nine hours a day.

79. Emmy Arnold to Hans-Hermann Arnold, 8 November 1937. BHA Coll. 0288_02.

80. Georg Barth and Hardy Arnold, 'The Hutterian Communities in five Centuries', *The Plough* 1, no. 1 (March 1938), 19–29.

81. The books they footnoted were: Ernst Troeltsch, *The Social Teaching of the Christian Churches* (London: George Allen & Unwin, 1931); John Horsch, *The Hutterian Brethren, 1528–1831* (Goshen, Ind.: Mennonite Historical Society, 1931); R. J. Smithson, *The Anabaptists* (London: James Clarke & Co., 1935); Carl Heath, *Social and Religious Heretics in Five Centuries* (London: Allenson, 1936); T. Edmunds, *Christian Freedom and Community* (Cardiff, 1937); and Toyohiko Kagawa, *Brotherhood Economics* (London: SCM, 1937).

82. In 1929 Eberhard Arnold discovered correspondence of Johannes Waldner with several leading Moravians in Russia in the Moravian archives in Herrnhut, Germany. The extract in *The Plough* was the first publication from these documents.

Josef Hofer's wife was given permission to see him after he died, and she found, to her horror, that the authorities had dressed him in the military uniform he had refused to wear. The Cotswold community wanted to tell 'the story of this martyrdom'.[83]

This positioning within the Hutterite movement continued in subsequent issues of *The Plough*. In the September 1938 issue there was a six-page extract from the diary of David Hofer about his experiences a year earlier when the Rhön Bruderhof was forcibly dissolved. It seemed, he concluded, as though he had 'come to Europe to experience what it means to be driven from one's house and home'.[84] The December 1938 *Plough* featured an article by Hardy Arnold on 'The Connections of Quakers to Hutterian Communities'. It offered historical research into a report in 1663 by William Moore and John Philly, two English Quakers, of a visit they had made to Hutterian communities in Transylvania and Austria. The Quaker report spoke of the great suffering of the Hutterites. In one area 'above two Hundred of the [Hutterite] Men' had been killed. The Hutterites were described by the two Quakers as 'a kind of Baptists, who lived in a Community, having, like the Primitive Christians, their Goods and Possessions in common, they also refused to Swear or Fight, and dwelt by Hundreds of them together in one Family'. Hardy Arnold suggested that comments by George Fox in 1669 could have been influenced by the Quakers' visit to the Hutterites.[85] Given the way in which the Cotswold Bruderhof had established significant Quaker relationships, this was an important article.

Carl Heath responded in the Spring 1939 *Plough*, noting that although George Fox 'suggested to the Friends a community of sorts, he does not appear to have pressed it'. Heath hoped *The Plough* would continue with its historical investigations.[86] Subsequent issues continued to cover Hutterite history. There was a further article detailing the cruel

83. Georg Barth and Hardy Arnold, 'The Hutterian Communities in Five Centuries' *The Plough* 1, no. 1 (March 1938), 27–28.

84. David Hofer, 'The Dissolution of the Rhoenbruderhof', *The Plough* 1, no. 3 (September 1938), 89–94. This includes two pages of photographs.

85. Hardy Arnold, 'The Connection of Quakers to the Hutterian Communities', *The Plough* 1, no. 4 (December 1938), 117–123. Hardy was drawing from Besse, *A Collection of the Sufferings of the People called Quakers*, 420–432, which had the report about the Hutterites. See also, as quoted in the *Plough* article, Heath, *Social and Religious Heretics in Five Centuries*, 119.

86. Carl Heath, 'The Connections of the Quakers with the Hutterian Communities', *The Plough* 2, no. 1 (Spring 1939), 27.

treatment of Hutterian conscientious objectors in the United States and the faith they had exhibited.[87] The Confession of Faith of Claus Felbinger, a Hutterite who was martyred in 1560, appeared in one issue.[88] *The Plough* was contributing to serious engagement with the Hutterian movement through the centuries as well as with contemporary movements.

Continuing Identity Issues

While making the Cotswold Bruderhof's Hutterian identity clear, Georg Barth and Hardy Arnold wanted to encourage the kind of community life in which there could be engagement with wider currents of thought and action. It was not surprising that Georg Barth wrote in the second issue of *The Plough* about 'work and handicraft', since this was an integral part of the Hutterite heritage.[89] However, it was not part of the American Hutterian approach to connect with someone like Eric Gill, the prominent Arts and Crafts figure, whose article on politics and brotherhood was published in *The Plough* in the following year.[90] Gill had made a spiritual journey from evangelical Free Church life as a teenager—he recalled in his autobiography that he held up his hand in a mission service and was 'saved'—to joining the Roman Catholic Church and erecting a chapel for Catholic worship within his community, Pigotts, near High Wycombe, Buckinghamshire. There was also a Catholic priest in the community. For Gill this environment represented a spiritual 'consummation'.[91]

In some areas Gill's beliefs had attractions for the Bruderhof. In 1936 he wrote a book, *The Necessity of Belief*, reflecting his desire, as he put it a decade earlier, for renewal in the world—including in art—to take place through a 'radical remedy', which was 'the conversion of the world to see the Faith'.[92] In 1937, in *Work and Property*, he argued against the

87. J. G. Ewert, 'Hutterian Brothers and Conscription', *The Plough* 2, no. 2 (Summer 1939), 40–45.

88. Claus Felbinger, 'The Church and the World', *The Plough* 2, no. 2 (Summer 1939), 36–40; no. 4 (Winter 1939), 113–19.

89. Georg Barth, 'Work and Handicraft in the Spiritual Culture of the Church', *The Plough* 1, no. 2 (July 1938), 57–60.

90. Eric Gill, 'Religion is Politics: Politics is Brotherhood: Brotherhood is Poverty', *The Plough* 2, no. 1 (Spring 1939).

91. Gill, *Autobiography*, 59, 246–47.

92. Gill, *Christianity and Art*, 16; Gill, *The Necessity of Belief*. Speaight's *The Life of Eric Gill* is valuable for its insights into Gill's faith.

rule of money and what he called the control of politics by bankers and financiers.[93] All of this had resonance for the Cotswold community. They were unaware of Gill's personal life, which was marked by extramarital and incestuous relationships, but it is surprising that they did not see some dissonance between themselves and Gill's art, which featured nudity and eroticism.[94] However, in 1940, towards the end of his life, Gill wrote in *Sacred and Secular* that Christianity was 'following Christ', who was 'God Himself incarnate'. For him, as for the Bruderhof, the church was 'a small minority, with a mission like that of the first Christians.'[95] There was surprising common ground.

There were other unusual associations. *The Plough* gave a very favourable appraisal in 1938 of *Ends and Means*, a book produced that year in which the widely-read novelist and philosopher Aldous Huxley (author of *Brave New World*) argued the pacifist case, while the same review was sharply critical of a book produced by the SCM and written by Frank Russell Barry, a leading Anglican theologian of the period. The review (unsigned) stated: 'Whereas Aldous Huxley, in his book, deals with the most important ethical problems of our time such as war and social injustice, Canon F. R. Barry in his book hardly touches on these issues.' Barry's book was on faith, worship, and Christian living. *The Plough* reviewer considered that after reading Barry's book it was understandable that Huxley had chosen 'rejection of Christianity as the basis of right action, in favour of Indian mysticism.'[96]

Later in 1938 *The Plough* drew attention to currents of Christian thought and action in Europe. An article by Karl Kilmso covered 'The Present Religious Situation in Sweden'. Along with highlighting the strong Christian Socialist movement and the high numbers of conscientious objectors in the country, he spoke about spiritual revivals which had produced Free Church communities, including Baptists, the Salvation Army and Pentecostals. The article focussed on the largest Free Church community, the Swedish Missionary Society, and on its most influential leader, Paul Peter Waldenström, whose theological thought had affected the nation. Kilmso, who was not a member of the Bruderhof, was pleased

93. Gill, *Work and Property*.

94. The fullest biography of Gill is MacCarthy, *Eric Gill*. See also Yorke, *Eric Gill: Man of Flesh and Spirit*.

95. Gill, *Sacred and Secular*, 147–149.

96. Review of Huxley, *Ends and Means*; and Barry, *What has Christianity to Say?* in *The Plough* 1, no. 1 (March 1938), 40.

that (as he saw it) most churches in Sweden had accepted Waldenström's view of the atonement, which was that Christ 'did not suffer instead of us. He could not bear the punishment for our sins because God had already forgiven us these.'[97] In the same *Plough* issue, Karl Keiderling, from the Bruderhof, wrote about work in prisons. He mentioned figures who were well known in the peace movement, such as Elizabeth Fry and Mathilda Wrede, but gave most attention to Friedrich Haas, a German Catholic who became a leading medical practitioner in Moscow, and whose later life was devoted to achieving far-reaching prison reform in Russia.[98]

While these broader currents were being explored in 1937 and 1938, the Cotswold community sought to respond constructively to the Hutterite call for adherence to the Orders. Writing to Hans-Hermann in November 1937, Hardy said that he and Edith had been spending a few days away from the community 'in order to relax and consider things deeply'. Hardy and Edith were well aware that the Cotswold community was attracting people from very varied backgrounds in Britain and that their situation was completely different from that of the Hutterian communities in North America. There had been much discussion in the Cotswold community about adopting the Hutterian Orders, and it was recognised that accepting what seemed like restrictive changes could only be done slowly. In the meantime, Hardy said, the community sought to attend to 'the pre-condition for real church life', which was 'a burning love to Christ and to the brothers', with outward changes as a secondary matter. It had been decided to appoint people to 'services and offices' in the community, and there was a willingness to 'elect by lot in the Hutterian way'; as it actually happened, however, the community came to a common recognition of whom to appoint to leadership roles, so use of the lot was unnecessary. For Hardy, the contribution of the Hutterian Brothers was not being rejected. Instead there was a concentration on areas where Hutterian thinking and the concerns of the Cotswold community coincided, such as baptism and the Lord's Supper, church marriage, and the Christian education of the children. In other cases, which Hardy spoke of as 'minor points', such as families having meals on their own instead of all meals being communal, there was not yet 'complete unity'. Hardy and Edith were convinced that things 'will become clear when we are open

97. Karl Kismo, 'The Present Religious Situation in Sweden', *The Plough* 1, no. 3 (September 1938), 83–85.

98. Karl Keiderling, 'I was in prison and ye visited me', *The Plough* 1, no. 3 (September 1938), 83–89.

and ready to recognize what God wants from us here, without in any way opposing the advice of the Brothers'.[99]

A letter from Emmy Arnold to Hans-Hermann, a few days after the letter from Hardy, offers insight into elements within the community in this period. She wrote of the wedding of Liesel Wegner and Hermann Arnold. First there had been the registry office wedding. There was then a celebration meal in a restaurant in a place where the Bruderhof was known: 'Since we buy a lot there, the owner gave us a bottle of Bordeaux wine'. At the community everything was 'very beautifully decorated in the dining room. The celebration began with many nice folk-songs. Red candles burned on the tables. Then the kindergarten children came with circle games. The bigger children then performed "The Emperor's New Clothes," which was very funny'. On the next day, Sunday, Hardy Arnold spoke to the newly married couple and to the whole community about 'Christ the Head'. There was a public ceremony when Hardy 'asked the Hutterian marriage questions of the two'. There was a bridal procession, with Liesel in her white dress with a myrtle garland. Hymns and folk-songs were sung.[100]

Emmy then turned in her letter to Hans-Hermann from joyful to painful issues, which mainly had to do with Hans Zumpe, who was no longer a 'Servant of the Word'. Hans had written a fourteen-page letter to David Hofer and Michael Waldner on 20 October confessing in detail what he now saw as his many mistakes and sins. Emmy commented that Hans' letter was 'somewhat too crass for me, that is, one can say, too unsparing toward himself'. Hans had asked for forgiveness in many areas, including for saying to the Brothers, 'I don't care a hoot about your orders'. Emmy hoped that 'the Brothers in their great love will forgive Hans his failings'. Emmy said she and others had faith that God could 'restore his inner being'. She, together with Georg and Hardy, talked to him almost every day.[101]

A letter received on 17 November 1937 from David Hofer and Joseph Kleinsasser, as Hutterian Elders, was addressed to Hans Zumpe but also included Hardy and Georg Barth. It stated that 'we want to forget everything that lies behind us, and look toward the goal that is extended

99. Hardy Arnold to Hans-Hermann Arnold, 3 November 1937. BHA Coll. 0304.

100. Emmy Arnold to Hans-Hermann Arnold, 8 November 1937. BHA Coll. 0288_02.

101. Emmy Arnold to Hans-Hermann Arnold, 8 November 1937. BHA Coll. 0288_02.

to us. And we ask, dear, faithful, heavenly Father forgive them, they have failed in Christian love, without their knowing it; especially dear Hans shall God forgive.'[102] A possible factor contributing to the positive response to Hans' repentant letter was sentiments Emmy had expressed. In a letter to David Hofer on 12 November 1937 she seemed to place the community in the hands of the Brothers. 'We are waiting for your advice and help', she wrote: 'I believe you understood the situation of our church better than we perhaps knew it ourselves at the time, for if we had then recognized everything as clearly as it now appears before our eyes, then everything would surely have turned out differently'. It was 'quite incomprehensible' to her why Hans Zumpe, 'who often expressed himself so positively among us about the Hutterians, now upon your visit became fearful that a disunity might arise through the encounter of new-Hutterdom with old-Hutterdom'. Emmy believed that Hans 'now recognizes his guilt very strongly and would give everything to have your visit only beginning now'. Emmy addressed the issue of identity, clearly wanting to go as far as she could in affirming Hutterian ways: 'We are now trying to become more Hutterian in some things. . . Starting on Monday, the daily schedule is to be arranged differently. We will try to have the prayer before supper, then a short, silent supper time, then an hour of talk with guests, until 8 o'clock'. There was even mention by Emmy of the possibility of Hans and his family going for a year to Canada 'to learn a lot from you'.[103] At this point Emmy was seeking to tie the community's future as closely as possible to the wider Hutterian movement.

Fragile Relationships

The idea of deepening relationships through further face-to-face fellowship was a good one, but it did not happen. Instead, communication was conducted by letter, and partly as a consequence the relationships remained fragile. Edith Arnold wrote to Hans-Hermann in February 1938 to say that she and Hardy wished all would feel 'how basically difficult the question with the Hutterians is, and that it cannot simply be a question of accepting points'. As she thought about the experiences of the Bruderhof in Germany in the 1920s, Edith was convinced that real unity with the

102. David Hofer and Joseph Kleinsasser to Hans Zumpe, 17 November 1937. BHA Coll. 0080.

103. Emmy Arnold to David Hofer, 12 November 1937. BHA Coll. 0288_02.

Hutterians 'cannot deny our God-given new beginning'. It was only 'deep in Christ', she continued, and in 'the breadth of Christ' that this tension over old and new could be resolved. Edith was evidently exploring how there could be spiritual integration. 'In true depths', she wrote, 'we shall recognize our weaknesses and also not undertake what is not given by the Spirit'. This also meant 'a persistent fight until we all, as a complete circle, are led to full unity'.[104]

A few weeks later Edith returned to some of the same themes, writing to Emmy Arnold. She began by affirming that it was 'wonderful to be able to live in community'. However, her hope was that God would give a 'truly clear and pure atmosphere' and this pure air might 'blow again in every corner of the Bruderhof, so human beings don't take up so much of the foreground'. When Edith looked at the life of the Cotswold community she felt that 'small things often occupy an awfully large place'. She was specific in identifying the problem of Hutterian practice. There was 'bickering over Hutterian points', and it seemed to her that 'unanimity of spirit, which should be the prerequisite for the fight, doesn't appear so important'. Having opened her heart in this way, Edith accepted that she might 'be stating it somewhat harshly', but she was disturbed that 'brotherly trust' was 'often very weak'.[105]

Fresh Hutterian impetus was felt in the Cotswold Bruderhof in early 1939 as members of the community began a new phase of publishing early Hutterite material. On 5 February 1939, Edith wrote to Hardy, who was then in hospital in London with throat problems, to say she was looking forward to working on a new edition of the Hutterian 'Chronicle'—which had been produced in the seventeenth century and told the early Hutterite story. She added that it was 'marvellous to work with you!' This kind of scholarly work, for Edith, was not divorced from active service. She saw the community's future tasks as 'enormous, and we have to ask God for real strength of spirit, soul, and body so we can truly serve poor people'.[106] Hardy replied to say he was feeling much better and looking forward to being back with Edith. He had hoped that work on a new edition of Peter Riedemann's 'Account of Our Religion, Doctrine and Faith' (1565) would proceed more quickly. Hardy was amazed by the Hutterite history of martyrdom in their first decades and their four-hundred-year

104. Edith Arnold to Hans-Hermann Arnold, 28 February 1938. BHA Coll. 0304.

105. Edith Arnold to Emmy Arnold, 4 April 1938. BHA Coll. 0304.

106. Edith Arnold to Hardy Arnold, 5 February 1939. BHA Coll. 0304.

existence. He was convinced, however, of 'the necessity of a renewal of the Spirit in the whole Hutterian movement', and wanted to affirm what Edith had said about 'being filled with and enveloped in the atmosphere of Jesus'.[107] It was Edith who drew attention a month later to the fact that their relationship with Kingsley Hall, with its mission of making Jesus known in a working-class environment, had faded. She was aware that working-class people could not readily travel to the Cotswold community, but she hoped that there could be reconnection and wondered if Hardy and Heini 'could do more in that line'.[108]

In Hardy's talk to the Cotswold community in March 1939, in which he reviewed the connections with Hutterian life, he emphasised the valuable contribution of the two Hutterite Brothers from North America during their time in Europe. His view at this point was that the Cotswold community had not sufficiently appreciated what the Brothers had brought. Hardy then explained that after the Brothers had returned home the Cotswold Bruderhof had assured them that the community was 'prepared to accept all that they wished to say to us through the Spirit'. The response from the Brothers, at the end of 1937, had been to set out eight 'points which lay on their hearts, and which they felt important for us'. Hardy enumerated these but was keen to put them in context, as being 'really very minute in comparison with the greatness of history and of all that unites us'.[109]

The Brothers had made these requests of the Cotswold community: to say grace aloud at mealtimes; to place the central administration of the Bruderhof in the hands of men; to open communal worship to all guests; to introduce a Sunday School for children; to note that the Hutterites elected people to community offices by majority vote; to encourage those who wanted to marry not to have long engagements; to take all meals communally, with men and women sitting on different sides of the room; and to standardise clothing. Hardy acknowledged there were different views in the community about these points; indeed they were still being discussed over a year after having first been set out. Some Cotswold members felt that 'we cannot accept these eight points without their being an inner experience'. Hardy recalled that Eberhard did not introduce Hutterian customs in Germany. The suggestion from Hardy was that it

107. Hardy Arnold to Edith Arnold, 7 February 1939. BHA Coll. 0304.

108. Edith Arnold to Emmy Arnold, 8 March 1939. BHA Coll. 0304.

109. Hardy Arnold, community meeting, Cotswold Bruderhof, 31 March 1939. BHA Coll. 0055.

was better to wait for 'their gradual growth within the whole circle'. The eight points were not, he argued, on the level of a command such as 'Love your neighbour'. He categorised the points as 'questions of the style or rhythm of life'. His conclusion was to 'allow God to lead and guide us'.[110]

At the end of 1939, Hardy Arnold corresponded with Johannes Maendel, a leader in a Hutterite colony in Manitoba. Hardy wrote enthusiastically about himself and Johannes being brothers in Christ who 'want to build our life on the same basis and foundation of truth'. In line with his vision of church life, Hardy prayed that God would lead 'in all things, so that everything that is wrong among you as among us may be overcome and eliminated'.[111] Johannes Maendel replied in January 1940, and in response Hardy raised issues which were evidently troubling him, as they had Eberhard, about mission and unity. Johannes Maendel wrote of the lack of mission among the North American Hutterites. Hardy agreed with that: 'You are right; you have no mission.' He saw the problem as linked with a deeper one: the fact that there was a lack of unity among the three Hutterite groups.[112] Hardy then referred to a circular letter from Julius Kubassek, which took the view that each Bruderhof in North America was too independent. Kubassek, who was from Hungary, had been converted from atheism to a commitment to Christ and had emigrated in 1925 to North America. In 1936 he made contact with the Hutterites in Alberta, Canada. Later, when he was in Ontario, a community grew around him and took the name the 'Community Farm of the Brethren'.[113] Hardy saw in Kubassek 'a faithful seeker of God' and hoped that there might be a 'full uniting soon' between him and the Hutterites.[114] It is likely that Kubassek, as someone who was not part of the ethnic Hutterian community, interested Hardy.

In June 1939, Joseph Kleinsasser and David Hofer, as Elders of the Hutterian Church in Manitoba, signed a document to confirm that David Hofer and Michael Waldner had ordained Georg Barth and Hardy

110. Hardy Arnold, community meeting, Cotswold Bruderhof, 31 March 1939. BHA Coll. 0055 .

111. Hardy Arnold to Johannes Maendel, 13 December 1939. BHA Coll. 0304.

112. Hardy Arnold to Johannes Maendel, 15 February 1940. BHA Coll. 0304.

113. Hostetler: *Hutterite Society*, 279; Janzen and Stanton, *The Hutterites in North America*, 253.

114. Hardy Arnold to Johannes Maendel, 15 February 1940. BHA Coll. 0304. The 'uniting' that Hardy hoped for did not happen.

Arnold to the ministry of the Hutterian Church on 13 September 1937.[115] However, this affirmation did not bring about any significant improvement in what was an increasingly fragile transatlantic relationship. In the course of correspondence in early 1940, Johannes Maendel commented to both Hardy and Heini Arnold about the situation in Europe, as he saw it, and the needs of the Cotswold community. He had evidently become tired of receiving requests for help, and he had stated that there could be no help because, as he said, 'we ourselves are too weak'. He also stated that if it was God's will for the members of the Cotswold community to die— which was seen as a possibility with the rise of Nazi aggression—they would be released from much suffering and would be with God. Hardy quoted these words back to Johannes Maendel and commented: 'This comfort is right and would also be helpful if you had done all you could to help us.' But Hardy expressed his disappointment that American Hutterites had 'failed to take a wonderful opportunity to serve God through brotherly love'. It had been Hardy's hope that fellow Hutterians would 'do everything, absolutely everything' to help brothers in need. He quoted James, in his epistle, chapter 2, verses 15–16, in a newer translation: 'Suppose some brother or sister is ill-clad and short of daily food; if any of you tells them, "Depart in peace! Get warm, get food," without supplying their bodily needs, what use is that?' Hardy was thankful for the help that had been given, but drew his letter to a conclusion on a sombre note: 'But woe to those who close their hearts to the working of this Spirit of love and out of greed and selfishness do not help their brothers.'[116] Being Hutterian had not produced the strong relationships that had been anticipated.

115. Statement signed by Joseph Kleinsasser and David Hofer, the Elders of the Hutterian Church in Canada, 2 June 1939, in Eberhard Arnold, *Brothers Unite*, 335.

116. Hardy Arnold to Johannes Maendel, 22 July 1940. BHA Coll. 0304.

7

Progress and Pressure

In the late 1930s the Cotswold community had as its main focus the challenges faced in the community's life in England. Numbers in the community were growing, but rather than being content with this the members wanted to try to make an increasing impact nationally. Locally and more widely there was a desire within the Bruderhof to make a difference, to make progress in the witness of the community. At the same time the community was facing considerable pressures. These began locally and became more political as war with Germany drew closer, and then became even more severe when war was declared. It was becoming increasingly difficult to sustain the life of an international community, especially one with a significant German element.

'To Extend this Work'

The continued growth of the community led, at the end of 1938, to the purchase of three hundred acres and a home farm on the borders of Gloucestershire and Wiltshire, which became the Oaksey Bruderhof. Oaksey Park was about five miles from the Cotswold community. Based on growth over the previous three years, it was anticipated that the Bruderhof would 'rapidly extend their activities at Oaksey'.[1] The announcement provoked what would become a lengthy local debate. At a meeting of the Cirencester Rotary Club, an influential local group of

1. 'A Wiltshire Manor', *Daily Telegraph*, 26 October 1938.

business and professional people, on 8 November, Hardy Arnold said (as reported in the Swindon *Evening Advertiser*) that he fully appreciated that when 'an unusual group of people settled in a rural district, there was bound to be some misunderstanding and misrepresentation'. Knowing the Rotary commitment to local communities, Hardy went on to speak of the economic benefits of the Bruderhof coming to Ashton Keynes. These included bringing trade to the local area, helping neighbouring farms, and providing employment to local workmen. Hardy stated that about £3,500 had been paid by the Bruderhof as wages to local builders, and a similar amount had been spent in Ashton Keynes, as Bruderhof members had bought food from local butchers, grocers and bakers. Funds, he said, had come from supporters of the community in Britain, America, and Holland, and from new members joining the community. Hardy sought to allay fears that the community's expansion into Oaksey meant that 'the local population will suffer'.[2]

Hardy took the opportunity to engage audiences in wide-ranging discussions, against a background of suspicion that the Bruderhof housed German spies.[3] He explained that in Germany in the 1930s, in an atmosphere of 'hatred and war', the Bruderhof had tried to keep alive a group 'which did not give way to the force and pressure of the State and which tried in a weak way to give clear witness even in a Fascist State'. Hardy discussed Christian beliefs, spiritual movements in the Middle Ages and the Reformation, and the Bruderhof's connections with a variety of Christian bodies. His technique was to assume that those listening to him were aware of Christian history, which might or might not have been the case, and to build sympathy for the Bruderhof cause. With farmers he discussed the Bruderhof's agricultural endeavours: 'We keep a T.T. [tuberculosis tested] herd of fifty cows and about 30 young cattle. Our poultry section, which is very successful, consists of about 3,000 laying birds. We also have 140 sheep and about 20 hives of bees.' For people interested in trade he spoke about the turning shop: 'We have four lathes there and we sold £900 gross in one year, and we hope to extend this work.' His talks also encompassed those involved in serious research. Describing this aspect of what went on at the Bruderhof, Hardy com-

2. 'Living the Simple Life', *Evening Advertiser* (Swindon), 9 November 1938.

3. Brinson and Dove, in *A Matter of Intelligence*, show the extent to which from 1933 the resources of the Security Service (MI5) were devoted to surveillance and investigation of German—and subsequently Austrian—anti-Nazi refugees, who were assumed to pose a danger as communists.

mented: 'We have among our members a number of academic people.'[4] It was difficult for locals to portray the Bruderhof as a dubious or even dangerous movement.

There was a continued need, however, to explain to local people the expansion of the Bruderhof. Oaksey residents had overwhelmingly supported a local petition against an Oaksey Bruderhof settlement.[5] In the light of this, the Cotswold community organised two public meetings in February 1939 in the village halls in Oaksey and Ashton Keynes. Publicity for the events was restrained in tone: 'Considerable interest and attention has been shown by the residents of North Wiltshire and Gloucestershire in the activities of the Cotswold Bruderhof.' The community's notices also stated that invitations had come for their members to speak to churches, Rotarians, and other organisations. Village hall meetings were convened so that Bruderhof members could 'meet their neighbours in order to give a full explanation of the objects and purpose of their life, and to give every opportunity for questions to be asked'.[6]

The *Gloucestershire Echo* of 16 February reported on the Oaksey public meeting. Interested people, the reporter said, filled the village hall, a large number having to stand. Arnold Mason was the principal speaker for the Bruderhof, and Bruce Sumner also spoke. They clearly wanted to show that the Cotswold community had British leaders. Arnold Mason offered a history of the Bruderhof and then turned to the issue of 'their recent decision to extend their activities by purchasing Oaksey Manor'. He assured farm workers currently employed on the Oaksey farm that they would be able to continue as employees until they found other work.[7] For a wider and more sympathetic audience, the issue of *The Plough* produced in parallel with these local meetings explained that the emphasis at Oaksey was on using three hundred acres for dairy purposes, and that the community intended to continue to produce milk, as they did at the Cotswold Bruderhof, but on a larger scale. With the purchase of Oaksey Park, it was possible to 'extend our work'.[8]

4. 'Cotswold Bruderhof', *Faringdon News*, 11 November 1938.

5. Petitioner to the editor, *Wilts and Gloucestershire Standard* (hereafter *Standard*), 25 February 1938.

6. Notice of Public Meetings, Printed by the Swindon Press, Ltd. BHA Coll. 0334.

7. *Gloucestershire Echo*, 16 February 1939.

8. Bruce Sumner, 'The Cotswold Bruderhof: A report of the events and activities in 1938', *The Plough* 2, no. 1 (Spring 1939), 21.

In the summer 1939 *Plough*, Heini Arnold gave some further background about Oaksey for the benefit of those interested in the dynamics of community life. He referred to Hutterian history, which he said had shown that a healthy Bruderhof community should number 150–200 adults and children. The reasons for this were both spiritual and economic. In the area of spiritual experience, Heini explained, 'each member should, if possible, know all the others and share all joys and sorrows'. When a community was too large this awareness was not possible. However, if the number was below 120, then certain individuals could be too dominant. On the question of economics, Heini suggested that the optimum number allowed for a 'favourable relationship between productive work, which accounts for the community's income, and the necessary household work such as cooking, baking, washing etc'. The size that was being commended from experience also worked well for educating children. However, Oaksey was not intended to house more than 60–70 people, and therefore some aspects of the two communities would be shared, such as the bakehouse and educational facilities.[9] The Bruderhof was able to take over the Oaksey estate and a farmhouse, with ten rooms, in spring 1939, when existing tenants moved out. There was excitement about moving to such a beautiful setting. In view of local sensitivities, careful discussions took place in the Cotswold community about who should form the initial group in this new community.[10]

In his report in the summer 1939 *Plough*, Heini also detailed tensions over the purchase. He spoke of how the plans for Oaksey had meant that the community had come up against 'strong opposition in the neighbourhood, especially from the wealthy landowners'.[11] They could exercise a strong influence. Nobility in the area feared that the community would drive out foxes. Lord Bathurst, who with his wife had been the owner of the *Morning Post* newspaper and was the largest property owner in the district, asked to see the Bruderhof about this. At the meeting, Lord Bathurst—his country seat was Bathurst Park—stated categorically that he did not want Oaksey purchased because it was a

9. J. Heinrich Arnold, 'The New Bruderhof Community at Oaksey', *The Plough* 2, no. 2 (Summer 1939), 51.

10. Emmy Arnold to Hans-Hermann Arnold, 16 March 1939. BHA Coll. 0288_02.

11. J. Heinrich Arnold, 'The New Bruderhof Community at Oaksey', *The Plough* 2, no. 2 (Summer 1939), 49–50.

popular fox-hunting farm.[12] Lord Apsley, a son of Lord Bathurst and Member of Parliament for Bristol Central, even raised the purchase of Oaksey as an issue in Parliament. He asked if the Home Secretary, Sir Samuel Hoare, knew that the Bruderhof was going to buy an estate 'in a rich farming district, where the standard of living is high' and was going to live there 'under primitive conditions'. The reply from Sir Samuel, who had received detailed background information from the Bruderhof, gave no ground to the Bruderhof's opponents. He could see no reason why the purchase should not take place.[13] There had been a deep-rooted feeling on the part of the Bruderhof that this extension to their work and witness should go ahead. Heini described how when Oaksey was taken over, the whole community went to pray that in this new setting 'only the spirit of brotherly justice might reign'.[14] When the main house was occupied, the community's school was transferred from Ashton Keynes to Oaksey.[15]

Coping with Criticism

The most sustained criticism of the expansion of the Bruderhof community came not from the aristocracy but from one individual who lived locally, W. B. Wilson, at Fairhaven Farm, Oaksey. When the intended purchase of Oaksey was reported, Wilson immediately opened correspondence in the *Wilts and Gloucestershire Standard* (the *Standard*). He wrote: 'There are many people in this district who, by virtue of their love for England as the home of the English, look with increasing anxiety on the encroachments of the Cotswold Bruderhof, and the growing incursion of aliens of all nationalities in our midst. The foreign population in this country everywhere creeps up silently in numbers.' Wilson wondered why 'over-populated England' should welcome all the rest of Europe's 'unwanted'. He also asked why people from abroad should take British jobs at a time when unemployment among British people was increasing. In relation to the Bruderhof, he asked on what grounds the community was allowed by the Home Office to be established, and how—since they

12. Arnold Mason, 'Early Memories'. BHA Coll. 0006.

13. 'Lord Apsley and the Cotswold Bruderhof', *Bristol Evening World*, 22 December 1938.

14. J. Heinrich Arnold, 'The New Bruderhof Community at Oaksey', *The Plough* 2, no. 2 (Summer 1939), 51.

15. Hardy Arnold, 'The History of the Cotswold and Oaksey Bruderhofs, 1936–41'. BHA Coll. 0304.

had no money—they could find thousands of pounds to buy farms and a manor house. He was also concerned about the location of the community. 'Why should these people, openly pacifists, come and settle down here in the midst of an armed camp with three large British aerodromes in close proximity?' Wilson accepted that people in Britain were free to choose to help others, but for him this could not be 'at the detriment of our own countrymen—not if you are a genuine Englishman!'[16] Wilson's fears—immigration, unemployment, and espionage—were common at the time. Yet out of approximately 400,000 refugees who fled Germany, Austria, and Czechoslovakia between 1933 and 1939, under 60,000 were admitted to Britain, with fourth-fifths, including 10,000 children, entering in the period between October 1938 and September 1939, most of these the victims of anti-Semitism.[17]

Two days after Wilson's letter appeared, Heini Arnold went to see him and found him 'polite', but in his attitude to the growth of the community 'cold and determined to fight'. Heini was convinced after the visit that 'even in so-called tolerant England, we must be persecuted for Christ's sake'.[18] The consequences of this for the community would reach further than anyone could see at that stage. Hardy Arnold and Arnold Mason then replied to Wilson's letter in the *Standard*. They began by expressing gratitude 'to the British Government and to our neighbours for the very friendly way in which our foreign members have been received and are constantly treated'. Foreign Bruderhof members had been surprised 'to experience so much sympathy and understanding after a long time of suffering under the National Socialist regime in Germany'. The letter went on to speak about aspects of Cotswold Bruderhof life, such as the 'Christian ideal of love and brotherhood', the fact that many British people were part of the community, and how the community engaged constructively with local traders. On the question of the Bruderhof being in a district where there were aerodromes, the letter pointed out that these did not exist when the community first settled there in 1936.[19] The intention of this letter was not so much to try to convince Wilson as to communicate with a wider audience.

16. W. B. Wilson to the editor, *Standard*, 5 November 1938.

17. Skran, *Refugees in Inter-War Europe*, 50; Sherman, *Island Refuge*, 264–65. Almost 10,000 were children on a special programme, the *Kindertransport*.

18. Heini Arnold to Hans-Hermann Arnold, 8 February 1939. BHA Coll. 0288_02.

19. E. C. H. Arnold and A. H. Mason to the editor, *Standard*, 12 November 1938.

Two other letters from local people, both supportive of the Bruder-hof, appeared in the 12 November *Standard*. Gertrude Wood, a member of the council of the Women's Guild of Empire, said that she had taken friends to the Cotswold Bruderhof on several occasions and had 'always come away with a feeling of admiration for these people who are inspired to live as they feel God would have us work—in true brotherhood one with another'.[20] The other supporter was Sir Thomas Bazley at Hatherop Castle. When the community became aware of help he was willing to offer, they kept in touch with him.[21] Sir Thomas was the founder of Mari-gold Health Foods, and Hatherop Castle housed a school for girls estab-lished by Sir Thomas' mother. In his letter to the *Standard* he noted that Britain sometimes criticised political dictatorships for their treatment of minorities: 'The least we can do is to accept a small proportion of those who have had to leave or are expelled owing to race or creed'.[22]

It is possible that at this point Wilson realised he could be portrayed as a bigot, and in his next letter he stated that he had 'the utmost sympa-thy for all who are persecuted and are robbed and ill used and made into refugees'. In the remainder of his letter, however, the sympathy was hardly evident. All his complaints about the Bruderhof were reiterated.[23] Not all were sympathetic to those who had been persecuted. H. W. J. Cuss from Cricklade (a village between Swindon and Cirencester) asserted that if refugees were not so readily accepted by Britain, then 'their own Powers would not be so ready to hound them out'. He was blunt in his opinion about why the Home Office should refuse permission for the Bruderhof to stay. They were 'foreigners and as such should not be given the right to farm British soil'.[24] Gertrude Wood, continuing the correspondence, pointed out to those opposing foreigners that the British had settled in many countries as foreigners, and R. H. Rimes, who knew the Bruderhof through his grain business, had 'read with shame' what Cuss had written about people 'only endeavouring to carry out their Christian beliefs in practice'.[25] Determined to have the last word, Wilson, who was Roman Catholic, asked about Bruderhof beliefs. He (mistakenly) understood

20. Gertrude Wood to the editor, *Standard*, 12 November 1938.
21. Heini Arnold to Hans-Hermann Arnold, 8 February 1939. BHA Coll. 0005.
22. Thomas S. Bazley to the editor, *Standard*, 12 November 1938.
23. W. B. Wilson to the editor, *Standard*, 19 November 1938.
24. H. W. J. Cuss to the editor, *Standard*, 19 November 1938.
25. Gertrude Wood and R. H. Rimes to the editor, *Standard*, 26 November 1938.

that to be a member 'you must forego any creed you have hitherto held, and any form of religion you have practised'. He saw such a requirement as 'a dangerous precedent to establish in a country known for its religious freedom'.[26]

At the end of 1938 the Bruderhof received censure from another quarter. This time the issue was registration of 'aliens'. British law contained no distinction between 'refugee' and 'alien'. Rights of entry, grants of asylum, and other matters relating to the refugee status of Bruderhof members fell under 'alien immigration'.[27] In December 1938 Arnold Mason was summoned to the Cricklade Police Court because he had failed to register four 'alien' members of the Bruderhof. All the foreign members had entered Britain by his invitation. Each of these four said they had handed their passport to the Bruderhof office, but they accepted responsibility for not being more insistent about registration. Arnold pleaded guilty and was fined £1.00 for each person not registered. He assured the court this would not happen again. The chairman of the court noted that this was the first time the Bruderhof had failed in registering and he was being lenient, but it was 'a serious offence'.[28]

The incident would not have been a matter of interest beyond the local area except for the fact that at the court hearing one of the Bruderhof members became involved in a misunderstanding over taking the oath. As was customary in the Bruderhof, and in Anabaptist tradition generally, he would not swear an oath, on the grounds that Jesus said, 'Do not swear at all'. The clerk of the court then showed him how he could affirm instead, but he initially refused, as affirmation involved raising the right hand in what could have been seen as a Nazi-like salute. National papers such as the *Daily Express* found this incident newsworthy. The *Express* gave its item the heading 'German refuses to give "Nazi salute" as court oath'.[29] *The Plough* later commented that the Bruderhof had discussed the issue and decided that no one would raise their hands in court. The incident, said *The Plough*, had been 'grossly exaggerated in the newspapers'.[30] Bruderhof members were under scrutiny.

26. W. B. Wilson to the editor, *Standard*, 3 December 1938.

27. London, 'Jewish Refugees, Anglo-Jewry and British Government Policy, 1930–1940', 164.

28. *Evening Advertiser*, 28 December 1938.

29. *Daily Express*, 29 December 1938.

30. 'Concerning the Bruderhof Communities', *The Plough* 2, no. 2 (Summer 1939), 61.

A *Daily Express* reporter seems to have decided that something involving foreigners and refugees was going on in the Cirencester area which was worth investigating. After some local interviews, a piece appeared in the *Express* which referred to 'Cirencester snobs' who did not want to receive evacuated children—from Germany and Austria—into their homes. W. B. Wilson was incensed, and wrote to the *Standard* about the lack of 'manners and breeding' of the *Express* representative. Instead of children going into private homes, Wilson suggested they should be housed in large centres. This gave him the ideal opportunity to suggest a centre: the Cotswold Bruderhof. It was Wilson's view that in the event of war the 'aliens and un-English Englishmen' in the community would be interned. They would be 'a hindrance and a burden', but at least the community's buildings would become available.[31] Although the language used about the community was deliberately dismissive, discussion about internment would become a serious issue.

A month later, in February 1939, local people were able to question Bruderhof members at the public meetings in Ashton Keynes and Oaksey. At Oaksey, where feelings had been expected to run high, the Swindon *Evening Advertiser* reported that 'very few questions were asked'.[32] The *Standard* gave more detail. Wilson asked the first question: 'Is it right to describe yourselves as refugees, or is it not right to say you were outlawed because you refused to obey the regulations of the one who is set in authority over Germany, who suspected you also, I imagine, of being more or less Communistic?' This was a gift for Arnold Mason, who replied that the Bruderhof would not allow Nazi teachings in their school and what they had said made it obvious they were not Communists. There were other questions: for example, why the Bruderhof bought property away from highways, to which Arnold responded by pointing out that the Ashton Keynes Bruderhof was beside the main road. Finally, Wilson asked what would happen to the Bruderhof if war broke out. Arnold replied: 'I have no idea, we should very much like to know.'[33]

---

31. W. B. Wilson to the editor, *Standard*, 28 January 1939.

32. 'Cotswold Bruderhof Members Reply to Critics', *Evening Advertiser*, 16 February 1939.

33. 'Life in Community', *Standard*, 18 February 1939.

Areas of Advance

Despite facing some local criticism, the Bruderhof felt in early 1939 that the community was making progress on several fronts. Hardy Arnold was delighted to report that while attending the centenary luncheon of the Anti-Slavery and Aborigine Protection Society in April 1939 he was able to speak to Sir Samuel Hoare.[34] Hardy followed this up with a lengthy letter to Sir Samuel in which he spoke of the Bruderhof's values, referred to Sir Samuel's understanding of their pacifist position—especially because the Home Secretary was 'a descendent of those brave Christians and local citizens, the Quakers'—and expressed concern: 'We trust that in the future critical days of international unrest your government will continue its friendly attitude towards us.' Having been compelled to leave Germany 'on account of our Christian refusal to participate in the un-Christian ways of the present German government', Hardy continued, 'and having been received in this country with so much friendliness, you can rest assured that the attitude of our members, whether British or non-British, is one of loyalty and gratitude to the British government in time of peace as much as in time of war'. Hardy talked of the desire by the community to 'serve this great nation and its government' by working on the land.[35] The Bruderhof hoped the Home Secretary would be able to indicate the government's attitude to the Bruderhof in the event of war, but Sir Samuel's reply was simply one of thanks for the information.[36] Heini Arnold subsequently wrote an important *Plough* article, 'Christ or Civilization? Here he argued against any attempt to 'stay within the injustice of civilization'.[37]

The purchase of Oaksey, which cost over £25,000, was made possible thanks to the Bruderhof's significant network. Gerald Vaughan's financial support was crucial, as was a large mortgage on very reasonable terms. Growth in the community overall, through the addition of new members, was such that in April 1939 Annemarie Arnold noted that Oaksey was filled to its capacity and that Ashton Keynes Bruderhof was

34. 'Concerning the Bruderhof Communities', *The Plough* 2, no. 2 (Summer 1939), 60.

35. Hardy Arnold to Sir Samuel Hoare, 27 April 1939. BHA Coll. 0055.

36. 'Concerning the Bruderhof Communities', *The Plough* 2, no. 2 (Summer 1939), 61.

37. J. Heinrich Arnold, 'Christ or Civilisation?', *The Plough* 3, no. 1 (Spring 1940), 19–21.

also full.[38] Writing in August 1939 to the Hutterian elder David Hofer, Emmy Arnold spoke in a similar vein about new people coming 'almost daily, seeking something different from the world and its ways'. At the same time, Emmy struck a sombre note. 'The world situation is so very serious; one hears a lot about the danger of war, about killing, poison gases, and so on.' War would not be declared until the following month, but Emmy anticipated that would happen. She wrote: 'We don't know who of us will survive the coming war.'[39] Annemarie, writing after war had been declared, took up the same theme: communal advance against a background of enormous uncertainty. She talked about 'great numbers of people' coming to experience Bruderhof life. By this time there were eighty people at Oaksey, making 320 in total in the two communities. Many of those coming were families. There were signs, Annemarie commented, that people had been 'awakened by the seriousness of the times and want to begin a new and different life'. There was continued outreach. 'Some of us', she said, 'go out to address meetings, and we receive many letters from people who are making serious enquiries'.[40]

Within the life of the Bruderhof, the year 1939, as Hardy Arnold saw it, was the 'most intensive year of activity' up to that point. He spoke of important elements in the inner as well as the outer life of the community. Six weddings had taken place that year.[41] An article in *The Friend* in July 1939 highlighted the range of the activities. Several of these were contributing to community income through the sale of produce. Farming had now increased to five hundred acres and was still increasing. A modern milking shed had been built at Oaksey, with an Alfa Laval milking machine. Beekeeping had increased to eighty hives. Rye bread was being baked in the community's bakery, and it was intended to purchase a grinding mill. Nine acres of potatoes had been planted, and there were beds of strawberries and blackcurrants. Orchards of apple and plum trees were being cultivated. In the printing area, the number of publications from Plough Publishing was increasing. The production of turned wooden articles had 'proved a successful branch of work carried on by the craftsmen of the Bruderhof'.[42]

38. Annemarie Arnold to her mother, 25 April 1939. BHA Coll. 0005.

39. Emmy Arnold to David Hofer, 11 August 1939. BHA Coll. 0288_02.

40. Annemarie Arnold to her mother, 31 October 1939. BHA Coll. 0005.

41. Hardy Arnold, 'The History of the Cotswold and Oaksey Bruderhofs, 1936–41'. BHA Coll. 0304.

42. 'Progress at the Bruderhof', *The Friend*, 21 July 1939.

Meanwhile, education and building community continued to be priorities. The aim of education, said the report in *The Friend*, was for children to 'develop naturally in an environment of love, in which both parents and teachers are united'. It was noted in the article that over the years many teachers had become members of the Bruderhof communities. As well as caring for the children of parents who were part of the Bruderhof, the community had also taken in other children, including a number of orphans and, recently, three unwanted babies. The needs being met were varied. Some unemployed men had spent time with the community. 'Such a life', the report commented, 'demands hard work from early morning until late at night.'[43]

As well as building up community life, there were continuing efforts to relate to wider streams of thought and action. The spring 1939 *Plough* carried a review by Kathleen Hamilton of *Heaven and Earth* (1938), by John Middleton Murry.[44] This was a demanding book, which, as Kathleen put it, tried to 'reveal the actual growth of the modern world through the minds of some great men who experienced in act or imagination the travail of its becoming'. Chaucer, Montaigne, Shakespeare, Cromwell, Milton, Rousseau, Goethe, Wordsworth, Shelley, Marx, and Morris all figured in the book. Through them, Kathleen said, 'we watch the change from the great wholeness of life of the Middle Ages to the rise of individualism in matters of religion, politics and economics'. This view of the Middle Ages was somewhat romantic, and Murry's vision for ecclesiastical renewal was certainly not in line with that of the Bruderhof. Nonetheless, Kathleen quoted with approval Murry's statement that the church was 'the community of men and women who recognise an authority independent of the secular state. . . the communion of those who are called out from secular society to acknowledge that their final allegiance lies elsewhere'.[45]

In the next *Plough*, Freda Bridgwater discussed a book by the outstanding Japanese Christian social reformer Toyohiko Kagawa, *Brotherhood Economics* (1936), in which he included comment on Hutterian communities in Brazil. In response to a letter from the Bruderhof asking for further details, Kagawa said he was relying on Brazilian sources. He also wrote: 'May God bless the Cotswold Bruderhof and its great devotion

43. 'Progress at the Bruderhof', *The Friend*, 21 July 1939.

44. John Middleton Murry, *Heaven and Earth* (London: Jonathan Cape, 1938).

45. Review, Kathleen Hamilton, *The Plough* 2, no. 1 (Spring 1939), 30–31.

to the cause of peace!'[46] Eric Gill's writings were of continuing interest to the Bruderhof. His *Work and Property* (1937) and *The Rich and the Poor: A Biblical Anthology* (1938) were reviewed in the winter 1939 *Plough*. George Vigar was pleased that Gill was encouraging 'an understanding of the proper meaning and function of Art' and noted religious influences: 'As a Catholic [Gill] has a feeling for the unity of life and Art which the Protestant seems to have lost.'[47] Further evidence of wider connections was seen in an informative review by Gertrud Hüssy of a handbook on Jewish village communal life.[48]

There was a determined intention within the Bruderhof that the activity which took place there should be sustained by strong spiritual life. On 26 July 1939, Hardy Arnold led a united Bruderhof meeting at which he spoke of the experience of various members of the two communities. He described how individuals had been 'accepted into the love of God and into his church'; had received a spiritual gift, which he called 'the baptism of the Holy Spirit'; or had taken the opportunity to 'begin anew' in the spiritual life. In particular, he spoke of the joy of welcoming Sylvia Walker into the novitiate, something delayed by illness. During the previous months she had known 'particularly great difficulties and hard struggles'. Hardy noted that 26 July was Eberhard Arnold's birthday, but for Hardy it was important to remember that what his father wanted was for people to carry on the work to which he had given himself. Hardy urged Christ-centredness: 'Christ is victorious!' He spoke of the 'terrible effect if a single man like Hitler or Stalin is possessed by an evil spirit', but there was a much more powerful effect when Christ was victorious in the hearts of individuals and when even a 'very small circle of people' joined together through the Holy Spirit. Hardy then turned to baptism, which was being administered as new members joined the community. 'The essential thing with baptism', he reiterated, 'is the baptism of the Spirit.' He spoke of the necessity of inner life: without that, the Bible itself and the Orders of Hutterite tradition could have a 'deadening effect', since they would be interpreted in a way that was lifeless. He concluded: 'We need the Spirit every hour, that it may blow the fire of love into us anew.'[49] This

46. Winifred Bridgwater, 'Hutterian Brothers in Brazil?', *The Plough* 2, no. 2 (Summer 1939), 52–53.

47. Review, George Vigar, *The Plough* 2, no. 4 (Winter 1939), 132.

48. Review, Gertrud Hüssy, *Handbook of the Jewish Communal Villages in Palestine* (Jerusalem: Keren Kayemeth Leisrael and Keren Hayesod, 1938).

49. Hardy Arnold, community meeting, Cotswold Bruderhof, 26 July 1939. BHA Coll. 0055.

message about the need for spiritual renewal was going to be of great relevance in the hard times ahead.

The Outbreak of War

As war grew closer in 1939, the issue of military conscription was introduced in the summer 1939 *Plough*, in relation to the Military Training Act of May 1939, under which all British men aged twenty and twenty-one who were fit and able were required to take six months' military training.[50] *Plough* commented that it was well known 'that under no circumstances will any member of our communities join the fighting forces or do any alternative form of service'. This had been confirmed at a Bruderhof meeting. All the English Bruderhof members were over twenty-one, but it was noted that 'some of the closer friends of the Bruderhof communities have refused to be conscripted, and have been put on the register of conscientious objectors'. This was the first time in Britain that conscription had been introduced in peacetime, and further developments were anticipated.[51] The annual Baptist Assembly in May 1939 gave serious consideration to the Military Training Act and passed a resolution on religious freedom which called on churches to stand by men convinced that in loyalty to Christ they should take no part in war. There was also a call to the government to fulfil the spirit as well as the letter of its pledge to treat conscientious objectors fairly.[52] *Peace News* reported in July 1939 that the Bruderhof was willing to take in any young men who shared its peace convictions.[53] At a Bruderhof meeting at the end of July, the outbreak of war was placed in a wider social context and was linked to challenges for Christian witness. Hardy Arnold recognised that 'many people live in fear and anxiety that soon a war will break out'. He also spoke of fears that 'the oppression of the working class' would increase. There could be a spread of 'lying, unfaithfulness, depravity, and impurity', but in the face of all this it was necessary to advocate 'the faith that Christ is victorious'.[54]

50. This anticipated much wider conscription in September 1939. See Danchev, 'The Army and the Home Front, 1939–1945', 298–315.

51. 'The Brothers and Conscription', *The Plough* 2, no. 2 (Summer 1939), 61.

52. 'Baptist Assembly', *Baptist Times*, 11 May 1939, 362.

53. 'Alternatives to Military Service', *Peace News*, 21 July 1939.

54. Hardy Arnold, community meeting, Cotswold Bruderhof, 26 July 1939. BHA Coll 0055.

In contrast with the belligerent outlook which had characterised much of mainstream British Christianity when the First World War began, the predominant mood at the beginning of the Second World War was one of restraint. Adrian Hastings suggests, 'For the Church, as for the nation as a whole, war was seen by September 1939 as inevitable and just, but it was entered into soberly and rather sadly'.[55] It is not the case, however, that everyone in the churches subscribed to the 'just war' theory. Ann Kramer speaks of the 'flourishing peace movement', which led in the period of the Second World War to approximately 62,000 conscientious objectors (COs) appearing before local tribunals to appeal for exemption from fighting.[56] From 1939 to 1940 membership of FoR in Britain grew from just over 9,000 to almost 12,000, and at the end of 1940 FoR had contact with 1,429 COs, of whom 528 had appeared before tribunals. Ninety-two had been granted unconditional exemption from all service connected with war, which was what Bruderhof members sought.[57] The Baptist Pacifist Fellowship (BPF) was also growing rapidly in this period, reaching 1,600 members by 1940. In the later 1930s annual Baptist Assemblies adopted anti-war resolutions, and the BPF, at its meeting on 13 February 1939, affirmed that 'to be part of the military machine was contrary to our Christian conscience'.[58]

Within denominations such as the Baptists, a specifically denominational fellowship could, as the FoR minutes recorded, help to bring churches 'to the conviction that the Christian way is the pacifist way'.[59] A typical Baptist CO, Harold Stead, aged twenty-six, appealing to the tribunal in May 1940, spoke of being guided by the teaching and life of Christ: 'He has primary claim to my allegiance'. Stead referred to the Sermon on the Mount and stated that Christ's Kingdom was 'to be built upon the basis of sacrificial love'. He continued: 'As one of many co-workers with Him in this Kingdom today, I can use no other force than the all-prevailing force of love.' In Christ, he said, 'there is no barrier of race,

55. Hastings, *History of English Christianity*, 373.

56. Kramer, *Conscientious Objectors of the Second World War*, 7–23.

57. Minutes of the General Committee of FoR, 30 and 31 December 1940. COLL MISC 0456/1/6.

58. Dekar, 'Twentieth-Century British Baptist Conscientious Objectors', 37–38; Minutes of Baptist Pacifist Fellowship, 13 February 1939. D/BPF Box 1. Papers held in the Angus Archive, Regent's Park College, Oxford.

59. Minutes of the General Committee of the FoR, 1–3 April 1940, 6. COLL MISC 0456/1/6, London School of Economics.

class or creed' and to participate in war 'inevitably separates me from those with whom Christ would have me live in brotherhood.' Stead was a Baptist lay preacher and a member of the BPF. His appeal was accepted.[60]

In an interview with the *Gloucester Echo*, published on 13 September 1939, after the outbreak of war, Hardy Arnold said that fighting was incompatible with Bruderhof beliefs, but he stressed the contribution of the community's farm work and linked this with a statement by the Minister of Agriculture about the importance of agriculture in war time.[61] The spring 1940 issue of *The Plough* reported that five Bruderhof members had at that stage been called up and had registered as COs. One, Philip Britts, had already appeared before a tribunal and had been granted unconditional exemption from military service. Bruce Sumner, Reginald Lacy, Walter Bennett, and Alan Stevenson were scheduled to appear in the near future.[62] The Bruderhof went to considerable lengths to establish a connection with Judge Wethered, who heard tribunal cases in Bristol. Ernest Wethered had a long and distinguished career as a barrister, county judge, public servant and educationalist. By March 1942 he had heard over 4,000 CO cases, and he wrote an unpublished analysis of the beliefs of the COs whose cases had come to him.[63] At first Arnold Mason and Stanley Fletcher, who attended Bristol tribunal hearings, felt that Judge Wethered was approaching his task without much understanding of COs. Stanley was given the task by the community of protesting to the judge about his initial treatment of cases, including those from the Bruderhof, and also of explaining Anabaptist convictions. The judge studied Bruderhof literature and saw how the community was dedicated to peace and brotherliness and how members worked without wages.[64]

On 2 July 1940, Bruderhof member Sydney Hindley took a Christocentric approach at his CO tribunal, similar to that of Harold Stead: 'I am convinced that the true way of life was shown by Jesus, and desire with

60. Application to Local Tribunal by a Person Provisionally Registered in the Register of Conscientious Objectors: Harold Arthur Dobson Stead. D/BPF Box 1. Papers held in the Angus Archive, Regent's Park College, Oxford.

61. 'Bruderhof and War', *Gloucestershire Echo*, 13 September 1939. See Andrew Rigby, 'Pacifist Communities in Britain in the Second World War', *Peace & Change* 15, no. 2, 107–122.

62. 'Our members and the Tribunals', *The Plough* 3, no. 1 (Spring 1940), 30.

63. Barker, *Conscience, Government and War*, 37–38. For more on COs, see Hayes, *Challenge of Conscience*; Goodall, *We will not go to War*.

64. Stanley Fletcher, 'Stanley Fletcher's Life Story'. BHA Coll. 0067; Arnold Mason, 'Early Memories'. BHA Coll. 0006.

my whole heart to follow him. I respect the State and will obey it in all things which are not contrary to the call of Jesus. He calls me to show my love to God not merely by loving my friends, but by loving my enemies also. He himself clearly revealed that love in his own life and teachings, and above all in his death. I cannot reconcile such love with the killing of my fellows, and therefore I cannot bear arms.' He then went on to speak of wanting to give his life to 'a creative, brotherly way of active service'. He explained that he 'joined the Society of Brothers nearly four years ago, and am now a full member'. He, too, was granted unconditional exemption from military service.[65] Also in July, Fred Goodwin applied for exemption using a number of the same themes. As recorded in the *Evening Advertiser*, he stated: 'As a Christian I refuse to do any kind of military service. I have had this conviction for about six years and this contributed to, rather, led me to join the Bruderhof community.' He expressed gratitude for freedoms granted to the Bruderhof in England and continued: 'As a member of the community it is my wish to obey the laws and to fulfil the wishes of the state so far as they do not contradict the obedience which I owe to God.' He believed the best help he could give to others consisted in 'taking my part in the witness of the community which is founded on the New Testament and the witness of the Early Christians'. He was also given complete exemption.[66] Nationally, unconditional exemption was only granted to COs by local tribunals in 2,900 cases.[67] The consideration afforded to the Bruderhof, with all applicants ultimately receiving unconditional exemption, was unusual.

As an international community, the Bruderhof was also unusual among British communities of the period. By 1940 British members (including children) had become the largest group, with almost as many German members, as well as Swiss, Dutch, French, Czech, Swedish, and one Italian member. Nationally, a procedure was instituted by the British government to place 'aliens' in the country in different categories. Tribunals were set up, and by the end of November 1939 these bodies had reviewed 35,000 'aliens'. There were three categories: those in A were deemed high security risks and were interned; those in B had restrictions placed on them because of doubts about their loyalty to Britain; and those in C were free, as their loyalty was not in question. In November 1939,

65. Sydney A. Hindley, 'Statement to the National Service (Armed Forces) Office'. BHA Coll. 0324.

66. 'Bruderhof Objector Granted Exemption', *Evening Advertiser*, 16 July 1940.

67. Kramer, *Conscientious Objectors of the Second World War*, 7.

only 348 'aliens' were interned. However, the status of aliens living in Britain deteriorated rapidly in the early months of 1940, and by the end of July 1940 about 30,000 were interned.[68] A three-person tribunal, with a translator, came to the Bruderhof to interview 'enemy aliens' (those from enemy countries) and to ascertain their 'friendliness' to Britain.[69]

Hella Römer's Alien Registration book gives insights into the experience of being a refugee and then an alien. She had landed at the port of Newhaven, Sussex, from the Alm, in October 1937, and was given permission to stay in Britain one month. This was extended on two occasions, and in August 1939 she was granted permission to stay indefinitely as a member of the Bruderhof, provided she did not take employment or engage in any occupation other than that authorised by the Home Secretary. On 5 October 1939, she appeared before the tribunal as an 'enemy alien', and after the hearing her registration book was stamped 'Refugee from Nazi Oppression' and she was exempted 'until further order' from internment.[70] Arnold Mason and Hardy Arnold had asked if they could be present at tribunal hearings. In certain cases, they 'protested politely' about inaccurate translations. The hearings, however, were sympathetic, and at the point at which the tribunal came to the community all the German members were granted the status of friendly aliens.[71]

Ernest Cooper at the Home Office continued to be supportive of the Bruderhof. This was significant in individual cases, such as that of Roger Allain, a Bruderhof member and French citizen who found himself in difficulties with the British authorities. On 23 September 1939, it was reported in the *Daily Herald* that Roger, who was then aged twenty-four, was recommended under the tribunal process for deportation to France. He had arrived in Britain in April 1938 with a passport that was valid until July, but he had not reported to the police until September 1939. By this time, he had married, and he and his English wife, Norah, had a child. Roger explained to those looking at his case that he was engaged in agricultural work as a member of the Bruderhof, that he was a conscientious objector, and that if he was deported to France, he would be in a country where there was no provision for pacifist beliefs.[72]

68. Lafitte, *The Internment of Aliens*, 89–93; Gillman, '*Collar the lot!*', 45.

69. 'Our members and the Tribunals', *The Plough* 3, no. 1 (Spring 1940), 30.

70. Charles Headland, 'Charles Headland Remembers Cotswold and Oaksey'. BHA Coll. 0118.

71. Arnold Mason, 'Early Memories'. BHA Coll. 0006.

72. 'Must go Home to France', *Daily Herald*, 23 September 1939.

This case illustrates the channels through which the Bruderhof was seeking to communicate. Although the initial recommendation was that Roger Allain should be deported, his case was remanded for Home Office investigation and for government order. With the help of Ernest Cooper's active involvement on behalf of the Bruderhof, Roger was allowed to stay. Pressures were clearly increasing, however, and in a conversation with Hardy Arnold in May 1940, Cooper was not optimistic about future possibilities.[73] Cooper's brother was behind a suggestion that the Bruderhof might consider building up a community in the Highlands of Scotland. Arnold Mason, Heini Arnold, and Alan Stevenson travelled north twice, but there were no indications that this move was feasible.[74] In any case, this would not have been a complete solution.

Increasing Local Opposition

On Sunday 3 September 1939, the day Britain entered the war, a man on a bicycle arrived at the entrance of the Cotswold Bruderhof, took off his jacket, and offered to fight any 'Germans'. The next day the local paid workers at the Bruderhof flew a Union Jack over their workplace.[75] In an effort to prevent anti-German sentiment from becoming a more serious problem for the Bruderhof, Hardy Arnold wrote a letter to the *Standard* which was published on 23 September 1939. He first expressed the communities 'feelings of love and gratitude to the British nation and its Government'. He then gave a brief history of how the community in Germany had been broken up in 1937 by what he called the 'pagan state', with property and land confiscated, resulting in the expulsion from Germany of its members. He was thankful to Britain for 'liberty of conscience' and for the 'tolerance' not shown by Hitler. Hardy spoke of the recent unprovoked attack by Hitler on Poland and went as far as to express loyalty to the British government as it, together with France, showed determination to 'resist any further acts of aggression'. It was a response that seemed to stretch pacifist convictions to the limit. Hardy then highlighted all that was being done by the Bruderhof to maximise agricultural production in order to help the neighbourhood. He concluded: 'May we repeat

73. Hardy Arnold to Edith Arnold, 23 May 1940. BHA Coll. 0304.

74. Arnold Mason, 'Early Memories'. BHA Coll. 0006.

75. Charles Headland, 'Charles Headland Remembers Cotswold and Oaksey'. BHA Coll. 0118.

that we entirely disapprove of the ways of the Nazi regime in Germany (which deprived us of our home and property) and that we, on the basis of Christian teaching, owe allegiance to the Government of Britain, to whose people and institutions we feel deeply attached and indebted?'[76]

During the autumn of 1939 there was relatively little public discussion locally about the Bruderhof, at least in the local press. Fritz Kanitz, an Austrian who had found refuge in Britain and had stayed for a short time with the Cotswold community, made clear in the Standard that he would be prepared to fight for Britain and this his views were 'rather different from those of a religious community of German origin in this district'. Kanitz was living at North End Farm, Ashton Keynes.[77] In November the North Wilts Herald reported on a talk that Stanley Fletcher had given to the Swindon Workers' Educational Association. The subject of the war did not feature in the newspaper report.[78] However, the community heard that rumours about its supposed German sympathies were circulating locally. One story was that the community had a submarine—kept in its small and landlocked gravel pit! Another rumour was that the community had chosen to go to Ashton Keynes to poison the Thames and thus London's water supply.[79]

Although some local people believed the Bruderhof was predominantly German, it was British people who were joining. The spring 1940 Plough reported that at the beginning of March twelve novices were taken into full membership. The present novitiate, it was reported, numbered nineteen, most of whom had come to the community in the previous few months. These new additions were British. There were by then 153 community members and would-be members, with 138 children and 35 guests and helpers, making a total of 318, of whom 84 were at Oaksey and 234 were at Ashton Keynes.[80] It may be that the appearance and dress of the Bruderhof members contributed to their being seen as 'alien'. A generally sympathetic article which appeared in February 1940 was headed 'A German Colony in Britain', and the reporter described meeting men with beards and wearing 'short breeches' and women in 'plain long gowns'. The reporter did not understand what was being said by those who spoke to

76. E. C. H. Arnold to the editor, Standard, 23 September 1939.

77. Fritz Kanitz to the editor, Standard, 30 September 1939.

78. 'Bruderhof and Religion', North Wilts Herald, 10 November 1939.

79. Charles Headland, 'Charles Headland Remembers Cotswold and Oaksey'. BHA Coll. 0118.

80. 'Growth of the communities', The Plough 3, no. 1 (Spring 1940), 29–30.

him in what he called 'deep guttural voices'. This article mentioned the possible internment of foreign members of the community.[81]

Anxiety about foreigners grew in 1940, with newspapers such as the *Daily Mail* saying police must round up every 'doubtful alien'.[82] The Bruderhof increasingly became a target for hostility. By this time, the community had bought two milk rounds in Swindon, and members were delivering milk from door to door, together with homemade bread, fresh eggs, and vegetables. On 22 April 1940, a letter appeared in the Swindon *Evening Advertiser* from Gordon Hollas, who stated: 'The Bruderhof consists of many nationalities, including Germans, and does not pay wages to its members. By this unfair competition it is threatening the future livelihood of many milk roundsmen.'[83] The following day Hardy and Arnold Mason wrote a 'Reply to Critics'. They pointed out that a number of milk rounds in Swindon were being offered for sale. The Bruderhof had bought two at the current prices. The letter emphasised that the Home Office and local authorities were aware of the nature of the Bruderhof's work and had encouraged them in the area of agriculture. In particular, the community had been urged by the Agricultural Committee to maximise food production. The letter invited people to visit the Bruderhof and noted that many hundreds of people in Swindon had been visitors and that talks had been given by Bruderhof members to groups in the town. The community reiterated what had been said by members repeatedly, that 'the oppressive and brutal spirit of Nazism is wrong'.[84] This did not, however, satisfy critics. A number of letters followed, questioning why British Bruderhof members did not fight Nazism, but instead were COs, and maintaining that acceptance by the community of a lower standard of living enabled it to 'maintain itself in competition with the more progressive elements of the national economy'.[85] One correspondent spoke of the Bruderhof's 'cabbage soup and camp bed' style of life.[86]

Several serious accusations were raised about the Bruderhof in May 1940 by A. F. Pressland, from Cirencester, who said in a letter to the *Evening Advertiser* that he had lived with the community for six weeks. He

81. 'A German Colony in Britain!', *Answers*, 3 February 1940.

82. Lafitte, *The Internment of Aliens*, 169–170.

83. Gordon Hollas to the editor, *Standard*, 22 April 1939.

84. 'Bruderhof Reply to Critics', *Standard*, 27 April 1939.

85. S. T. Ball and W. Ibberson Jones to the editor, *Standard*, 24 and 27 April 1939.

86. 'Sphinx' to the editor, *Standard*, 29 April 1939.

alleged that the Bruderhof scorned the English working classes, insisted on guests paying for their own keep and working every day including most Sundays, had bedrooms which could not be locked from inside, operated a 'Gestapo' punishment regime which included solitary confinement, and exploited Jewish young people living in the community.[87] A reply was published from Bruce Sumner, Heini Arnold, Cyril Harries, Arnold Mason, and Hardy Arnold. They were 'grieved that a man can spread such deliberate lies and gross misrepresentations and distortions of facts'. They continued: 'Those thousands who have been our guests during the past four years know as well as he does, that we have nothing to hide, and that his allegations are untrue, not only in detail but even in substance'. Readers were again invited to visit: 'Our doors are open, they can stay as long as they wish without any charges, sharing our work, our meals, our meetings'. The letter stated that the community had 'the deepest love for the working class people and many of our members come from the so called working classes', that there was no Gestapo regime or solitary confinement, that work was voluntarily offered, with none on Sundays except for unavoidable duties, and that rooms could be locked from inside and outside.[88]

The rebuttal of Pressland's charges was backed up by others. Geoffrey and Phyllis Welham, who had on several occasions been guests of the Bruderhof, offered an entirely different view. For them the community was 'the first place we have found absolute brotherhood and love'.[89] Werner Weiss wrote on behalf of the (twenty) Jewish young people living in the community to say that 'Hitler drove us out of Germany and we are happy we have found in the Bruderhof a settlement prepared to give a good training for our proposed work in Palestine in the future'. He concluded: 'Contrary to Mr Pressland's assertions we have no complaint against the Bruderhof's attitude towards us'.[90]

Although two more letters from Pressland were published, they simply continued his litany of complaints about the inner life of the Bruderhof.[91] More significant were letters voicing nationalistic sentiments. A letter on 15 May to the *Evening Advertiser*, signed 'Briton', began: 'I believe

87. A. F. Pressland to the editor, *Evening Advertiser*, 3 May 1940.

88. Society of Brothers to the editor, *Evening Advertiser*, 4 May 1940.

89. Mr and Mrs G. T. Welham to the editor, *Evening Advertiser*, 4 May 1940.

90. Werner Weiss to the editor, *Evening Advertiser*, 4 May 1940.

91. A. F. Pressland to the editor, *Evening Advertiser*, 11 May 1940; A. F. Pressland to the editor, *Standard*, 18 May 1940.

I am voicing the opinion of the majority of English men when I say that it is time the Bruderhof was abolished and its occupants told to seek shelter elsewhere.' The letter condemned 'unfair trading' in Swindon by the Bruderhof.[92] The 'unfair trading' theme continued. On 18 May, Edith Harris from Swindon wrote about the Bruderhof 'hitting our tradespeople'.[93] Controversy continued, with correspondents such as Lionel Howse calling on 20 May for 'drastic action'.[94] One friend of the community overheard a conversation in a pub about plans to set fire to the Bruderhof.[95] By contrast with many letters, Leslie Mobey from Swindon wrote: 'I ask the citizens of Swindon to end this petty criticism of the Bruderhof before it becomes persecution, and when that begins it is impossible to stop it.' He then referred to pacifism: 'At this time it is easy to criticize members of the Bruderhof because they will not fight. However they have always held these pacifist views, both in Germany and elsewhere.'[96] Support also came from the vicar of St Paul's Church, Swindon, C. F. Harmon, who described the Bruderhof as 'avowedly Christian, pacifist and anti-Hitler, and as such deserving of our sympathy and respect'. He asked pointedly: 'What would Jesus do?'[97] The tide of local opinion, however, had moved. An 'Ex-Serviceman' wrote on 31 May about 'British cowards' joining the community.[98] A week later, W. H. Harris from Swindon proposed a boycott of Bruderhof products.[99] As reported in *The Plough*, the result was that a major part of the community's income was lost.[100] Behind the scenes, enquiries were being made about leaving Britain.

National Pressures

Alongside the local pressures on the Bruderhof there were also continued national developments. On 16 May 1940, the *Evening Advertiser* carried a report with the heading 'Bruderhof members may be interned'.[101] This

92. 'Briton' to the editor, *Evening Advertiser*, 15 May 1940.
93. Edith M. Harris to the editor, *Evening Advertiser*, 18 May 1940.
94. Lionel Howse to the editor, *Evening Advertiser*, 20 May 1940.
95. Arnold Mason, 'Early Memories'. BHA Coll. 0006.
96. Leslie Mobey to the editor, *Evening Advertiser*, 20 May 1940.
97. C. F. Harman to the editor, *Evening Advertiser*, 20 May 1940.
98. 'Ex-Serviceman' to the editor, *Evening Advertiser*, 31 May 1940.
99. W. H. Harris to the editor, *North Wilts Herald*, 7 June 1940.
100. 'Economic Repercussions', *The Plough* 3, no. 2 (Summer 1940), 56.
101. 'Bruderhof members may be interned', *Evening Advertiser*, 16 May 1940.

did not in fact apply to inland areas of Britain, and the following day the Advertiser carried a piece in which Stanley Fletcher, on behalf of the Bruderhof, explained that its members were not affected.[102] W. B. Wilson again entered the fray and told the *Gloucestershire Echo* that a request he had made to the Home Office to look into the Bruderhof had been acknowledged and he had been told the matter would be considered. The *Echo* article on this, of 21 May, reported that a petition had been signed by residents of Ashton Keynes for presentation to the Home Secretary, Sir John Anderson (who had succeeded Sir Samuel Hoare), protesting against the freedom allowed to German members of the Bruderhof. Arnold Mason, for the community, was quoted as stating that 'the Home Office is fully informed about us'.[103] Three days later the protest by residents was reported nationally, in the *Daily Telegraph*.[104] Sir John Anderson was aware of this press campaign directed against all aliens.[105] National feeling was growing, with the fall of France and the Low Countries in May 1940 creating panic in Britain over the possible existence of 'Fifth Columnists'. R. H. Wells, vicar of Ashton Keynes, said he was receiving letters almost every day from senior military personnel asking what was going to be done about the Bruderhof. He quoted one letter about internment orders, from a major-general, which said: 'I hope the new regulations will apply to the Bruderhof . . . We cannot afford any Fifth Column, for it is a life and death struggle.'[106]

In an attempt to put their case at a higher level, members of the Bruderhof sent a deputation, led by Arnold Mason, to the Swindon Conservative MP, W. W. Wakefield. On 25 May, the day after the visit, the *Evening Advertiser* headline was: 'Swindon's M. P. Tells Bruderhof He Has No Sympathy for Them.' Wakefield told the deputation bluntly: 'We are engaged in a life and death struggle and you do nothing but hide behind our soldiers, sailors and airmen'.[107] The attempt to win over the MP had a negative impact, since national newspapers such as the *Daily Herald* printed the story of how Wakefield, 'a former England rugger captain', had told the Bruderhof that they were—and this was the *Herald* head-

102. 'Bruderhof passed by', *Evening Advertiser*, 17 May 1940.

103. 'Protest to Home Office over Bruderhof', *Gloucestershire Echo*, 21 May 1940.

104. 'German Colony in the Cotswolds', *The Daily Telegraph*, 24 May 1940.

105. Peter and Leni Gillman, *'Collar the Lot'*, 79–80.

106. R. H. Wells to the editor, *Evening Advertiser*, 25 May 1940.

107. 'Swindon's M. P. Tells Bruderhof He Has No Sympathy For Them', *Evening Advertiser*, 25 May 1940.

ing—'Hiding Behind Our Fighters'.[108] A reporter from the *Daily Express* followed up and visited the Bruderhof. The Express report appeared on 27 May. In Ashton Keynes the reporter was told by Julian Mordaunt, who was prominent in local life, that he and others had written to the government 'urging the danger of allowing aliens to be at large in such an area'. At the Bruderhof, the reporter spoke to Stanley Fletcher, who stated: 'We strongly refute the suggestion that there may be spies in our midst. It would be impossible. We know each other's hearts so well that we should soon find out.'[109] There was satisfaction locally when German Bruderhof members were placed under restrictions that included a curfew. Without special permission, they could not travel more than five miles.[110] Bruderhof members affirmed this as realistic.[111] One member, however, Manfried Kaiser, refused to be bound by this condition and was interned in the Isle of Man. He was later deported to a camp in Canada.[112] Over seven thousand 'aliens' were deported in the period of mass internment. Captain Victor Cazalet, MP for Chippenham, who argued that many internees were refugees, described their treatment as a 'bespattered page in our history'.[113]

The Bruderhof continued to feature in the national press in June 1940. The *Daily Express*, which maintained its interest in the community, reported on 5 June that police had arrested a British member of the community.[114] This was the case of Freda Bridgwater, who had married a German, August Dyroff, and had therefore become an 'enemy alien'.[115] Freda's release from the Isle of Man was brought about through a direct appeal made by Arnold Mason, on behalf of the Bruderhof, to Sir Alexander Maxwell, the Permanent Under-Secretary of State in the Home Office. Maxwell's father was a Congregational minister, and he had sym-

108. 'Hiding Behind Our Fighters', *Daily Herald*, 27 May 1940.

109. 'Germans in Colony Alarm', *Daily Express*, 27 May 1940.

110. Hardy Arnold, 'The History of the Cotswold and Oaksey Bruderhofs, 1936–1941'. BHA Coll. 0304.

111. 'Curfew Pleases Germans', *Evening Standard*, 25 May 1940.

112. He remained an advocate of the community, and someone he met during his internment, Hugo Brinkmann, subsequently found his way to the Bruderhof. See Charles Headland, 'Charles Headland Remembers Cotswold and Oaksey'. BHA Coll. 0118.

113. For more see Stent, *A Bespattered Page?*.

114. 'Police Raid', *Daily Express*, 5 June 1940.

115. See the Introduction.

pathy with those suffering for their conscience. He worked closely with the Home Secretary and took advice from Ernest Cooper; there was a desire in the Home Office to maintain a balance of liberty and law and order.[116] Freda's release, at a time of mass internment and deportation of aliens, illustrates the conflicting pressures on the Home Office and the different perspectives about issues of identity.[117] On the one hand there were voices such as Victor Cazalet, who chaired an all-party committee of MPs pressing the government to recognise that many of the 'aliens' were in fact resolutely anti-Nazi. The secretary of this committee was Eleanor Rathbone, sometimes described as the Member of Parliament for refugees.[118] On the other hand, when Winston Churchill became Prime Minister in March 1940 there was a strong move towards internment. Churchill's statement, 'Collar the Lot', came as a result of Italy entering the war. Those 'collared' included many Jewish refugees. Maxwell had the task of carrying out what had become government policy.[119]

The Bruderhof situation was discussed in a debate in the House of Lords on 12 June 1940. George Bell, bishop of Chichester, argued in the debate that the approach to internment was misguided. His view was that it was demanded neither by national security nor justice.[120] Lord Methuen, of Crosham Court, three miles from Chippenham, Wiltshire, reported on how he and a friend had visited the Bruderhof: 'We were shown everything that we wanted to see and every question was quite obviously answered sincerely and fully.' Although Lord Methuen did not doubt 'the sincerity and the good faith of the leaders of any German peace organisation which has settled here since the coming into power of the National-Socialist régime in Germany', he believed 'such centres'—the Bruderhof being in fact the only one—should be subject to 'local internment, and have police or even a military guard billeted on the spot'. He described local feeling as 'running very high'. Edward Cavendish, Duke of Devonshire, spoke on behalf of the government. In response to the bishop's speech he said he knew the vast majority of those who had come into Britain were genuine refugees, but he added that a few might not be

116. Gillman, 'Collar the Lot', 92–93.

117. Pistol, 'Enemy Alien and Refugee', 37–52.

118. Sherman, Island Refuge, 184.

119. Gillman, 'Collar the Lot', 168.

120. For Bell's wider protests against injustice in this period, see Chandler, George Bell, Bishop of Chichester.

genuine.[121] For the benefit of the House, he described the community: 'It consists of pacifists and conscientious objectors, a number of them Germans. They live in a community, they take no wages, they live off the produce of their land, and sell the rest.' The Duke had been part of the British Intelligence Service, and commenting on accusations that German members of the community were Fifth Columnists he stated wryly that someone whose English was limited and wore a long beard and dressing gown would be 'the last person I should dream of employing as a German spy'. The possibility of interning the whole community *in situ* had been discussed, but he was against this as from the agricultural point of view there would be a loss of 'a producing asset'.[122]

Following the debate in the House of Lords about internment, a question was raised about the Bruderhof by an MP in the House of Commons. Captain Alan Graham asked whether the whole community of the 'German Peace Bruderhof' at Ashton Keynes had been interned. Osbert Peake, the Under-Secretary of State at the Home Office, replied that the question of the best method of dealing with the members of the community was being considered. He added that the government had received 'a great deal of advice' regarding the community and was reviewing the options. Peake pointed out that only 40 percent of the members of the community were either German or Austrian, and that the community was making a valuable contribution to the production of food.[123] Nancy Astor, who was the first woman to become an MP in the House of Commons, also contributed to the debate. The Bruderhof had written to her on 7 June to ask for her help with possible emigration to the United States—she had been born in America—and she immediately wrote to the American ambassador.[124] She also arranged for Arnold Mason and Hardy Arnold to be in the public gallery of the House, and she spoke to her fellow-MPs about the community as one 'whose sole concern is Christianity', with its members 'a great asset to the country instead of a

121. Stent, *A Bespattered Page?*, 80–81. Stent's quotation indicates the sympathetic note the Duke of Devonshire struck about the Bruderhof.

122. Parliamentary Debates, House of Lords Official Report 116, no. 58, 12 June 1940.

123. House of Commons Reports, London, 26 June 1940. Hansard, Vol. 362, cc443–4.

124. Hardy Arnold to Viscountess Astor, 7 June 1940; Nancy Astor to Hardy Arnold, 10 June 1940. BHA Coll. 0055. Nancy Astor was a friend of Eleanor Rathbone and was therefore aware of the wider refugee issue.

liability'. Osbert Peake agreed that this was a pacifist community driven out of Germany, and he used the remark from the House of Lords, which was greeted with laughter in the Commons, that 'members all wear brown dressing-gowns and beards and are for that reason unlikely to be employed by the enemy'.[125]

The day after this debate a letter appeared in the *Wiltshire Gazette* from Victor Cazalet, who had been in contact with Peake about refugees. Cazalet said that for some years he had been interested in the Bruderhof and had visited their farms. Despite their having different beliefs from his, he respected 'the sincerity of their views, and the deep and real simplicity of their Christian faith'. He believed tolerance of a minority 'should still be a British characteristic which we should cultivate and maintain'.[126] In the eyes of the Bruderhof, however, it seemed increasingly unlikely that their way of practising the Christian faith could be sustained in the British context of the time. Moves began to be made to seek to leave the country.

125. House of Commons Reports, London, 26 June 1940. Hansard, Vol. 362, cc443–4.

126. V. A. Cazalet to the editor, *Wiltshire Gazette*, 27 June 1940.

8

Moving On

Having found sanctuary in Britain in 1936, by the summer of 1940 the Bruderhof was facing another move. Emigration planning began to take shape in May 1940, with a visit by Bruderhof representatives to Ernest Cooper at the Home Office.[1] On 8 June, four days before the debate in the House of Lords about refugees, the Bruderhof wrote to C. A. C. J. Hendrick, who was the Secretary to the Leader of the House of Lords, Lord Caldecote, asking the government to continue its policy of tolerance of the religious convictions of the community. If this was not possible, the community was ready 'to join our sisters and brothers [the Hutterites] in North America'. For this to happen, it would be necessary for the British government and the government of either Canada or the United States to grant the necessary permits.[2] Over the summer of 1940 the Bruderhof's contacts in British government circles indicated that the situation was such that the community's German members would have to leave the country if they were going to avoid the mass internment of aliens that was taking place. In response, the community requested time to allow the entire group to leave Britain. This was agreed.[3]

1. Arnold Mason, 'Early Memories'. BHA Coll. 0006.

2. The Society of Brothers to C.A.C.J. Hendrick, 8 June 1940. BHA Coll. 0055.

3. Hardy Arnold, 'The History of the Cotswold and Oaksey Bruderhofs, 1936–1941'.

Seeking Sanctuary

Although plans were now being made to emigrate, members continued their pacifist witness to those with whom they were in contact in Britain. Witness continued at tribunals. In August 1940 the *Evening Advertiser* reported that at a tribunal twin brothers Charles and Robert Headland, 'who several years ago decided to withdraw from the everyday world and throw in their lot with the Society of Brothers, Ashton Keynes, were granted unconditional exemption from military service'. Both the brothers spoke in their statements (oral and written) of how they had been in the Peace Pledge Union (PPU). For Charles, joining the Bruderhof involved discovering 'a positive expression of what I had been seeking'. His witness was that 'in this practical, brotherly life on the land I have found the true discipleship of Christ'.[4] However, as the community embraced moving on, Charles' work on the land would give way in the following year and a half to a different way of life in which his skills as an accountant would be crucial.[5]

In the search for refuge abroad, the Bruderhof first sought to join the Hutterites in Canada, where most Hutterite communities were located, or perhaps in the USA. Sir Evelyn Wrench of the Overseas League, an organisation through which he wanted to express his Christian vision for internationalism, was interested in the Bruderhof and wrote to L. B. Pearson, Official Secretary, Canada House, on 28 May 1940. He affirmed: 'It is so rare nowadays to meet whole-hearted idealists who live up to their convictions'.[6] It was also rare for pacifists in Britain to make efforts to leave the country, since many saw themselves as witnesses to their countrymen, but Pearson agreed to forward the Bruderhof's request for permission to emigrate and join the Hutterites to the Canadian government in Ottawa. Later the Bruderhof were told that Ottawa was not prepared to give consideration to the request. Through various friends in Britain the Bruderhof then approached a number of countries, including Australia, New Zealand, South Africa, British Guiana, Jamaica, and the Windward Islands. When all these efforts failed, it was decided that there would be a better prospect of success if one or two community members travelled

4. 'Twins Exempted', *Evening Advertiser*, 28 August 1940.

5. Charles Headland, 'Charles Headland remembers Cotswold and Oaksey'. BHA Coll. 0118.

6. Sir Evelyn Wrench to L. B. Pearson, 28 May 1940. BHA Coll. 0055. Evelyn Wrench published a nostalgic and much misunderstood book, *I Loved Germany*.

to North America, where, in cooperation with the Hutterites, they could make direct contact with the Canadian or American governments.[7] An unexpected opportunity occurred through one of the Jewish young people, Pauli Fischel, at the Cotswold Bruderhof. His parents had been able to travel to Venezuela, and a request came for someone from the community to accompany Pauli to join them. The shipping route was via New York, and it was agreed that Hans Meier would travel with Pauli, which would give Hans time to make contacts in America.[8]

Another member of the community, Guy Johnson, from Birmingham, who, it was thought, could use his skills as a lawyer in any negotiations, was able to travel with Hans Meier. Guy had recently been granted exemption from military service by Judge Wethered, having explained that from 1934 onwards he had been a pacifist, involved in the FoR and the PPU, and that he had given up his work as a solicitor and joined the Bruderhof.[9] The normal ruling in such cases of exemption was that Bruderhof COs would work in the community, especially in farming. Guy, however, later asked if he could receive a visa to visit Jamaica, where his uncle was a Methodist bishop, and most unusually this request was granted. The journey to Jamaica involved going via New York. Hans and Guy visited the American consul in Bristol and were given ninety-day transit visas for the United States.[10] The journey to New York was on the Cunard White Star Liner *Scythia*, an old passenger boat, and it involved twelve days of zigzagging, under war conditions, across the Atlantic. This was the early period of the Battle of the Atlantic.[11]

After arriving on 12 August 1940, they met with a Jewish committee to discuss arrangements for Pauli Fischel. The committee members were satisfied with the care that had been provided for Pauli but decided that they would take responsibility for Pauli's onward journey to Venezuela. The priority for Hans and Guy now became following up with North American contacts—in Canada and the USA—who might be able to help with the emigration of the community from Britain.[12] The most promis-

7. Arnold Mason, 'Early Memories'. BHA Coll. 0006.

8. Hans Meier, 'Journey of Guy Johnson and Hans Meier to North America, 1940'. BHA Coll. 0007.

9. 'Bruderhof Conscientious Objector', *Wiltshire Telegraph*, 1 June 1940.

10. Hans Meier, 'Journey of Guy Johnson and Hans Meier to North America, 1940'. BHA Coll. 0007.

11. See Dimbleby, *The Battle of the Atlantic*.

12. Hans Meier, 'Journey of Guy Johnson and Hans Meier to North America, 1940'. BHA Coll. 0007.

ing contact was Orie Miller, a founder and well-travelled leader of the Mennonite Central Committee (MCC). Emmy Arnold and Hans Zumpe had met Miller in 1936 at a Mennonite conference in Amsterdam. They had also spoken to Harold Bender there.[13] At the conference, it had become apparent that German Mennonite congregations were not prepared to stand up against the Nazis with regard to military service. However, eighteen Mennonite leaders, including Harold Bender and Orie Miller, together with Emmy and Hans from the Bruderhof, signed a declaration opposing 'the sin of war' and committing themselves to the 'proclamation of the gospel of peace'.[14]

Orie Miller offered the service of the MCC, and he and his wife welcomed Hans Meier and Guy Johnson to their home, near Lancaster, Pennsylvania.[15] Miller's view was that a Quaker body, the American Friends Service Committee (AFSC), which was active in helping refugees from Nazi Germany, would have more access to the government of the United States than the Mennonites did. He mentioned exploring settling in Paraguay, a country where the MCC had contacts with the government. However, at this point the hope still was that the Bruderhof could join the North American Hutterites. Hans and Guy met an AFSC representative in Philadelphia, who gave them a contact in the State Department in Washington, DC. They were able to have a meeting at the State Department and were referred on to the senator from South Dakota, William Bulow, who knew Michael Waldner, the elder at the Bon Homme Hutterite Colony, who had played an important role when he visited the European Bruderhofs. The senator, who had German ancestry, was sympathetic and fondly recalled having visited Bon Homme to enjoy beer with Michael Waldner during Prohibition.[16]

The attempts through the AFSC to gain a hearing in Washington D.C. proved unsuccessful, however, and Clarence Pickett, one of the founders of the AFSC, subsequently arranged for Hans and Guy to go to Pendle Hill, the Quaker centre in Pennsylvania. They met a number of people, some of whom Hans knew from Germany. An informal breakfast meeting was also arranged with Eleanor Roosevelt, the wife of the President, who knew about the Bruderhof through Pickett, and she wrote about this

13. Barth, *An Embassy Besieged*, 266.

14. Barth, *No Lasting Home*, xiv–xv, 195–98.

15. For Orie Miller see Sharp, *Calling to Fulfill*.

16. Hans Meier, 'Journey of Guy Johnson and Hans Meier to North America, 1940'. BHA Coll. 0007.

meeting in her 'My Day' column in the *New York Post*. She appeared to have enjoyed meeting her 'unusual visitors', from a group—as she put it—that believed in living 'in real brotherhood', and she reported that the group 'wishes to bring over its members to join those in this country'. The issue of pacifism was not mentioned. 'It is evident', she continued, with her interest in democracy, 'that they would be model citizens and their conception of democracy is certainly a pure and practical one.'[17]

Efforts were also made in Canada. Hopes were raised when Jean Lasserre, the son of Henri Lasserre, who remained deeply interested in the Bruderhof, contacted Hans and Guy to suggest a meeting in Ottawa. Jean Lasserre was active in the French-speaking FoR. Hans and Guy left for Ottawa, to find that two Hutterites had been at Government House the day before but had left, having been told there was no prospect of Bruderhof members from England entering Canada. There was nothing more for Hans and Guy to do in Ottawa, and they took the next train to Toronto, where Jean Lasserre gave them hospitality and then took them to meet David Hofer, whom they were delighted to see again, and another Hutterian leader, Joseph Kleinsasser. The information from these leaders was discouraging. They had been told by a senior official that the Canadian government already had 'sufficient troubles with the Hutterians already in Canada, and therefore they did not wish to have any more enter the country'. From the Hutterite perspective, Canadians were generally more nationalistic than people in England. A community made up largely of Germans and English pacifists was not going to garner support. The Bruderhof had a supportive letter from a member of the Gladstone family to the Canadian Prime Minister, Mackenzie King. However, the Hutterite view was that trying to use this would not achieve anything.[18] In the meantime it was becoming clear that a positive response from the Department of State in Washington, DC, was not likely to be forthcoming.[19] Efforts in North America had reached a dead end.

17. Roosevelt, 'My Day', *New York Post*, 24 September 1940.

18. Hans Meier, 'Journey of Guy Johnson and Hans Meier to North America, 1940'. BHA Coll. 0007.

19. Arnold Mason, 'Early Memories'. BHA Coll. 0006.

A Refuge in Paraguay

When Orie Miller heard of the Bruderhof's failures, he approached the
Paraguayan ambassador to the United States—who was the son-in-law
of the President of Paraguay—on behalf of the Bruderhof, and the ambassador then invited Hans Meier to see him. The result of this contact
was an invitation to the Bruderhof to settle in the Paraguayan Chaco,
or Western Region, a semi-arid part of the country where Mennonites
had colonies.[20] Unsurprisingly, there was no instant enthusiasm for the
Paraguay option on the part of the Bruderhof. Emmy Arnold recalled
the feelings: 'At first this idea seemed very strange to us; we knew next to
nothing about that country. We obtained reading matter about it, and everything seemed very remote to us. To live among monkeys and parrots.
We also read about the people there—the Indians and the half-Indian
and half-Spanish people—about the diseases, the isolation, the insects.'
But the community also realised that there was no security to be found
by remaining in Europe. 'How often', said Emmy, 'did we hear the heavily
armed planes above us at night when everything was blacked out; then
we would hear the bombs crashing and bursting, and the alarm, the signal to go to the air-raid cellars.'[21] There were certain features about Paraguay that were appealing. It was made clear to the Bruderhof that they
would be welcome under the same laws as the Mennonites: freedom of
religion, freedom of education, and freedom from military service were
guaranteed. In any case, this appeared to be the only option on offer. The
Cotswold community instructed Hans and Guy to press ahead.[22]

Some of the Mennonites of the Chaco had left Canada and gone
to Paraguay after the First World War, when there was strong Canadian
anti-German sentiment. Others had arrived from Russia in the 1920s and
1930s, escaping from Stalinist terror. Orie Miller wrote to Jacob Siemens,
the MCC representative in Paraguay, to explain: 'You have no doubt
heard of the small Hutterite group in England, which formerly lived in
Germany and Liechtenstein. . . They are a nonresistant group who live
in two communities in England and now number about 300.' Miller explained about the failed attempts by the Bruderhof to emigrate to Canada

20. For Mennonite experiences, see Dueck, *To Build a Homeland: Home in a
Strange Land*.

21. Emmy Arnold, 'The Beginning and Early Years of the Bruderhof Communities'. BHA Coll. 0288.

22. Arnold Mason, 'Early Memories'. BHA Coll. 0006.

or the United States, and continued: 'The group has therefore decided to accept our help in going to Paraguay for settlement in the Chaco.' The MCC committed itself to serving the Bruderhof in every way possible. They were to be given the choice of any land that was available.[23]

It was agreed that Hans Meier would make his way to Paraguay. Before he did so he took part in a meeting of the MCC in Chicago, which as well as Mennonite representatives included Michael Waldner of the Bon Homme Hutterite Colony and Daniel Wipf of the Rockport Hutterite Colony. At this meeting, assistance from both Mennonites and Hutterites was affirmed.[24] The Cotswold Bruderhof then contacted the Paraguayan consulate in London and dealt with May Stork, who proved very helpful. She came to talk to the Cotswold community personally to help speed up the issue of visas and related questions.[25]

The first group to leave Britain for Paraguay did so on 24 November 1940. The initial hope had been to travel third class on Royal Mail ships, but all these ships had been requisitioned for transporting troops. The only option was to travel first class on ships of the Blue Star Line, which meant paying fares at three times the price of Royal Mail fares.[26] The night before this first group left there was a meeting of the community. Heini Arnold spoke of the deep emotion involved in 'parting from our 80 brothers and sisters' and the wish 'that we may be united again'. The main theme of his talk was the building up of the church. He spoke optimistically of 'the joy of a new building up to be given to us in the new land of Paraguay'. For him the particular place—whether England or Paraguay—was not important. What was crucial was that the church should be a 'city on a hill', with a witness to the nations. Heini quoted Micah 4:1–7, regarding the mountain of the Lord's temple being established and all nations coming to it. He continued: 'Since Jesus has been on the earth, a story has begun that has embraced more and more people.' It began 'with single individuals and then embraced nations, as Micah says, and it shall ultimately embrace the whole earth'. The vision being set before the community by Heini was an eschatological one, grounded in

23. Barth, *No Lasting Home*, 27–30.

24. Meier, *Solange das Licht brennt*, 82–86.

25. Chalres Headland, 'Charles Headland remembers Cotswold and Oaksey'. BHA Coll. 0118.

26. Hardy Arnold, 'The History of the Cotswold and Oaksey Bruderhofs, 1936–1941'. BHA Coll. 0304.

the atonement: the 'ultimate reconciliation' of humanity to God through 'the blood of Jesus'.[27]

The next day the group left by train for Liverpool to board the *Andalucia Star*. This group included several Arnold family members—Emmy, Hardy and Edith and their children, Hans-Hermann and Gertrud and their children—and a number of long-term and experienced Bruderhof members, together with their children. These included Adolf and Martha Braun, Alfred and Gretel Gneiting, Fritz and Sekunda Kleiner, and Kurt and Marianne Zimmermann.[28] At a community meeting in the evening after the group had left, Heini spoke of how the farewells at the station, with so much singing taking place, were 'a witness of brotherhood'.[29]

As this was happening, arrangements had been made to sell Oaksey. It was sold for £16,637, including plant, machinery, furniture, and livestock.[30] From October 1940 on, all those from the Oaksey Bruderhof had to be accommodated at the Cotswold Bruderhof. Another urgent issue was selling the Cotswold site. The money from the sale of the properties needed to be sufficient to provide the community with funds to emigrate: to pay for sea passages and to begin again in a new country. A director of Friends of the Bruderhof Ltd., A. P. I. Cotterell, was interested, along with members of the Wessex Pacifist Community Council, in settling a group of about a hundred COs in an agricultural project and saw the Cotswold Bruderhof as a distinct possibility.[31] On 23 November, D. J. Weight, one of the promoters of this idea, wrote to Arnold Mason to say that he had discussed with representatives from the PPU, the Friends Service Committee, the Methodist Peace Fellowship, and the International Commission the practicalities of purchasing the Cotswold property. The proposals were, he said, 'sympathetically not to say enthusiastically received'. The Mennonites also wanted to help to get the property 'into the right hands'.[32] This attempt to find financing was done privately as the

27. Heini Arnold, community meeting, Cotswold Bruderhof, 23 November 1940. BHA Coll. 0055.

28. Barth, *No Lasting Home*, 186–87.

29. Heini Arnold, community meeting, Cotswold Bruderhof, 24 November 1940. BHA Coll. 0055.

30. Report 'Society of Brothers, Accounts and Report, 1936–1943'. BHA Coll. 0334.

31. Charles Headland, 'Charles Headland remembers Cotswold and Oaksey'. BHA Coll. 0118; Arnold Mason, 'Early Memories'. BHA Coll. 0006.

32. D. J. Weight to Arnold Mason, 23 November 1940. BHA Coll. 0334.

Bruderhof did not want public appeals.[33] The view within the Bruderhof was that the scheme was unlikely to be able to raise the money needed. At this stage the Home Office became involved. On 7 December Arnold Mason wrote to Weight to say that the community had received a visit from a Home Office inspector with a view to their being purchased for a Home Office approved school.[34] A complication was that the Cotswold property was recorded in a register in London of properties which could be not sold without the approval of the authorities. The Home Office and also the London County Council registered claims.[35]

By the end of 1940 the first Bruderhof group to leave Britain had arrived in Paraguay and had met up with Hans Meier and Guy Johnson, who had separately travelled from the United States to South America. A new and challenging period in the life of the Bruderhof had begun. Their departure from England and arrival in Paraguay were covered in different ways in the local and national press. The local *Wilts and Gloucestershire Standard* stated on 11 January 1941 that 'the German members of the colony have left the country and the colony is dispersed'. In a generous comment, it added that allegations by some local people of subversive foreign activity on the part of the community had never been proved and that the group that had emigrated would have 'much to give to the country that accepts them'.[36] A different viewpoint was found in the *Daily Express*. It focussed on one of the English members, Cyril Davies. He was reported as being twenty-three, a young medical doctor and former public schoolboy and cadet officer, and his mother was quoted as saying that she did not agree with his being allowed to 'desert the country which gave him his chance'. She continued: 'I went out to work to help pay for my son's education, which cost a great deal of money'. She had, she said, implored Cyril to do something to help his country as a civilian doctor, but in her view 'he seemed completely under the spell of the foreigners who run the community'.[37]

33. A. P. I. Cotterell to Arnold Mason, 29 November 1940. BHA Coll. 0334.

34. This type of school was for young people who were seen as being in need of reform.

35. Arnold Mason to D. J. Weight, 7 December 1940. BHA Coll. 0344.

36. 'The Cotswold Bruderhof', *Wilts and Gloucestershire Standard*, 11 January 1941.

37. 'Conchie (registered to fight) goes away with Germans to South America', *Daily Express*, 29 January 1941.

Moving In and Moving Out

Despite the later part of 1940 and the early months of 1941 being a time of great upheaval for the Cotswold community, new people continued to join. The novitiate list for September 1940 had twenty names, all of them British.[38] Three of these—Phyllis Bateman, Cyril Davies and John Hinde—were part of the initial group to go to Paraguay. Not all of these twenty novices, however, subsequently joined the community as full members. Charles and Muriel Wright, for example, although they greatly appreciated their time at the Cotswold Bruderhof, moved on.[39] But most remained with the community. One of those who visited the Cotswold Bruderhof at this stage was Kate Streatfeild, who noted that many of those who came to the community to explore what was right for them became convinced that this was indeed their calling, 'and they then consistently followed this calling, in spite of very great pressure from family, friends, churches, employers etc'.[40]

Kate signalled her own intention to join the community, and on 26 October 1940, as she was in the process of leaving her job as a housing manager and selling her house, Hans-Hermann Arnold wrote to her to indicate that 'the majority of members will leave shortly for Paraguay, to build up there a new community of love and brotherhood'. He added that this news was not being made public, but the community wanted Kate to know about the plans in view of her 'vocation of living this life with us'.[41] Kate replied immediately to say she would like 'very much to go out [to Paraguay] with the community'.[42] Although her letter seemed to convey confidence in the future, Stanley Fletcher, aware of the challenges, assured Kate that there was support for her from the community 'especially in an inner way', and particularly regarding any misgivings she might have about Paraguay.[43]

38. Household list, 5 September 1940. BHA Coll. 0055.

39. I am grateful to my friend and colleague at Spurgeon's College, Dr. Nigel Wright, Charles and Muriel's son, for this information. I am also indebted to Nigel for the Foreword to this book, in which he includes family details.

40. Kate Cavanna (formerly Streatfeild), 'Memories'. BHA Coll. 0341.

41. Hans-Hermann Arnold to Kathleen Streatfeild, 26 October 1940. BHA Coll. 0334.

42. Kate Streatfeild to Hans-Hermann Arnold, 30 October 1941. BHA Coll. 0334.

43. Stanley Fletcher to Kate Streatfeild, 1 November 1940. BHA Coll. 0334.

As it sought to manage an influx of new people, the Cotswold community was arranging to bring its continued life in England to an end. On 20 December 1940 Charles Headland and Heini Arnold visited the Home Office in London to clarify a number of issues. By that stage the Home Office had begun to discuss a definite interest that was being shown in the Cotswold property by the London Police Court Mission (LPCM), which was part of the probation service and was involved in running hostels connected with rehabilitation. Charles Headland wrote on 24 December to C. P. Hill at the Home Office to thank him for the time spent with him four days previously and to confirm the core issue raised in the conversation. The community, he said, was happy to move forward with the LPCM and realised 'this stage of the negotiation must take its due course'.[44] He could not have imagined how extended the 'due course' would be. The proposal was for the LPCM to turn the Cotswold property into an approved school, with the advantage of the property being that boys who had got into serious difficulties with the police could get not only schooling there and but also an agricultural training.

The LPCM decided to buy the property. From this point John Gittings, an innovative educationalist then working at the Home Office Children's Department, became a frequent and a friendly visitor to the Cotswold community.[45] The negotiations with the LPCM about the selling price, however, proved very difficult, culminating in a conference at the Home Office with all interested parties. C. P. Hill asked the community to bring to the meeting what would be their minimum selling price. Arnold Mason, who had the benefit of advice within the community from Robert Headland, a land agent, told Hill that the Bruderhof needed £40,000 pounds to meet all loan liabilities, the cost of the journeys by ship to Paraguay, and about £20 per head for each of the members as they settled in Paraguay, an amount which was seen as very modest. The LPCM, for their part, said that the district valuer's price for the buildings and land was £38,500. After discussion £39,500 was agreed.[46]

As negotiations were completed, fares to Paraguay had to be paid. The Home Office then helped in a highly significant way by making very

44. Charles Headland to C. P. Hill, Home Office, 24 December 1940. BHA Coll. 0334.

45. 'Obituary: John Gittings', *The Independent*, 7 November 1996.

46. Charles Headland, 'Charles Headland remembers Cotswold and Oaksey'. BHA Coll. 0118; Arnold Mason, 'Early Memories'. BHA Coll. 0006.

unusual arrangements with Thomas Aggett of the Blue Star Line.[47] The agreement was that all Bruderhof members would be able to travel on a credit basis for a period of time, until the community received payment on the Cotswold sale.[48] By the end of January 1941 it became clear that the sale to the LPCM was going to take considerable time. Over the course of more than a year Charles Headland, using his accountancy experience, was deeply involved. He had to write numerous letters to Thomas Aggett appealing for yet another extension to the credit arrangements because of further delays with the sale. Such exceptional procedures in war time would not have been possible without the firm backing of the British government. The community recognized, however, its financial insecurity. There was also considerable uncertainty over the dates when sailings were to take place.[49]

On 12 January 1941 a small group of six men left on the Blue Star's *Tuscan Star*.[50] By the time this group arrived in Paraguay, the community had decided to move from the Chaco to better land in east Paraguay. The new property was called Primavera.[51] Meanwhile the largest group to leave at one time, numbering 159, had made all the necessary preparations for what they thought was their imminent departure. Almost on the eve of the departure date, the news was received at the Bruderhof that the sailing had been postponed for security reasons. The shipping company's agents gave no details. Everything about voyages was kept secret, because of the danger that some shipping information would enable German submarines to learn of the movement of boats. At last, however, there was confirmation that the Blue Star liner *Avila Star* was definitely sailing from Liverpool in the early part of February.[52] The group sailed on 7 February 1941.

47. As an indication of the size of the Blue Star Line, by 1939 the company had thirty-eight vessels.

48. Charles Headland, 'Charles Headland remembers Cotswold and Oaksey'. BHA Coll. 0118.

49. Arnold Mason, 'Early Memories'. BHA Coll. 0006.

50. Five of these were German and one, Francis Beels from Birmingham, was British. In the following year, in September 1942, the *Tuscan Star* was sunk by a German U-boat.

51. Barth, *No Lasting Home*, 57–68.

52. Charles Headland, 'Charles Headland remembers Cotswold and Oaksey'. BHA Coll. 0118. The *Avila Star* was sunk in July 1942.

Prior to this major event, two Cotswold community meetings took place. At each, Heini Arnold was the main speaker. On 2 February Heini took up the themes of fellowship, forgiveness, and joyful hope. He quoted from Blumhardt—as he did several times—who said that waiting in hope was 'not laziness', but was 'active participation in what God is doing'. It involved listening to God and looking at the signs of the time.[53] After Heini's talk, several members spoke about their experiences. Harry Barron, a recent member who was ready to go with his wife Edith to Paraguay, had spoken to some friends of his in Manchester. Harry had noted 'a real movement amongst the pacifists towards community'.[54] Another contributor was Philip Britts, a horticulturalist and a poet who before joining the Bruderhof had been active in the PPU and had conducted Bible studies on peace.[55] As he thought about experience in the Bruderhof, he was deeply impressed by 'a God who can bring people together from the ends of the earth and forge them together into one body'. Linked with this focus on spiritual experience, Käthe Arnold spoke about prayer, George Vigar reflected on unity, Kate Streatfeild wanted to 'live the life more fully', and Milton Myers foresaw difficulties but hoped the community would be 'bound together' in shared spirituality.[56] The last two speakers were Chris Caine and Joan Britts. Chris had previously been strongly anti-Christian, but through an experience within the Bruderhof he 'was flooded with a love to Christ'.[57] His message concerned the 'sharpness and greatness of the fight' involved in real spiritual experience. Joan Britts' concern was to bring people 'some message of hope and forgiveness'.[58] A second community meeting was held two days later, with Heini stressing the call of God, which meant that 'the love of Christ is so deep in us that we have only one purpose in life, the purpose of God'.[59]

53. Heini Arnold, community meeting, Cotswold Bruderhof, 2 February 1941. BHA Coll. 0055.

54. Harry Barron, community meeting, Cotswold Bruderhof, 2 February 1941. BHA Coll. 0055.

55. *Evening Advertiser*, 27 February 1940.

56. Various speakers, community meeting, Cotswold Bruderhof, 2 February 1941. BHA Coll. 0055.

57. Chris Caine, 'Chris Caine's Life Story'. BHA Coll. 0047.

58. Various speakers, community meeting, Cotswold Bruderhof, 2 February 1941. BHA Coll. 0055.

59. Heini Arnold, community meeting, Cotswold Bruderhof, 4 February 1941. BHA Coll. 0055.

With the departure of this very large group on 7 February, the community was reduced to less than a third of its previous size. Eleven more people left on 14 February on the *Andalucia Star*. One of these, Phyllis Rabbitts (later Woolston), a nurse who had joined the community a year before, wrote about the departure. Like others at the Cotswold community, she had followed with concern the groups that had already gone to Paraguay. She wrote about meeting for worship, with prayer that God would 'care for our loved ones far off in Paraguay', and how on that particular Sunday, before the close of the meeting, a cable had arrived with good news. The Cotswold community members were full of joy and thankfulness and, Phyllis wrote, 'felt so strongly God's leading'.[60] On 13 February 1941 Phyllis wrote to two of her friends, Minnie and John: 'My going this week is very unexpected but I'm taking the place of another whose exit papers are not through yet but also it is felt that a nurse is needed with these who are going.' Ten others living in the community were travelling with her, including three elderly people, two of whom, the Sondheimers, were Jewish refugees whom the Bruderhof had helped to escape from Germany.[61]

Two weeks later Phyllis gave a further explanation to her two friends about what being in the Bruderhof had meant to her. She felt she was standing 'on the brink of something deep, holy and unfathomed, something which is God's'. She continued: 'We are not a sect—but just a body of broken men and women who have felt deeply mankind's great need and this deep realization of our share in this guilt. . . And when a point of utter despair comes to one, then God's Spirit comes in like a flood and His truths can be revealed.' She spoke of how she had learned that 'unity penetrates every aspect of our lives, sacred and secular, worship and work become one'.[62] The difficult task for the future would be to maintain this unity.

Twelve more from the community travelled to South America on 20 March 1941 on the *Empire Star*. This group included Philip and Joan Britts, Paul Cavanna, Robert and Dorothy Headland, and Kate Streatfeild.[63] The loss of so many people who had all been fully involved in community work created problems, in particular the massive challenge

60. Phyllis Woolston (formerly Rabbitts), 'From England to Paraguay'. BHA Coll. 0316.

61. Phyllis Rabbitts to Minnie and John, 13 February 1941. BHA Coll. 0316.

62. Phyllis Rabbitts to Minnie and John, 28 January 1941. BHA Coll. 0316.

63. Barth, *No Lasting Home*, 189.

of sustaining five hundred acres of farmland with a considerable amount of livestock. A farm could not be shut down and started up again. There was also the question of the spring cultivations and sowing. When the LPCM had decided to buy the Cotswold property, they had agreed that it would be right to make arrangements for the carrying on of the existing farm work as far as possible, in cooperation with the Bruderhof members who had not yet emigrated. To add to the challenges, the County War Agricultural Executive Committee (CWAEC) requested that forty acres of potatoes be planted.[64]

Through the initiative of John Gittings, an appointment was made by the LPCM of a retired farmer from Leicestershire to take on the overall responsibility of the farm work.[65] There was also some practical help available from new members. Among these were Johnny Robinson, who was a county agricultural adviser, and his wife, Betty. Johnny soon observed that work on the farm was being done by people who had few agricultural skills. One of these was Gwynn Evans, whom Johnny was amazed to discover was an Anglican clergyman and also an all-round sportsman—a Cambridge Blue. The way in which members of the community were willing to take on any task despite their previous background was, for Johnny, profoundly impressive. He had not been sympathetic to the Christian faith, but he saw in the Bruderhof the outworking of Christian ideals in a 'levelling up' that was, he said, 'beyond my wildest dreams'. Seeing Christian love in action brought him to personal Christian faith and to commitment to the community.[66]

The leaving date for the last large group—ultimately numbering sixty-three—to embark for Paraguay was 23 April 1941, on the *Avila Star*. Twenty extra exit permits were requested by the community. Those on this additional list included two doctors, Marjorie Parker-Gray and Ruth Cassell. When Arnold Mason submitted the list to the Home Office, Sir Alexander Maxwell was away. In his absence, Assistant Under-Secretary Frank Newsam emphatically refused Home Office approval for additional permits. Understandably, he cited the need of the country at a time of national emergency. In a remarkable development, however, this verdict was reconsidered. Maxwell initially took Newsam's side, pointing out that when Bruderhof members had been granted exit permits

64. For wider background see Short, *The Battle of the Fields*.

65. Charles Headland, 'Charles Headland remembers Cotswold and Oaksey'. BHA Coll. 0118.

66. Johnny Robinson, 'Johnny's Journey'. BHA Coll. 0239.

the Home Office had not expected the community to recruit even more members. The response from Arnold Mason was that this was not what had happened. Rather, people had come to the community having heard of its way of life. In what he called 'a quite exceptional measure', Maxwell overturned Newsam's decision, but stressed that no further Bruderhof requests for exit permits would be granted.[67] The group left, and the remaining Cotswold community amounted to nine people, of whom three, Stanley Fletcher and Charles and Hella Headland, were full Bruderhof members.[68]

Struggles to Sell

Before the last group's departure, Stanley Fletcher and Charles Headland were given power of attorney so that they could act on behalf of the Bruderhof in England. The legal aspect of this arrangement was conducted with assistance from Peter Cavanna. At this point Peter had only just come to the community. He had become involved in peace movements in the later 1930s, and in his work as a solicitor began to feel deeply the injustices he saw associated with aspects of the legal system. He wanted to find a better way.[69] Within the community, he was drawn into the negotiations about the sale of the Cotswold property. The legal issues were dealt with by Kingsford, Dorman & Co., located in the Strand, London. Mr Shepherd, a partner in the firm, assured Stanley and Charles that all was in order. He anticipated that the sale would go through in a few weeks' time, mortgages and loans would be paid off, and creditors—especially the Blue Star Line—would receive what was owed them. This proved to be hopelessly optimistic. D. L. Bateson, the acting solicitor for the LPCM, had various questions, including regarding arrangements for power of attorney. His stance was quite aggressive, whereas Shepherd, acting for the community, was rather quiet and gentle, to such an extent that a measure of assertiveness to try to counter Bateson had to come from Stanley and Charles. The issue was complicated by the fact that, in addition to being the solicitor in the case, Bateson was also chairman of the LPCM and had

67. Arnold Mason, 'Early Memories'; Arnold and Gladys Mason, 'Memories'. BHA Coll. 0006.

68. Charles Headland, 'Charles Headland remembers Cotswold and Oaksey'. BHA Coll. 0118.

69. Peter Cavanna, 'Peter Cavanna's Memories'. BHA Coll. 0341.

a personal interest in making a thorough investigation of every detail of the conveyancing.[70]

A letter arrived in early May 1941 from Shepherd to say that the LPCM had now signed the contract for sale, and that this document could be picked up from his office. This seemed promising. Stanley and Charles travelled by train to Paddington Station, walked down the Strand from Trafalgar Square, and turned down Essex Street, at the bottom of which was the solicitor's office. As they turned into this street they noticed the air was filled with the acrid fumes of burning. Water hoses were being deployed and there was general confusion. There had been an air raid. They picked their way through the rubble, and when they reached the bottom of the street it seemed as if all that remained of the solicitor's office was a pile of ruins. They had no idea what had happened until a few days later when Shepherd told them that the attack had come at night, so that nobody had been in the offices, and that the contract was in the firm's strong room, underneath the debris.[71]

It took six weeks to rescue the relevant documents. In the meantime, it was difficult to keep the community in Primavera, Paraguay, abreast of these delays. Letters took about three months to get through. Cables were preferable. After the apparent progress with the Cotswold sale before the summer, some serious difficulties arose in September. The LPCM threatened to make a request to the Home Office that the Cotswold property be requisitioned on account of the delays.[72] The Charity Commissioners were brought into the process. There was talk of the possibility that the sale might not go through until March 1942.[73]

October 1941 brought further struggles for Stanley Fletcher and Charles Headland. Conveyancing documents were sent by the LPCM to Paraguay for the signature of the Bruderhof trustees, despite the local

70. For these memories see Charles Headland, 'Charles Headland remembers Cotswold and Oaksey'. BHA Coll. 0118; Stanley Fletcher, 'The Time between the Cotswold and Wheathill Bruderhof, April 1941–March 1942'. BHA Coll. 0067.

71. Charles Headland, 'Charles Headland remembers Cotswold and Oaksey'. BHA Coll. 0118; Stanley Fletcher, 'The Time between the Cotswold and Wheathill Bruderhof, April 1941–March 1942'. BHA Coll. 0067.

72. John Martin Robinson, in *Requisitioned: The British Country House in the Second World War* (London: Aurum Press, 2014), looks at twenty houses around Britain requisitioned for varied purposes.

73. Charles Headland, 'Charles Headland remembers Cotswold and Oaksey'. BHA Coll. 0118; Stanley Fletcher, 'The Time between the Cotswold and Wheathill Bruderhof, April 1941–March 1942'. BHA Coll. 0067.

power of attorney arrangements previously made, and at the end of the
month a cable arrived from the Primavera community in Paraguay advis-
ing that everything connected with the sale should be left in the hands
of Kingsford, Dorman & Co., and that all those community members
who had exit permits should embark on the next available boat for South
America. It was understandable that if it was now the case that giving
Stanley and Charles the power of attorney was not acceptable to the buy-
ers, there was no point in them remaining in England. However, the cable
left those members and others still in England with a dilemma.

A committed group had begun to gather around the three Bruderhof members. One of these, Belinda Manley, had picked up a copy of the
Bruderhof's *Children in Community* in a bookshop and wanted to find
out more. She was a pacifist and, as a teacher, was deeply concerned for
the education of children, and she came to the view that community was
a crucial element which had been missing in her search up to that point.
She had read about Eric Gill's community and then visited the Bruderhof
as a guest. She found about twenty people there, joined in daily worship,
meals, work and discussions, and came to the conclusion that 'the life
as the Bruderhof lived it' was right, although a struggle continued for
several months, in spring 1941 she became a novice.[74]

The problem with the instruction from Primavera to leave England
was that by October 1941 there were at least a dozen people, like Belinda,
who did not have permission to leave the country but who had given up
everything to join the Bruderhof. The issue of what to do for them was
a serious question of conscience. They needed either permission to leave
from the Home Office, or for some form of community life to continue in
England. Stanley and Charles decided to send a cable to Paraguay setting
out how they saw the current situation.[75]

In order to explore the first option, Stanley and Charles went to see
Sir Alexander Maxwell at the Home Office, in the hope that he, perhaps
with support from Ernest Cooper, might be able to continue to aid the
community. They discussed with him the ongoing situation with the
LPCM. However, they were aware that asking for permission for more
people to leave the country was not going to be regarded favourably. As
could have been predicted, Maxwell was annoyed about the request. He
again said that it seemed new Bruderhof members were being recruited.

74. Manley, *Through Streets Broad and Narrow*, 20–27.

75. Charles Headland, 'Charles Headland remembers Cotswold and Oaksey'.
BHA Coll. 0118.

Stanley explained once more that the community had in no way sought out these new people. While this was true from one perspective, when Belinda Manley came to the end of her initial stay with the Bruderhof, Stanley said to her: 'Just remember that if you have really seen what our life is about and feel it is right as you said, you will find that it will never leave you. However far you run away from it, you cannot escape it.'[76]

Sir Alexander asked Stanley for a list of the new people with all their personal details, and a document was prepared and given to him. Any hopes that had been raised, however, were soon dashed. When Maxwell saw that the list consisted of young people of military age he was adamant that he could not help. He explained that he could not possibly show the list to the Home Secretary.[77] Later, in correspondence with Arnold Mason, Maxwell reiterated his view that it was 'unfortunate' (his real feelings were probably stronger) that during the unexpectedly long period in which legal issues were discussed, Stanley Fletcher 'and the other Brothers' had gathered around them 'a number of fresh adherents'. Maxwell told Arnold Mason that he found this to be 'contrary to the purpose and spirit of the arrangement which I made with you'. He continued: 'The object of the special arrangement made with you was to enable your adherents to remain together as a united body and to go together to Paraguay. On the plea that all your adherents should be treated alike, permission was secured as a quite exceptional measure—despite the general restrictions on all subjects who are liable to be called upon for national service.'[78]

Around this same time, the Home Office, in conjunction with the LPCM, made a payment of £6,000 (with the remainder to follow) towards the Cotswold property and demanded that the Bruderhof vacate the property. A further cable was sent to Primavera, asking for advice. On 22 February 1942, a reply was received from Primavera which expressed complete understanding of the situation. This communication was received with great enthusiasm. There was still hope in Paraguay that exit permits might be forthcoming, but in the meantime Stanley Fletcher was given authority to undertake whatever community tasks in England seemed right. This took away the uncertainty of the previous period.[79]

76. Manley, *Through Streets Broad and Narrow*, 25.

77. The larger issue with which the British authorities were dealing was exit permits being sought by young Irish men: Wood, *Britain, Ireland and the Second World War*, 142.

78. Sir Alexander Maxwell to Arnold Mason, 15 May 1942. BHA Coll. 0055.

79. Stanley Fletcher, 'The Time between the Cotswold and Wheathill Bruderhof,

Struggles in Seeking Direction

Prior to these events, it had been hard at times to find a direction. Individuals had struggled. Hella Headland felt the whole departure and separation very deeply, especially as it reminded her of her experiences four years before when the Rhön came to a forced end. Others who were part of the small community at this point were Norman Price, from Wales, who was in the novitiate, and five others—May Davis, Muriel Marsh, Eric Phillips, Bernard Robertshaw, and Arthur Woolston—who were at that stage helping in the community and who had all asked to join the novitiate. In the case of Eric Phillips, he had hoped that his wife, Kathleen, with their small son, would join the community, but this did not happen. On 10 July 1941, Eric and Bernard Robertshaw left on the *Andalucia Star* for Paraguay.[80] Arthur Woolston wrote that when Eric left his wife behind this was 'a very, very hard situation for both of them'. As the issue of the effect on some marriages of one partner joining the Bruderhof was discussed, Arthur and others discovered that Stanley Fletcher's wife had also refused to join the community.[81] In 1945 Mr Justice Denning was to grant his wife, Irene Fletcher, a divorce from Stanley on the grounds that it was unreasonable for a husband to expect his wife to live in the community 'unless she feels called to do so'. For his part, Stanley denied deserting her. The case was widely reported in the British national press.[82]

During May and June 1941, a number of people arrived at Ashton Keynes hoping to join the community. Each had their own struggles. Wilfred Crossley, who had been a musician, then a tramp, and then a member of another community, decided to return to the Bruderhof, where he had been before. He now thought it had been a mistake to leave. He was followed by Dick Whitty, who had also been at the Bruderhof previously. As a serious Roman Catholic who at one time had studied for the Catholic priesthood, Dick Whitty had gone through a crisis, and he now considered his life should be with the Bruderhof. Norah Caine, whose husband Chris, with their son David, had already settled in Paraguay,

---

April 1941–March 1942'. BHA Coll. 0067; Charles Headland, 'A History of the Founding of the Wheathill Bruderhof'. BAH Coll. 0118.

80. In October 1942, the *Andalucia Star* was torpedoed by a German submarine and sunk.

81. Arthur Woolston, 'Arthur Woolston's Story'. BHA Coll. 0316.

82. For example, the *News Chronicle*, 8 February 1945; *The Daily Telegraph*, 8 February 1945.

also arrived at Ashton Keynes, to confirm that with their young baby, Robin, she now wished to join her family and the community in Primavera. She had previously had serious reservations about whether this was right for her.[83]

By this time part of the Cotswold property was occupied by the LPCM-run school, and the small Bruderhof community group was given some paid work by the school, mostly looking after the buildings and the farm. Initially the small group operated largely in what had been the Bruderhof houses where children's activities had taken place. In the summer of 1941, however, there were further additions to the group and the community moved as a self-contained unit into the old printing house. This accommodated most of them, with a fairly large room to spare for a dining room, and also a room for an office. Among those who joined in this period were Peter Rutherford, and a couple, Jack and Annie Ellison. Jack had taken leave from his job as a bus conductor.[84]

In September Norah Caine and baby Robin, together with May Davis, left for Paraguay. Earlier in the year May Davis, who was one of the Scott family of the *Manchester Guardian*,[85] and her husband Harry, had visited the Cotswold Bruderhof together and had been impressed by the experiences. Both of them were trained ceramists, having studied with the well-known studio potter and art teacher Bernard Leach, of St Ives, Cornwall, who was regarded as the father of studio pottery.[86] Subsequent to their Bruderhof visit, Harry Davis had been teaching ceramics in West Africa, at Achimota School in Ghana (then the Gold Coast), and despite his best efforts he could not get back to Britain quickly. However, he and May jointly agreed that they would meet in Paraguay. May's skills in brick-making and pottery were judged to be needed in Primavera. Later Harry was able to join her there.

The steamer carrying Norah, Robin, and May left from Tilbury Docks, London, on 13 September, and went up the east coast of Britain, docking at Leith, the port for Edinburgh, where it stayed some time. The journey to Edinburgh was a dangerous one, with attacks from German aircraft and bombs dropped round the ship. When the community

83. Charles Headland, 'Charles Headland remembers Cotswold and Oaksey'. BHA Coll. 0118.

84. Arthur Woolston, 'Arthur Woolston's Story'. BHA Coll. 0316,

85. See Ellis, *Trust Ownership and the Future of News*, 138–142. The Scotts were a newspaper-owning family. From 1936 the Scott Trust owned the *Manchester Guardian*.

86. Bernard Leach wrote *A Potter's Book* (London: Faber & Faber, 1940).

received a letter with news of the frightening trip and the likelihood of a few days spent docked in Leith, it was decided that Stanley Fletcher and Hella Headland would go up to Scotland to try to visit the ship. This did not turn out to be possible. They were not allowed by military authorities to go anywhere near where the ship was moored. However, some messages of encouragement were exchanged. Later the steamer left and travelled all the way around the north of Scotland and eventually out to the North Atlantic, to arrive safely some weeks later in South America.[87]

May Davis' sister, Olive Scott, had also visited the Bruderhof and had been challenged by the life of the community. Along with them, Laurence Scott, their brother, visited and was interested but did not join. Olive was at that time a student in Galashiels, in the borders of Scotland, and was engaged to Bill, who was a church organist in Galashiels. After her visit, Olive left Ashton Keynes determined to return when she had worked through the issue of her engagement. There were also struggles due to the opposition of her parents. Having settled back in her course in Galashiels in October 1941 it seemed she was having second thoughts about the community. Stanley Fletcher and Hella Headland decided to travel to Scotland to talk to her. They stayed two days, and on the second day, a Sunday, Stanley felt it was wrong to continue the conversations. But a dramatic turn of events was in store. Olive went to church that Sunday evening. The Bible reading in the service was from Paul's letter to the Corinthians, in which Paul contrasts the wisdom of God with the wisdom of the world. Olive took this as indicating a direction for her. Olive and Bill both made their way to Ashton Keynes. Bill believed the community was cutting itself off from the struggles of humanity. Further drama followed. Olive's father, John Scott, arrived at Ashton Keynes and announced, 'You will get my daughter only over my dead body!' He was offered a guest room and stayed two days, refusing all the food he was offered. He had long talks with Olive, and towards the end of the second day he told Stanley he had become convinced that Olive had made her own decision and he could not stand in her way. Later, he and his wife became supportive of the community.[88]

87. Charles Headland, 'Charles Headland remembers Cotswold and Oaksey'. BHA Coll. 0118; Stanley Fletcher, 'The Time between the Cotswold and Wheathill Bruderhof, April 1941–March 1942'. BAH Coll. 0067.

88. Stanley Fletcher, 'The Time between the Cotswold and Wheathill Bruderhof, April 1941–March 1942'. BHA Coll. 0067; Arthur Woolston, 'The Last Days at the Cotswold Bruderhof'. BHA Coll. 0316.

Among those who had ongoing contact with the community and who were seeking direction in this period were Ken and Julie Gough, who had been part of a PPU group with Arthur Woolston. The Goughs were friendly with Robert and Olwen Rimes, who knew the community through the Rimes' grain business in Cirencester, and with Geoffrey and Phyllis Welham, who had defended the community in the newspaper. These couples wanted communal life but they did not want to go with the Bruderhof to Paraguay. Arising out of the aspirations they had, the Rimes and the Welhams, together with another couple, John and Peggy Bazeley, bought a farm and set up the Adam's Cot community. Their beliefs about religion were quite disparate, which eventually caused tensions. For a time, George Ineson, who had been part of a community influenced by the novelist D. H. Lawrence, was drawn to Adam's Cot. George and Connie Ineson had also been at High House, Bromsash.[89] The three main couples in Adam's Cot were to join the Bruderhof. Ineson moved on, and later, having become a Roman Catholic, established a Catholic community at Whitley Court, near Prinknash Abbey, on the edge of the Cotswolds. In the book about his experiences, *Community Journey*, he spoke of the example of the Bruderhof.[90] Three members from the High House group, Mary Cawsey and Kenneth and Barbara Greenyer, joined the Bruderhof.[91] The Cotswold community continued to offer direction to those seeking an expression of Christian communal life.

A Renewed Community

During the last two months of 1941 a number of people either arrived at the community or, having already been living as part of the community, took steps of commitment. Each had made their own journey, often involving struggle. Belinda Manley, for example, although she was impressed by the Bruderhof's *Children in Community*, wondered if the religious terminology of the book could communicate with the social issues of the day.[92] Mari Attwater (later Marsden) was similarly influenced by reading Bruderhof publications. She was part of a circle of artists and

89. Peggy Bazeley, 'The Life Story of Peggy Bazeley'. BHA Coll. 0318.

90. Ineson, *Community Journey*, 25, 43–49; Armytage, *Heavens Below*, 417.

91. Charles Headland, 'Charles Headland remembers Cotswold and Oaksey'. BHA Coll. 0118.

92. Manley, *Through Streets Broad and Narrow*, 20.

teachers in the south of England who wanted to work out their ideals, including in the area of advocating peace. After making visits to Ashton Keynes, and trying community with other friends, Mari became part of the Bruderhof on Advent Sunday 1941.[93] Immediately after this, several guests arrived. One of these, Robert Horniman, a friend of Mari Attwater's, was from the Horniman tea family and was a member of the PPU. He entered into serious discussions about community life but was not convinced. A further guest was Stanley Salt, who had worked at the Dick Sheppard Centre, and was about to take a post helping evacuated children. For him, this post was his calling. Another, Fred Kemp, had been visiting communities in England, and Arthur Woolston knew him from Elmsett. His background was in farming, in Sussex, and this was valuable at Ashton Keynes.[94]

The community sought to offer new dimensions of life to those who joined, and at the same time the new members enriched the community and contributed to ongoing renewal. Eileen Taylor (later Robertshaw), who joined in December 1941, brought fresh inspiration through her knowledge of radical movements in England in the seventeenth century. Eileen had known the Bruderhof through her sister and brother-in-law, Margaret and Fred Goodwin, and when she started as a student at St Hugh's College in Oxford University she heard a talk by Christopher Hill, whose first book, *The English Revolution 1640*, was published in 1940.[95] Through Hill, who was to become a renowned historian in the Marxist tradition, Eileen—who already had a keen interest in socialism—learned about the Diggers or True Levellers, a seventeenth-century group that believed in community of property and in equality of all people. A group of Oxford students, including Eileen, made plans to compile a book of the writings of Gerard Winstanley, the main Digger leader, and they copied out old manuscripts from various universities, during the summer of 1940. A volume, *The Works of Gerard Winstanley*, edited and with an introduction by Sabine, was published in 1941.[96] Eileen was involved in producing a small collection of extracts from Winstanley. A book Hans-Hermann Arnold had studied, *The Levellers and the English Revolution*, by Henry Holorenshaw, was passed around at Ashton Keynes. Interest in

93. Mari Marsden, 'Memories by Mari Marsden'. BHA Coll. 0197.

94. Arthur Woolston, 'Arthur Woolston's Story'. BHA Coll. 0316.

95. Christopher Hill, *The English Revolution 1640* (London: Lawrence & Wishart, 1940).

96. Sabine, ed., *The Works of Gerard Winstanley*.

the Diggers grew within the community, especially because the move-ment had drawn from the teaching of Jesus, and the group at Ashton Keynes started learning and singing songs such as Winstanley's call to 'Stand up now, stand up now', with its line announcing that 'the gentry must come down, and the poor shall wear the crown'.[97]

This period saw joys and difficulties. One of the joys was that Charles and Hella Headland were able to adopt a child. They went to Croydon to bring back Elizabeth, who was six months old. She was welcomed into the community in December 1941. In another family development, to Ei-leen Taylor's surprise her mother, Vera, who was a widow, also joined the community for a time. Eileen realised that she 'now needed to strive not only for a right relationship with these unknown people [in the commu-nity], but with mother, too'. Eileen also realised that she herself 'still had no personal relationship with Jesus'. Her journey involved reading verses from Paul's letter to the Philippians which included the words 'that I may know Him and the power of His resurrection, and the fellowship of His sufferings' (Phil. 3:7–11). In February 1942 Eileen was baptised.[98] There were also family difficulties. For example, Harry Fossard, a CO working in Halifax, came to the community in early 1942 but his wife Nellie was not drawn to the Bruderhof way of life. There was sympathy for Harry, who it was said was living with a 'divided heart', and sadness, but the community at that time believed in readiness to leave family members.[99]

Because of the growth in the numbers of people staying, includ-ing guests who came to visit, the community decided to take over three empty rooms in the attic of the workshop. The leaders of the approved school were highly annoyed—even though they had still not paid for the Cotswold property—and cut off all the community's supply of vegetables and milk.[100] Christmas 1941 was celebrated at Ashton Keynes by a com-mitted circle of nineteen people, plus guests. In preparation for the fes-tivities, Dick Whitty and Arthur Woolston went out on bicycles in search of branches and holly. Near Cirencester they found an ample supply of foliage and berries on a large tree down a lane. They lopped off as much foliage, with berries, as they could get in a sack, but just as they were about to leave a burly policeman cycled down the lane and told them they

97. Arthur Woolston, 'Arthur Woolston's Story'. BHA Coll. 0316.

98. Eileen Robertshaw, 'Life Story'. BHA Coll. 0308.

99. Stanley Fletcher, 'The Time between the Cotswold and Wheathill Bruderhof, April 1941–March 1942'. BHA Coll. 0067.

100. Arthur Woolston, 'Arthur Woolston's Story'. BHA Coll. 0316.

were stealing from the Earl of Bathurst. The policeman explained that the Earl's horse racing track crossed the road at this point. After Dick and Arthur explained about the community, the policeman allowed them to keep half their spoils. Over the Christmas period, although the group was now almost entirely British (the exception being Hella Headland), some German traditions were still sung. On Christmas Eve, everyone gathered to sing carols, eat together, and then walk in a procession, still singing, to the dining room, where a tree was lit up with candles. On Christmas Day the community sang at breakfast, dinner, and supper many of the carols in *The Oxford Book of Carols*. Stanley Fletcher spoke about Christmases in the Cotswold Bruderhof, and Hella described times at the Rhön.[101]

During January and February several new members joined the novitiate. A letter from Primavera affirmed the task in England: to build up a new Bruderhof.[102] Early in 1942, therefore, members began to seek a suitable new farm. With the money coming from the sale of the Cotswold property it was now possible to make a purchase. On one of these journeys Wilfred Crossley, who was part of the novitiate and who knew farming areas well, and Charles Headland, were in Ludlow and found out about Lower Bromdon Farm, which had plenty of accommodation, much of it run-down, and almost two hundred acres of farming land. Although the land was poor quality, they felt that this could be the right location. Hella Headland and Belinda Manley viewed the farm, and their feeling was that the community did not need to look further.[103] Stanley Fletcher also made a trip and confirmed that this was the right place.[104] There was excitement at the movement taking place.

On 9 March 1942 the contract for the new farm was signed, and soon the whole group from Ashton Keynes had settled at what would become the Wheathill Bruderhof. There was one child, and there were nineteen adults, nine women and ten men—Stanley Fletcher, Hella and Charles Headland with Elizabeth, Jack and Annie Ellison, Peter Rutherford, Norman Price, Wilfred Crossley, Douglas Turner, Harry Fossard, Dick Whitty, Fred Kemp, Olive Scott, Mari Attwater, Mary Cawsey, Vera

101. Arthur Woolston, 'Arthur Woolston's Story'. BHA Coll. 0316.

102. Stanley Fletcher, 'The Time between the Cotswold and Wheathill Bruderhof, April 1941–March 1942'. BHA Coll. 0067.

103. Manley, *Through Streets Broad and Narrow*, 32.

104. Stanley Fletcher, 'The Time between the Cotswold and Wheathill Bruderhof, April 1941–March 1942'. BHA Coll. 0067.

Taylor, Eileen Taylor, Muriel Marsh, and Belinda Manley.[105] Most were relatively new members.[106] Almost immediately others began to express interest in joining, and Kenneth and Barbara Greenyer, with their daughter Ann, did so in April.

Because of the lack of experienced members, there were plans to send leaders from Primavera to Wheathill. Heini and Annemarie Arnold were considered, but it must have been no surprise when they did not receive visas. Sydney and Marjorie Hindley were able to come, although Sir Alexander Maxwell was most unhappy about the request, telling Arnold Mason on 15 May 1942 that bringing members back to England would 'make it appear that the arguments by which permission for their departure was obtained were fallacious and that the special concession granted to the Brotherhood has proved to be unjustified'. He did not see the justification for a new Bruderhof community in England.[107] Nonetheless, this is what happened. That constitutes a separate story.

105. Charles Headland, 'Charles Headland remembers Cotswold and Oaksey'. BHA Coll. 0118.

106. Eileen Robertshaw, 'Life Story'. BHA Coll. 0308.

107. Sir Alexander Maxwell to Stanley Fletcher, 15 May 1942. BHA Coll. 0055.

Conclusion

The story of the community that became known as the Bruderhof began with experiences of spiritual renewal in the early twentieth century. Eberhard and Emmy Arnold, together with and her sister Else von Hollander, were the main shaping forces in the emergence of the Bruderhof. All became committed to spiritual renewal, especially during the years 1905–07. This commitment involved connections with international movements, such as the Salvation Army, the YMCA, the Keswick holiness movement, Pentecostalism, and the Student Christian Movement. There were, however, tensions about the way in which renewal should be worked out in ecclesial terms. This led to Eberhard, Emmy, Else and others to break with the Lutheran Church and to be baptised as believers. The example of the Anabaptists of the sixteenth century became increasingly important as their ideas evolved. Although international connections flourished in the period before the First World War, the war brought division and destruction. For Eberhard Arnold, the hatred unleashed during the war also contributed to his embracing pacifism. Following the end of the war, intentional involvement in international work began again and slowly deepened.

The links between the Bruderhof and Britain, which culminated in the establishment of the Cotswold community in 1936, owed a great deal to Quakers from England who offered help to children in Germany after the First World War. Eberhard Arnold came to know and respect the Quakers for their combination of spiritual and social involvement. The community which came into being in 1920 at Sannerz saw itself as linked to wider movements for peace and spiritual renewal. Eberhard became part of the international Fellowship of Reconciliation. These links, especially at a personal level with Quakers such as John Stephens, led to Hardy Arnold spending a year as a student at Birmingham University. It

214

was during this time that it became evident that a number of people in Britain were ready to listen to the Bruderhof message, brought through Hardy Arnold, about communal Christian living. The follow-up to the year Hardy Arnold spent in England was a visit by Eberhard and Hardy, during which existing connections were deepened and new connections were made. By this time the witness of the Bruderhof in Germany was coming under increasing threat. The crisis reached a climax with the closure of the community in Germany. The Bruderhof had in the meantime established a community in Wiltshire and this now became the centre of the communal peace witness of the Bruderhof.

Dennis Hardy suggests in *Utopian England* that the experience of communities in England in the early decades of the twentieth century was one of 'mixed fortune'. Looking at their limitations, he notes that most of the communities were small, 'typically with memberships numbered in single figures, and ephemeral'. He sees another limitation as a marked lack of political engagement. Thirdly, he sees the communities as intellectually weak.[1] The experience of the Cotswold Bruderhof does not support this argument, something that Dennis Hardy partly recognises. He acknowledges the influence of the Bruderhof, suggesting that it became the focal point 'for a much wider range of spiritually related experiments in a troubled period'.[2] While most communities in this period were small, the Bruderhof reached a significant size, and those who joined were almost all younger people and many were well educated. On the question of political involvement, the Bruderhof was aware that its German members were living in a host country and had been received as refugees. They expressed thankfulness for the tolerance they knew in Britain, compared with the repression they had experienced in Germany. At the same time, they found ways to involve themselves in movements such as the PPU and FoR, significant groups which opposed militarism. Finally, through *The Plough* and other publications, the Bruderhof engaged in vigorous intellectual endeavours.

As it shared in wider witness, the Cotswold community was intent on building up its own communal life. There were rhythms of work and worship, and there were determined efforts to make the community financially viable, which meant seeking help from friends. At the heart of the community, however, was the consciousness that each person was

1. Hardy, *Utopian England*, 271–73.
2. Hardy, *Utopian England*, 272.

called to follow Christ and to do this together. In this journey of discipleship, the Christian year was important. As Kathleen Hamilton described of the first Sunday of Advent, the whole community, except the smaller children, met outside the dining room at 8.30am. They then filed in 'singing a glorious Advent song'. The dining room was decorated with pine twigs and there were red candles. One candle was lit for the first Sunday of Advent. There were readings from Isaiah and other Old Testament prophets about the coming of the Messiah. Songs were sung about the light and warmth of God's truth and love and how this light was to shine in the world.[3]

This wide spiritual vision was somewhat at odds with the outlook of the Hutterites in North America, despite the fact that since 1930 the Bruderhof in Europe had been part of the Hutterian movement. In the period of greatest crisis for the community in Germany, two Hutterite Elders who were in Europe at the time gave valuable assistance. Nonetheless, there were serious tensions at the Cotswold Bruderhof in the time the Hutterite Brothers were there, because of the desire of those who were in the community to be active in witness, a vision that the North American Hutterites had lost. Despite these differences of view, when the Second World War began and anti-German feeling grew in Britain, the Cotswold community began to investigate whether it would be possible to emigrate to North America to become part of Hutterite life there. This proved not to be possible, and at a time when the community was continuing to grow and exercise influence in Britain, the only option, if it was to remain an international community, was to emigrate to Paraguay.

Phyllis Rabbitts, a recent British member of the community, summed up this period: 'The idea of the whole community being transferred from one country to another in war time was something one could not grasp. It seemed too great a miracle. War had been waged between England and Germany for just over a year when the first group of the community left on November 24th, 1940 for Paraguay'. She continued: 'We had realized for many months the insecurity of our position in England as there was so much hate growing in the hearts of the general populace. This could be understood because we had many German members, also the pacifism of our English members roused a bitter spirit in nationalistic minds. Although the Government of England and local officials were tolerant and understanding, our economic position was getting acute because of

3. Kathleen Hamilton to her mother, 1 December 1937. BHA Coll. 0115.

the local hostility which crippled the business side of our life.' The community as a whole felt 'a definite leading from God that we should leave the country'. A 'well-built up Bruderhof' was being left behind, the fruit of five years of 'struggle and hard work'. But now, it seemed, 'the time had come to lay down one's tools and leave all this and to pick them up again in another country which we could not choose for ourselves'.[4]

Almost a century after its beginning in Sannerz, the Bruderhof consists of over 2,900 men, women, and children—families and single people—living in twenty-three intentional communities of differing sizes, most in Europe and North America. Communities have flourished again in Britain. There is a sense of the international nature of the movement. In 2012 the Bruderhof produced a document, *Foundations of Our Faith and Calling*, which was 'the outcome of discussion and study within the Bruderhof communities about the basis of our life together'. There was an extended exercise of drafting and redrafting of the text that concluded in June 2012 when all Bruderhof members worldwide adopted the text.[5]

This book is not intended to be a theological evaluation of the beliefs or spirituality of the Bruderhof.[6] Nor is its investigation of the period between 1936 and 1942 comprehensive. More could be done, for example, by looking at Home Office files. However, what this book has sought to do is to bring to life a period in which an international Christian community witnessed to the reality of the message of Christ at a time of great upheaval and to address the very hard decisions it had to make in order to remain united as a community. As Phyllis Rabbitts put it, referring to the move from Britain to South America, this was 'madness from a human and worldly standpoint', but the risk was 'for God's cause and He was leading, therefore we could do it'.[7] Although the future would be far more complicated than anyone could have foreseen, this sums up well the spirit that energised the Cotswold community.

4. Phyllis Woolston, 'From England to Paraguay'. BHA Coll. 0316.

5. *Foundations of Our Faith and Calling*.

6. For Bruderhof spirituality see Randall, '*Church community is a gift of the Holy Spirit*'.

7. Phyllis Woolston, 'From England to Paraguay'. BHA Coll. 0316.

Bibliography

Manuscripts of the Bruderhof Historical Archive (BHA) in Walden, New York

The following collections of Personal Papers from the Bruderhof Historical Archive (BHA) were consulted for this research. For other documents from the BHA, complete citations are given in the footnotes. Page numbers are not used in the citation of unpublished manuscripts from BHA. Shortened versions of the names of some of the documents listed below are used in the footnotes.

Arnold, Clara, 'His Way: Pictures from Eberhard Arnold's Childhood and Youth Put Together from His Own Notes and My Memories', 1936. BHA Coll. 0288_05.

Arnold, Eberhard, and Emmy Arnold, Correspondence. BHA Coll. 0288_02.

Arnold Emmy, 'The Beginning and Early Years of the Bruderhof Communities'. Unpublished portions of memoir published as *Torches Together*, 1963. BHA Coll. 0288.

Arnold, Hans-Hermann, and Gertrud Arnold, Correspondence. BHA Coll. 0190.

Arnold, Hardy, 'The History of the Cotswold and Oaksey Bruderhofs, 1936–1941'. Unpublished memoir, ca 1981. BHA Coll. 0304.

Arnold, Heini, and Annemarie Arnold, Correspondence. BHA Coll. 0005.

Arnold, Hermann, 'Almbruderhof 1935–Cotswold 1936'. Unpublished memoir, 1970. BHA Coll. 0015.

Bazeley, Peggy, 'The Life Story of Peggy Bazeley'. Unpublished memoir, ca. 2003. BHA Coll. 0318.

Caine, Chris, 'Chris Caine's Life Story'. Unpublished memoir, 1987. BHA Coll. 0047.

Cavanna, Kate, 'Memories'. Unpublished memoir, ca. 1970. BHA Coll. 0341.

Cavanna, Peter, 'Peter Cavanna's Memories'. Unpublished memoir, ca. 1970. BHA Coll. 0341.

Dyroff, Winifred, 'The Cotswold Bruderhof'. Unpublished memoir, 1970. BHA Coll. 0066

Dyroff, Winifred, 'Recollections of My Early Years'. Unpublished memoir, ca. 1997. BHA Coll. 0066.

Dyroff, Winifred, 'Telling about Cotswold'. Unpublished memoir, 1992. BHA Coll. 0066.

Fletcher, Stanley, 'Stanley Fletcher tells his Life Story'. Unpublished memoir, ca. 1974. BHA Coll. 0067.

Fletcher, Stanley, 'Tramp Preachers'. Unpublished interview, 1965. BHA Coll. 0067.

Fletcher, Stanley, 'The Time between the Cotswold and Wheathill Bruderhof, April 1941–March 1942'. Unpublished memoir, ca. 1970. BHA Coll. 0067.

Goodwin, Margaret, 'Margaret Goodwin tells of Fred Goodwin'. Unpublished memoir, 1992. BHA Coll. 0102.

Hasenberg, Kathleen, 'My Story'. Unpublished memoir, ca. 1992. BHA Coll. 0115.

Headland, Charles, 'A History of the Founding of the Wheathill Bruderhof'. Letter to communities in Paraguay, 1946. BHA Coll. 0118.

Headland, Charles, 'Charles Headland remembers Cotswold and Oaksey, July 1937 to April 1941'. Unpublished memoir, ca. 1970. BHA Coll. 0118.

Headland, Charles, 'Life Story'. Unpublished memoir, ca. 1993. BHA Coll. 0118.

Hinde, John, 'John Hinde's Life Story'. Unpublished memoir, ca. 2000. BHA Coll. 0395.

Hinde, John, 'Memories of Cotswold'. Unpublished memoir, 1970. BHA Coll. 0395.

Hindley, Marjorie, 'Marjorie Hindley's Memories'. Unpublished memoir, 1974. BHA Coll. 0324.

Hindley, Sydney A. 'Statement to the National Service (Armed Forces) Office', 2 July, 1940 BHA Coll. 0324

Hofer, David, 'Diary of David Hofer Vetter'. Unpublished translation of Hofer, David, *Reise nach Europa 1937*. Eli, Manitoba: James Valley Book Center, 1990; translation BHA Staff, 1977. BHA Coll. 0484.

Land, Ruth, 'Ruth Land memory book'. Unpublished memoir, ca 2010. BHA Coll. 0346.

Marsden, Mari, 'Memories by Mari Marsden'. Unpublished memoir, 1970. BHA Coll. 0197.

Mason, Arnold, 'Arnold Mason tells about his life'. Community meeting, Rhön Bruderhof, 11 October 1935. BHA Coll. 0006.

Mason, Arnold, 'Early Memories'. Unpublished memoir, ca 1984. BHA Coll. 0006.

Mason, Arnold and Gladys Mason, 'Memories'. Unpublished memoir, 1971. BHA Coll. 0006.

Meier, Hans, 'Journey of Guy Johnson and Hans Meier to North America, 1940'. Unpublished memoir, 1973. BHA Coll. 0007.

Paul, Tommy, 'Life Story of Tommy Paul'. Unpublished memoir, ca. 1996. BHA Coll. 0219.

Robertshaw, Eileen, 'Life Story'. Unpublished memoir, ca. 1974. BHA Coll. 0308.

Robinson, Johnny, 'Johnny's Journey'. Unpublished memoir, ca. 1993. BHA Coll. 0239.

Stangl, Rachel, 'Life of Oma Ivy'. Unpublished memoir, ca. 2002. BHA Coll. 0252.

Stevenson, Alan, 'Bruderhof Memories'. Unpublished memoir, ca. 1991. BHA Coll. 0314.

Stevenson, Alan, 'Something of My Life'. Unpublished memoir, ca. 1990. BHA Coll. 0314.

Stevenson, Nellie, 'Life Story'. Unpublished memoir, 1990. BHA Coll. 0314.

Trapnell, Nancy, 'Memories of Cotswold and Paraguay'. Unpublished memoir, 2002. BHA Coll. 0347.

Trapnell, Nancy, 'Nancy Trapnell tells about her father'. Unpublished memoir, 1996. BHA Coll. 0273.

Wegner, Gerd, 'Memories'. Unpublished memoir, ca. 1970. BHA Coll. 0475.

Woolston, Arthur, 'Arthur Woolston's Story'. Unpublished memoir, ca. 2002. BHA Coll. 0316.

Woolston, Arthur, 'The Last Days at the Cotswold Bruderhof', unpublished memoir, 1941. BHA Coll. 0316.

Woolston, Phyllis, 'From England to Paraguay'. Unpublished memoir, 1941. BHA Coll. 0316.

Zimmermann, Kurt, 'To My Dear Annemarie: A Short Survey of our Life Together within the Communal Life'. Unpublished memoir, 1934–1938. BHA Coll. 0319, Box 1, Folder 1–2.

Archive of the Fellowship of Reconciliation, London School of Economics and Political Science, Houghton St, London, WC2A 2AE

Minutes of the Executive Committee of the Fellowship of Reconciliation, 11 April 1935, COLL MISC 0456/3/5.

Minutes of the International Committee of the Fellowship of Reconciliation, 1 June 1920, COLL MISC 0456/5/5.

Minutes of the International Committee of the Fellowship of Reconciliation, 7 November 1921, COLL MISC 0456/5/5.

Minutes of the General Committee of the Fellowship of Reconciliation, 15 and 16 March 1937. COLL MISC 0456/1/6.

Minutes of the General Committee of the Fellowship of Reconciliation, 14 and 15 June 1937. COLL MISC 0456/1/6.

Minutes of the General Committee of the Fellowship of Reconciliation, 14 and 15 March 1938. COLL MISC 0456/1/6.

Minutes of the General Committee of the Fellowship of Reconciliation, 21 June 1938. COLL MISC 0456/1/6.

Minutes of the General Committee of the Fellowship of Reconciliation 1–3 April 1940. COLL MISC 0456/1/6.

Minutes of the General Committee of the Fellowship of Reconciliation, 30 and 31 December 1940. COLL MISC 0456/1/6.

Muriel Lester Archive, Bishopsgate Institute, London, EC2M 4QH

Muriel Lester Diary, 1897–1906, LESTER 1/1/2.

Minutes of a Kingsley Hall Meeting, 28 March 1937, LESTER 1/1/5.

Kingsley Hall Constitution, LESTER 7/2/9.

Parliamentary Papers

Parliamentary Debates, House of Lords Official Report, Vol. 116, No. 58, Wednesday 12 June 1940.

House of Commons Reports, London, 26 June 1940. Hansard, Vol. 362, cc443–4.

Archive of the Evangelical Alliance, 176 Copenhagen Street, London, N1 0ST

Minutes of the Evangelical Alliance Executive Council, 13 December 1883.

Minutes of the Evangelical Alliance Executive Council, 11 July 1895.

Evangelical Alliance Quarterly

Angus Archive, Regent's Park College, Oxford

Application to Local Tribunal by a Person Provisionally Registered in the Register of Conscientious Objectors: Harold Arthur Dobson Stead. D/BPF Box 1.

Minutes of Baptist Pacifist Fellowship, 13 February 1939. D/BPF Box 1.

Books

Allain, Roger, *The Community that Failed* (San Francisco: Carrier Pigeon Press, 1992).

Armstrong, C. J. R., *Evelyn Underhill, 1875–1941: An Introduction to her Life and Writings* (Grand Rapids: Eerdmans, 1976).

Armytage, W. H. G., *Heavens Below: Utopian Experiments in England, 1560–1960* (Abingdon: Routledge, rev. ed., 2007).

Arnold, Annemarie, *Anni: Letters and Writings of Annemarie Wächter* (Rifton, NY and Robertsbridge: Plough Publishing, 2010).

Arnold, Eberhard, *Brothers Unite: An Account of the Uniting of Eberhard Arnold and the Rhön Bruderhof with the Hutterian Church* (Rifton, NY: Plough Publishing House, 1988).

Arnold, Eberhard, *The Early Christians after the Death of the Apostles* (Ashton Keynes: Plough Publishing House, 1939).

Arnold, Eberhard, *Innerland: A Guide into the Heart of the Gospel* (Rifton, NY, and Robertsbridge: Plough Publishing House, 2011).

Arnold, Eberhard, *Salt and Light: Living the Sermon on the Mount* (Rifton, NY, and Robertsbridge: Plough Publishing House, 1998).

Arnold, Eberhard, *Why We Live in Community* (Robertsbridge: Plough Publishing House, 1995).

Arnold, Eberhard and Emmy von Hollander, *Love Letters* (Rifton, NY, and Robertsbridge: Plough Publishing House, 2007)

Arnold, Emmy, *A Joyful Pilgrimage: My Life in Community* (Rifton, NY: Plough Publishing House, 1999).

Arnold, Emmy, *Torches Together* (Rifton, NY: Plough Publishing House, 1964).

Backhouse, James, *The Life and Correspondence of William and Alice Ellis of Airton* (London: Charles Gilpin, 1849).

Barclay, Oliver, *Whatever Happened to the Jesus Lane Lot?* (Leicester: Inter-Varsity Press, 1977).

Barker, Rachel, *Conscience, Government and War: Conscientious Objection in Great Britain, 1939–45* (London: Routledge and Kegan Paul, 1982).

Barratt, Thomas, *When the Fire Fell: and an Outline of My Life* (Oslo: Hansen & Sønner, 1927).

Barrett, Clive, *Subversive Peacemakers* (Cambridge: Lutterworth Press, 2014).

Barry, F. R., *What Has Christianity to Say?* (London: Student Christian Movement, 1937).

Barth, Emmy, *An Embassy Besieged: The Story of a Christian Community in Nazi Germany* (Eugene, OR: Cascade Books, 2010).

Barth, Emmy, *No Lasting Home* (Rifton, NY, and Robertsbridge: Plough Publishing House, 2009).

Barth, Karl, 'Friedrich Naumann and Christoph Blumhardt', in *The Beginnings of Dialectic Theology*, ed. James M. Robinson, trans. K. R. Crom (Richmond, VA: John Knox, 1968).

Baum, Markus, *Against the Wind: Eberhard Arnold and the Bruderhof*, translated and edited by the Bruderhof Communities (Rifton, NY, and Robertsbridge: Plough Publishing House, 1998).

Bebbington, D. W., *Evangelicalism in Modern Britain: A History from the 1730s to the 1980s* (London: Routledge, 1995).

Begbie, Harold, *The Life of General William Booth*, Vol. II (New York: The Macmillan Company, 1920).

Berghahn, Marion, *Continental Britons: German Jewish Refugees from Nazi Germany* (New York: Berghahn Books, 2007).

Besse, Joseph, *A Collection of the Sufferings of the People called Quakers* (London, 1752), Vol. II, 420–432.

Binfield, Clyde, *George Williams and the Y.M.C.A.* (London: Heinemann, 1973).

Bingham, Jane, *The Cotswolds: A Cultural History* (Oxford: Oxford University Press, 2009).

Bloch-Hoell, Nils, *The Pentecostal Movement: Its Origin, Development, and Distinctive Character* (London: Allen & Unwin, 1964).

Bohlken-Zumpe, Elizabeth, *Torches Extinguished: Memories of a Communal Bruderhof Childhood in Paraguay, Europe and the USA* (San Francisco: Carrier Pigeon Press, 1993).

Bonhoeffer, Dietrich, *Life Together*, originally *Gemeinsames Leben* (Christian Kaiser Verlag, 1939).

Boobbyer, Philip, *The Spiritual Vision of Frank Buchman* (Pennsylvania State University: Penn State University Press, 2013).

Borries, Achim von, *Quiet Helpers: Quaker Service in Postwar Germany* (London: Quaker Home Service, 2000).

Boyd, Robin, *The Witness of the Student Christian Movement* (London: SPCK, 2007).

Brinson, Charmain, and Dove, Richard, *A Matter of Intelligence: MI5 and the Surveillance of Anti-Nazi Refugees 1933–50* (Manchester: Manchester University Press, 2014).

Brittain, Vera, *The Rebel Passion: A Short History of Some Pioneer Peacemakers* (London: Allen, 1964).

Brock, Peter, and Nigel Young, *Pacifism in the Twentieth Century* (Syracuse: Syracuse University Press, 1999).

Brown, Anthony, *Hazard Unlimited: The Story of Lloyd's of London* (London: Peter Davies, 1978).

Ceadel, Martin, *Pacifism in Britain, 1914–1945: The Defining of a Faith* (Oxford: Clarendon Press, 1980).

Ceadel, Martin, *Semi-Detached Idealists: The British Peace Movement and International Relations, 1854–1945* (Oxford: Oxford University Press, 2000).

Cesarani, David, ed., *The Making of Modern Anglo-Jewry* (Oxford: Blackwell, 1990).

Chandler, Andrew, *George Bell, Bishop of Chichester: Church, State, and Resistance in the Age of Dictatorship* (Grand Rapids: Eerdmans, 2016).

Chappell, Connery, *Island of Barbed Wire: Internment on the Isle of Man in World War Two* (London: Robert Hale, 1984).

Clements, Keith, *Bonhoeffer and Britain* (London: Churches Together in Britain and Ireland, 2006).

Clements, Keith, ed., *London, 1933–1935: Dietrich Bonhoeffer Works, vol. 13* (Minneapolis, MN: Fortress Press, 2007).

Community in Britain (Cotswold Bruderhof Press, Ashton Keynes: Community Service Committee, 1938).

Community in Britain (London: Community Service Committee, 1940).

Davis, Robert, *Woodbrooke, 1903–1953* (London: Bannisdale Press, 1953).

Dimbleby, Jonathan, *The Battle of the Atlantic* (London: Viking, 2015).

Dueck, David, *To Build a Homeland: Home in a Strange Land* (*Winnipeg: Mennonite Historical Society of Canada, 1981*).

Eberhard Arnold: Modern Spiritual Masters Series (Maryknoll, NY: Orbis Books, 2000).

Ellis, Gavin, *Trust Ownership and the Future of News: Media Moguls and White Knights* (London: Palgrave Macmillan, 2014)

Evans, Eifion, *The Welsh Revival of 1904* (Port Talbot: Evangelical Movement of Wales, 1969).

Fawell, Ruth, *Joan Mary Fry* (London: Friends House Service Committee, 1959).

Fischer, Hans, *Jakob Huter* (Newton, KS: Mennonite Publication Office, 1956).

Foundations of Our Faith and Calling, (Rifton, NY, and Robertsbridge: Plough Publishing House, 2012).

Fry, Joan Mary, *An Appeal to Help the Members of the Alm Bruderhof* (London: privately printed, 1935).

Fry, Joan Mary, ed., *Christ and Peace* (London: Headley, 1915).

Fry, Joan Mary, *In Downcast Germany: 1919–1933* (London: E. G. Dunstan, 1944).

Furneaux, Rupert, *Massacre at Amritsar* (London: Allen & Unwin, 1963).

Gibbard, Noel, *On the Wings of the Dove* (Bryntirion, Bridgend: Bryntirion Press, 2002).

Gill, Eric, *Christianity and Art* (Abergavenny: Francis Walterson, 1927).

Gill, Eric, *Eric Gill: Autobiography* (London: Right Book Club, 1944).

Gill, Eric, *The Necessity of Belief: An Enquiry into the Nature of Human Certainty, the Causes of Scepticism and the Grounds of Morality, and a Justification of the Doctrine That the End is the Beginning* (London: Faber & Faber, 1936).

Gill, Eric, *Sacred and Secular Essays* (London: J. M. Dent & Sons, 1940).

Gill, Eric, *Work and Property* (London: J. M. Dent & Co., 1937).

Gillman, Peter and Leni, '*Collar the lot!': How Britain Interned and Expelled its Wartime Refugees* (London; New York: Quartet Books, 1980).

Goodall, Felicity, *We Will Not Go to War* (Stroud: The History Press, 2010).

Grant, J. W., *Free Churchmanship in England, 1870–1940* (London: Independent Press, 1955).

Gregg, Richard, *The Power of Non-Violence* (London: Routledge, 1935).

Hardy, Dennis, *Utopian England: Community Experiments, 1900–1945* (New York: Routledge, 2000).

Hastings, Adrian, *History of English Christianity, 1920–2000* (London: SCM, 2001).

Hayes, Denis, *Challenge of Conscience: The Story of the Conscientious Objectors of 1939–1949* (London: George Allen & Unwin, 1949).

Heal, Oliver S., *Sir Ambrose Heal and the Heal Cabinet Factory, 1897–1939* (Wetherby: Oblong Creative Ltd., 2014).

Heath, Carl, *Social and Religious Heretics in Five Centuries* (London: Allenson, 1936).

Heath, Richard, *Anabaptism* (London: Alexander and Shepheard, 1895).

Heath, Richard, *Social Democracy: Does It Mean Darkness or Light?* (Letchworth: Garden City Press, 1910).

Hill, Christopher, *The English Revolution 1640* (London: Lawrence & Wishart, 1940).

Hollenweger, Walter J., *The Pentecostals* (London: SCM, 1972).

Holliday, Aaron, ed., *FoR: 100 Years of Nonviolence* (Oxford: Fellowship of Reconciliation, 2014).

Holmes, Janice, *Religious Revivals in Britain and Ireland, 1859–1905* (Dublin: Irish Academic Press, 2011).

Holmes, Miriam Arnold, *Cast Out in the World* (San Francisco: Carrier Pigeon Press, 1997).

Hostetler, John A., *Hutterite Society* (Baltimore, MD: Johns Hopkins University Press, 1974).

Housman, Laurence, *The Unexpected Years* (London: Jonathan Cape, 1936).

Hudson, Kenneth, *Towards Precision Shoemaking, C. & J. Clark Limited and the Development of the British Shoe Industry* (Newton Abbot: David and Charles, 1968).

Hughes, William R., *Indomitable Friend: The Life of Corder Catchpool* (London: G. Allen & Unwin, 1956).

Hunt, Tristram, *Building Jerusalem: The Rise and Fall of the Victorian City* (London: Weidenfeld and Nicolson, 2005).

Hutterian Brethren, ed., *The Chronicle of the Hutterian Brethren, Volume I* (Rifton, NY: Plough Publishing House, 1987).

Huxley, Aldous, *Ends and Means* (London: Chatto and Windus, 1938).

Huxley, Aldous, and Dick Sheppard, *100,000 Say No!* (London: Peace Pledge Union, 1936).

Ineson, George, *Community Journey* (London: Sheed & Ward, 1956).

Janzen, Rod, and Max Stanton, *The Hutterites in North America* (Baltimore, MD: Johns Hopkins University Press, 2010).

Janzen, Rod, *The Prairie People: Forgotten Anabaptists* (Hanover, NH: University Press of New England, 1999).

Joad, C. E. M., *'Defence' That Is No Defence: A Message to Every Citizen* (London: National Peace Council, 1937).

Joseph, Fiona, *Beatrice: The Cadbury Heiress Who Gave Away Her Fortune* (Birmingham: Foxwell Press, 2012).

Katz, Yossi, and John Lehr, *Inside the Ark: The Hutterites* in Canada and the United States (Regina, SK: Canadian Plains Research Centre Press, 2012).

Kemplay, John, *The Paintings of John Duncan: A Scottish Symbolist* (San Francisco: Pomegranate, 2009).

Kennedy, Thomas C., *The Hound of Conscience: A History of the Non-Conscription Fellowship* (Fayetteville: University of Arkansas Press, 1981).

Klassen, J. P., *The Economics of Anabaptists* (The Hague: Mouton and Co., 1964).

Koven, Seth, *The Match Girl and the Heiress* (Princeton and Oxford: Princeton University Press, 2014).

Kramer, Ann, *Conscientious Objectors of the Second World War: Refusing to Fight* (Barnsley: Pen & Sword Social History, 2013).

Lafitte, François, *The Internment of Aliens* (London: Libris, 1988. First published 1940).

Lamb, Edwin, *The Social Work of the Salvation Army* (CreateSpace Independent Publishing Platform, reprint from early twentieth century, 2016).

Lester, Muriel, *It Occurred to Me* (New York: Harper Brothers, 1937).

London, Louise, *Whitehall and the Jews, 1933–1948* (Cambridge: Cambridge University Press, 2000).

Lynch, Cecelia, *Beyond Appeasement: Interpreting Interwar Peace Movements in World Politics* (London: Cornell University Press, 1999).

MacCarthy, Fiona, *Eric Gill* (London: Faber & Faber, 1989).

Manley, Belinda, *Through Streets Broad and Narrow* (San Francisco: Carrier Pigeon Press, 1995).

Marsh, Charles, *Strange Glory: A Life of Dietrich Bonhoeffer* (New York: Alfred A. Knopf, 2014).

Meier, Hans, *Solange das Licht brennt: Lebensbericht eines Mitgliedes der neuhutterischen Bruderhof-Gemeinschaft*, (Klosters 1990).

Mommsen, Peter, *Homage to a Broken Man* (Rifton, NY, and Robertsbridge: Plough Publishing House, 2004).

Morrison, Sybil, *I Renounce War: The Story of the Peace Pledge Union* (London: Sheppard Press, 1962).

Mow, Merrill, *Torches Rekindled* (Rifton, NY: Plough Publishing House, 1989).

Murdoch, Norman H., *Origins of the Salvation Army* (Knoxville: University of Tennessee Press, 1996).

Murry, John Middleton, *Heaven and Earth* (London: Jonathan Cape, 1938).

Nauerth, Thomas, *Zeugnis, Liebe und Widerstand: Der Rhönbruderhof 1933–1937* (Paderborn: Schöningh, 2018).

Oved, Yaacov, *The Witness of the Brothers: A History of the Bruderhof* (New Brunswick and London: Transaction Publishers, 1996).

Packull, Werner, *Hutterite Beginnings: Communitarian Experiments during the Reformation* (Baltimore, MD: Johns Hopkins University Press, 1995).

Page, Jesse, *The Christianity of the Continent* (London: S. W. Partridge & Co., 1906).

Peel, Mark, *The Last Wesleyan: A Life of Donald Soper* (Lancaster: Scotforth Books, 2008).

Pleil, Nadine Moonje, *Free from Bondage* (San Francisco: Carrier Pigeon Press, 1994).

Prasad, Devi, *War is a Crime against Humanity: The Story of War Resisters' International* (London: War Resisters' International, 2005).

Price, Charles, and Ian Randall, *Transforming Keswick* (Carlisle: Paternoster, 2000).

Pugh, Michael, *Liberal Internationalism* (Basingstoke: Palgrave Macmillan, 2012).

Railton, G. S., *Lieut.-Col. Jacob Junker of Germany* (London: Salvation Army Publishing Department, 1903).

Randall, I. M. *'Church community is a gift of the Holy Spirit:' The spirituality of the Bruderhof community* (Oxford: Centre for Baptist History and Heritage, 2014).

Randall, I. M., *The English Baptists of the Twentieth Century* (Didcot: Baptist Historical Society, 2005).

Randall, I. M., *Evangelical Experiences: A Study in the Spirituality of English Evangelicalism, 1918–1939* (Carlisle: Paternoster, 1999).

Randall, I. M., and David Hilborn, *One Body in Christ: The History and Significance of the Evangelical Alliance* (Carlisle: Paternoster Press, 2001).

Richards, Edith, *Private View of a Public Man: The Life of Leyton Richards* (London: Allen and Unwin, 1950).

Riedemann, Peter, *Confession of Faith: Account of Our Religion, Doctrine, and Faith, Given by Peter Rideman of the Brothers Whom Men Call Hutterians* (Rifton, NY: Plough Publishing House, 1970). Previously published in 1950 by Hodder and Stoughton.

Roberts, R. Ellis, *H.R.L. Sheppard: Life and Letters* (London: John Murray, 1942).

Robinson, John Martin, *Requisitioned: The British Country House in the Second World War* (London: Aurum Press, 2014).

Robinson, Stuart, *Fertile Field: An Outline History of the Guild of Gloucestershire Craftsmen and the Crafts in Gloucestershire* (Gloucester: Guild of Gloucester Craftsmen, 1983).

Rouse, Ruth, *The World's Student Christian Federation* (London: SCM, 1948).

Rubin, Julius H., *The Other Side of Joy: Religious Melancholy among the Bruderhof* (New York: Oxford University Press, 2000).

Rubin, Julius H., *Religious Melancholy and Protestant Experience in America* (New York: Oxford University Press, 1993).

Sabine, George H., ed., *The Works of Gerard Winstanley* (Ithaca, NY: Cornell University Press, 1941).

Sandall, Robert, *The History of the Salvation Army*, Vol. III (London: Thomas Nelson, 1955).

Schill, Ray, *Workshop of the World: Birmingham's Industrial Legacy* (Stroud: The History Press, 2006).

Schmidgall, Paul, *European Pentecostalism: Its Origins, Development, and Future* (Cleveland, Tennessee: CPT Press, 2013).

Schmitt, Hans A., *Quakers and Nazis: Inner Light in Outer Darkness* (Columbia: University of Missouri Press, 1997).

Sharp, John E., *Calling to Fulfill: The Orie O. Miller Story* (Harrisonburg, Va.: Herald Press, 2015).

Sherman, A. J., *Island Refuge*, 2nd edn. (New York: Frank Cass & Co., 1994).

Short, Brian, *The Battle of the Fields: Rural Community and Authority in Britain During the Second Word War* (Woodbridge: The Boydell Press, 2014).

Skran, Claudena, *Refugees in Inter-War Europe: The Emergence of a Regime* (Oxford: Clarendon Press, 1995).

Snyder, C. A., *Anabaptist History and Theology: An Introduction* (Kitchener, Ontario: Pandora Press, 1995).

Speaight, Robert, *The Life of Eric Gill* (London: Methuen & Co., 1966).

Stayer, James M., *The German Peasants' War and Anabaptist Community of Goods* (Montreal: McGill-Queen's University Press, 1991).

Stent, Ronald, *A Bespattered Page?: The Internment of His Majesty's 'Most Loyal Enemy Aliens'* (London: Deutsch, 1980).

Steiner, Zara, *The Triumph of the Dark: European International History, 1933–1939* (Oxford: Oxford University Press, 2011).

Stevenson, Lilian, *Mathilda Wrede of Finland: Friend of Prisoners* (London: George Allen & Unwin, 1925).

Tatlow, Tissington, *The Story of the Student Christian Movement* of Great Britain and Ireland (London: SCM Press, 1933).

Tyldesley, Michael, *No Heavenly Delusion?* (Liverpool: Liverpool University Press, 2003).

Verduin, L., *The Reformers and Their Stepchildren* (Grand Rapids, MI: William B. Eerdmans, 1964).

Von Borries, Achim, *Quiet Helpers: Quaker Service in Postwar Germany* (London: Quaker Home Service, 2000).

Wallis, Jill, *Mother of World Peace: The Life of Muriel Lester* (Enfield Lock, Middlesex: Hisarlik Press, 1993).

Wallis, Jill, *Valiant for Peace* (London: Fellowship of Reconciliation, 1991).

Watson, Thomas, *Pioneer in Community: Henri Lasserre's Contribution to the Fully Cooperative Society* (Toronto: Ryerson Press, 1949).

Weir, John, 'London', in Reid, William, ed., *Authentic Records of Revival, Now in Progress in the United Kingdom* (London: James Nisbet & Co., 1860).

Wellock, Wilfred, *Off the Beaten Track: Adventures in the Art of Living*, 2nd edn. (Rajghat: Sarva Seva Sangh Prakashan, *1963*).

Whitworth, John McKelvie, *God's Blueprints. A Sociological Study of Three Utopian Sects* (London: Routledge & Kegan Paul Ltd., 1975).

Wood, H. G., *John William Hoyland of Kingswood* (London: SPCK, 1931).

Wood, Ian S., *Britain, Ireland and the Second World War* (Edinburgh: Edinburgh University Press, 2010).

Wrench, Evelyn, *I Loved Germany* (London: *Michael Joseph* and Ryerson, *1940)*.

Yorke, Malcolm, *Eric Gill: Man of Flesh and Spirit* (London: Constable & Co., 1981).

Zablocki, Benjamin D., *The Joyful Community: An Account of the Bruderhof: A Communal Movement Now in Its Third Generation* (Chicago: University of Chicago Press, 1971).

Zündel, Friedrich, *Pastor Johann Christoph Blumhardt: An Account fo His Life* (Eugene, Oregon: Cascade Books, 2010).

Articles, Essays, and Chapters

Adam, Dejan, '"The Practical, Visible Witness of Discipleship": The Life and Convictions of Hans Meier (1902–1992)', in K. G. Jones and I. M. Randall, eds., *Counter-Cultural Communities: Baptistic Life in Twentieth-Century Europe* (Milton Keynes: Paternoster, 2008), 285–342.

Arnold, E. C. H. [Hardy], 'The Fate of a Christian Experiment', *The Spectator,* 11 June 1937, 11.

Armytage, W. H. G., 'The Wheathill Bruderhof, 1942–9', *American Journal of Economics and Sociology* 18/3 (1959), 285–294.

Bender, H. S., 'The Anabaptist Vision', *Church History* 13 (March 1944), 3–24.

Briggs, John H. Y., 'Richard Heath, 1831–1912: From Suburban Baptist to Radical Discipleship by Way of Anabaptism', in J. H. Y. Briggs and A. R. Cross, eds., *Freedom and the Powers* (Didcot: The Baptist Historical Society, 2014), 69–84.

Browne, S. G., Obituary: Ernest Muir, 1880–1974. *International Journal of Leprosy*, http://ila.ilsl.br/pdfs/v42n4a14.pdf, accessed 24 January 2016.

Clements, Keith W., 'An Alliance for International Friendship: Sentiment, Reality, Hope', in Paul S. Fiddes, ed., *'A World-Order of Love': Baptists and the Peace Movements of 1914* (Oxford: Centre for Baptist History and Heritage, 2017), 9–29.

Clements, Keith W., 'Baptists and the Outbreak of the First World War', *Baptist Quarterly*, 26/2 (1975), 74–92.

Danchev, Alex, 'The Army and the Home Front, 1939–1945', in O. Chandler and I. Beckett, eds., *The Oxford History of the British Army* (Oxford: Oxford University Press, 1996), 298–315.

Dekar, Paul R., 'Muriel Lester, 1883–1968: Baptist Saint?', *Baptist Quarterly*, 34/7 (1992), 337–345.

Dekar, Paul R., 'Twentieth-Century British Baptist Conscientious Objectors', *Baptist Quarterly* 35/1 (1993), 35–44.

Durnbaugh, Donald F., 'Relocation of the German Bruderhof to England, South America, and North America', *Communal Societies* 11 (1991).Finlayson, Geoffrey, 'A Moving Frontier: Voluntarism and the State in British Social Welfare 1911–1949', *Twentieth Century British History* 1/2 (1990), 183–206.

Friedmann, Robert, 'An Epistle Concerning Communal Life. A Hutterite Manifesto of 1650 and Its Modern Paraphrase', *The Mennonite Quarterly Review* (October 1960), 249–254.

Glasgow, Eric, 'A History of the Birmingham University Library', *Library Review* 51/7, 373–378.

Goodhew, David, 'The Rise of the Cambridge Inter-Collegiate Christian Union, 1910–1971', *Journal of Ecclesiastical History* 54/1 (January 2003), 62–88.

Holthaus, Stephen, 'Friedrich Wilhelm Baedeker (1823–1906): His Life', in Tim Grass, ed., *Witness in Many Lands* (Troon: Brethren Archivists and Historians Network, 2013), 59–72.

Janzen, Rod, 'The Hutterites and the Bruderhof: The Relationship between an Old Older Religious Society and a Twentieth-Century Communal Group', *MQR* 79 (October 2005), 505–544.

London, Louise, 'Jewish Refugees, Anglo-Jewry and British Government Policy, 1930–1940', in David Cesarani, ed., *The Making of Modern Anglo-Jewry* (Oxford: Blackwell, 1990), 163–190.

Parker, Linda, '"Shell-Shocked Prophets": Anglican Army Chaplains and Post-War Reform in the Church of England', in Snape, Michael, and Edward Madigan, eds., *The Clergy in Khaki* (Aldershot: Ashgate, 2013), 183–97.

Pistol, Rachel, 'Enemy Alien and Refugee: Conflicting Identities in Great Britain during the Second World War', *Journal of Contemporary History* 16 (2015), 37–52.

Randall, I. M., 'Austere Ritual: The Reformation of Worship in Inter-War Congregationalism', in R. N. Swanson, ed., *Studies in Church History*, 35 (Woodbridge: The Boydell Press, 1999), 432–446.

Randall, I. M., 'Evangelical Spirituality, Science, and Mission: A Study of Charles Raven (1885–1964), Regius Professor of Divinity, Cambridge University', in *Anglican and Episcopal History* 84/1 (2015), 20–48.

Rigby, Andrew, 'Pacifist Communities in Britain in the Second World War', *Peace & Change* 15/2, 107–122.

Roosevelt, Eleanor, 'My Day', *New York Post*, 24 September 1940.

Rusch, J. B., 'Swiss Forebodings', in *The Living Age: The World in Review*, May 1938, 202–203.

Simpson, Carl, 'The Development of the Pentecostal and Charismatic Movements in the Germanic Countries', in William K. Kay and Anne E. Dyer, eds., *European Pentecostalism* (Leiden: Brill, 2011), 61–83.

Sun, T. H., 'The Madras Meeting on Rural Work', *West China Missionary News* (March, 1939), 125–129.

Van der Laan, Cornelis, 'The Proceedings of the Leaders' Meetings (1908–1911) and of the International Pentecostal Council (1912–1914)', *Bulletin of the European Pentecostal Theological Association* 6/3 (1987), 76–96.

Newspapers, Magazines, and Journals

Answers
Baptist Times
Bath and Wilts Chronicle and Herald
Bristol Evening World
British Weekly
The Brotherhood of the Way
Carrs Lane Journal
The Christian Pacifist
Coventry Herald
Daily Express
Daily Herald
Daily Telegraph
Evening Advertiser
Evening Standard
Faringdon News
The Friend
Gloucestershire Echo
The Life of Faith
Manchester Guardian
The Methodist Church Record: The Organ of the Swansea and Gower Circuits
Natal Mercury
News Chronicle
North Wilts Herald
Peace News
The Plough
The Spectator
The Times
Wilts and Gloucestershire Standard
Wiltshire Gazette

Theses

Lofton, Bonnie Price, 'On the Survival of Mennonite Community in Modern-Day America: Lessons from History, Communities, and Artists', Drew University DLitt (2012).

Vollmer, Antje, 'The *Neuwerk* Movement', unpublished translation of: *Die Neuwerkbewegung 1919–1935. Ein Beitrag zur Geschichte der Jugendbewegung, des Religiösen Sozialismus und der Arbeiterbildung*, (Augsburg, 1973). Translation BHA Staff. This dissertation has since been published as: Vollmer, Antje, *Die Neuwerk Bewegung: Zischen Jugendbewegung und religiösem Sozialismus* (Freiburg: Herder, 2016); page numbers refer to the English translation.

Index